'59: Summer of the Sox
The Year the World Series Came to Chicago

by Bob Vanderberg

Sports Publishing, Inc.
www.SportsPublishingInc.com

Page layout and design: Erin J. Prescher
Dust jacket and photo insert design: Terry N. Hayden
Edited by: David Hamburg

Thanks to the following for use of photos: UPI/Corbis-Bettmann, Chicago Tribune, AP/Wide World Photos and Bob Vanderberg

ISBN: 1-58261-036-3
Library of Congress Catalog Card Number: 99-60324

Sports Publishing, Inc.

This book is dedicated to the memory of Jacob Nelson Fox, American League Most Valuable Player of 1959 and the heart of the Chicago White Sox for more than a decade. It is also dedicated to all the members of the 1959 White Sox, those who have departed and those still among us, especially Early Wynn, who across three decades battled American League hitters, and who now battles that most insidious of afflictions, Alzheimer's Disease.

Finally, and above all, this book is dedicated to my father, who in my early years taught me to laugh at the Cubs, hate the Yankees and love God, writing and the White Sox.

"Have 40 years really come and gone since this magic carpet ride? *59: Summer of the Sox* reawakens the up-the-middle brilliance of Looie and Nellie, the arrival of Big Klu and the defiance of Early Wynn. It gives you a front-row seat to a year of South Side baseball that was joyous, intriguing, spellbinding and, yes, heartbreaking. Go Go Sox!"

—Chet Coppock, Fox Sports Chicago

"When I was a kid, I would have traded my family for Luis Aparicio and Nellie Fox. We took the bus past the Union Stockyards to Comiskey Park. Vanderberg saves you the trouble of commuting. If you want to know about Chicago and the White Sox and the way baseball is supposed to be played on the South Side, read this one."

—John Kass, columnist, *Chicago Tribune*

"Bob Vanderberg's book on the White Sox of the summer of '59 is a literary time machine that transports the reader back to another place. Turn the pages and let your mind and senses wander. Smell that bluish cloud of White Owl smoke dancing over the infield on a sultry summer night, cut by just a bit of the "bloom" of the Yards creeping in over left field. Watch Nellie, cheek bulging, choking up on a bottle bat from the land of Bunyan. Wait quietly in the ninth, while Billy toes the rubber, nods to Sherm and deftly delivers a horsehide laser over the inside corner. Bob Vanderberg, by virtue of this remarkable volume, becomes both the Boswell and the Merlin of the South Side."

—Louis Hegeman, Chicago attorney, co-founder of The Nellie Fox Society and attorney for Ted Williams in the Hall-of-Fame movement on behalf of Shoeless Joe Jackson

"For those Sox fans who were there in '59, and for those who learned about it from fathers and grandfathers, this is *the* Memory Book. This is proof that a Chicago team played in a World Series."

—Bill Gleason, "The Sports Writers on TV" and "voice" of the South Side

TABLE OF CONTENTS

ACKNOWLEDGMENTS

In writing this book, I depended a good deal on recollections of the book's heroes—the 1959 White Sox. I will always be indebted to club vice president Chuck Comiskey, manager Al Lopez, pitching coach Ray Berres, and the players who, over the years, were happy to share their memories: Luis Aparicio, Earl Battey, Johnny Callison, Larry Doby, Dick Donovan, Sam Esposito, Ted Kluszewski, Turk Lown, Jim Landis, Barry Latman, Jim McAnany, Billy Pierce, Jim Rivera, John Romano, Bob Shaw, Lou Skizas, Al Smith and Gerry Staley. And to Bill Veeck, whose generosity with his time and his memories long ago established a standard that too many in sports management today do not even approach.

For sharing their memories, a heart-felt thank you goes to two men who in 1959 were relatively new on the baseball beat, but who today are nationally known: Jack Kuenster, who covered the '59 Sox in the first half of the season for the *Chicago Daily News*, and Jerome Holtzman, who covered the second half for the *Chicago Sun-Times*.

Thanks also to Mike Pearson at Sports Publishing, Inc. for believing in the idea and shepherding the project through to its completion. For encouragement and memories, thanks to Leo Golembiewski, coach of the University of Arizona's nationally ranked ice hockey team but first and foremost a White Sox fan. Thanks to *Chicago Tribune* colleagues Al Solomon, Jim Binkley and Rich LaSusa for their suggestions, their editing and their encouraging words. And to Steve Marino, Rich Rott, Michael Mahaley and John Kieverts in the *Tribune's* library for help with microfilm and photographs.

I must thank, somewhat belatedly, the Oak Park playgrounds' "Baseball School" for taking a couple busloads of 10-, 11- and 12-year olds to Comiskey Park one June afternoon in 1959 to watch Barry Latman beat Washington for his first victory of the year. And thanks to my father for taking my brothers and me to countless Sox games, including some in '59, among them Nellie Fox Night.

Finally, thanks to my wife, Trish, and son, Brad, for their patience and understanding in the face of long nights at the word processor and calls to everywhere from Upper Saddle River, New Jersey, to Playa Del Rey, California, and from Tampa, Florida, to Vancouver, Washington.

FOREWORD

by Mike Veeck

They call them the formative years. I don't call them anything
except magical. Especially 1959. The year the Yankees didn't win the
pennant. But my beloved White Sox did.

What a time. Luis Aparicio would walk and then steal second.
Nelson Fox would single and drive him in. Then the Go-Go Sox
wouldn't score for another three innings. At least that's what my dad
always said. But the Sox represented the South Side—they were the
South Side. From Hyde Park to South Holland, they represented the
working-class city of big shoulders.

Comiskey Park, the venerable building destined to become the
dowager queen of stadiums until her demise in 1991, was the Land of
Oz to a youngster. "Big Klu," Ted Kluszewski, was the Cowardly Lion,
Earl Torgeson the Tin Man, Mary Frances (my mother) was Dorothy.
And, of course, the Wizard, the joy behind the curtain, cajoling,
encouraging and plotting—along with the graceful Senor, Al Lopez—
was my dad, Bill Veeck.

There was the collapse of the Indians and their manager, Joe
Gordon ("Our normal game will beat the Sox"). Mayor Daley, Richard
the First, the City's most famous Sox fan; Jack Brickhouse; the Com-
mander, Bob Elson; Jerome Holtzman; Bill Gleason; the Pied Piper,
Dave Condon; John Carmichael; Warren Brown—giants to a lad of
8 1/2 who hoped to be able to stay up late enough to hear the last innings
on WCFL before waking under the covers to the Voice of Labor and
Gene Chandler singing "The Duke of Earl."

The memories come washing over me in wave after wave of emo-
tion. A Jim Landis baseball card. Al Smith and the famous beer. Gerry
Staley and Turk Lown. Barry Latman and Bob Shaw. These were my
heroes. They were my obsession. In short, these living baseball cards
were my life.

Like the hero in Robert Coover's *The Universal Baseball Association, J. Henry Waugh, Proprietor*, I was immersed in my love of the
White Stockings when they won the pennant in Cleveland. In the

excitement, my dad and Dizzy Trout, on their way back to Chicago from Bloomington, Illinois, drove off the highway.

Fast-forward to the World Series. Lt. John L. Sullivan busted a counterfeit ring (single-handedly, to hear it years later). Nat Cole forgot the words to the National Anthem and made up better words than Francis Scott Key ever dreamed of.

Sitting on the steps under the press box with my mom ("Honey, dad can sell all of the seats," was her explanation) as Big Klu hit two monster shots. The joy was cataclysmic.

Alas, it was not to last. Wills, Gilliam, Neal and the unlikely Larry Sherry derailed the dream short of a world championship.

I cried. But, I remember. The other day, I was in Vegas, killing some time between speeches. I walked up to a roulette wheel. I put my money on 24. You know why? Not because it was Willie Mays' number, but because in that year of 1959, my favorite player of all time, Early Wynn, wore number 24.

She spun the wheel. Number 24. I won all over again.

Mike Veeck
Senior Vice President
Sales & Marketing
Tampa Bay Devil Rays

INTRODUCTION

That the Chicago White Sox have chosen to grace their followers with an American League championship only once every 40 years is one of baseball's remarkable oddities. But those of us who still swear allegiance to the Pale Hose at least can say that we have not become smug because of constant, taken-for-granted success and thus are better human beings because of it.

My father was born in 1919, only months before one of the great teams in baseball history, led by Shoeless Joe Jackson, Eddie Collins, Buck Weaver and Eddie Cicotte, steamrolled the American League—only to have eight members of that club conspire with gamblers to lose the World Series to the Cincinnati Reds. Then my dad patiently waited until 1959 before the White Sox won their next American League pennant, beating out the Cleveland Indians by five games and their perennial tormentors, the New York Yankees, by an amazing 15. Having accomplished that goal, though, the Sox went out and lost the World Series in six games to the Los Angeles Dodgers. At least, this time, they didn't lose it on purpose.

Now, my father and I confidently look forward to the 1999 season and another pennant, because another 40-year cycle will have been completed and also, more important, this is the year "the Looie Curse" will be lifted. "The Looie Curse," to the uninitiated, is the spell cast by Luis Aparicio, the Hall-of-Fame shortstop and one of the most crucial components of the '59 pennant-winning team, when he was traded to the Baltimore Orioles after the 1962 season. Angry with management because of a contract squabble and unhappy to be leaving the only organization in which he had played, he declared: "It took the White Sox 40 years to win their last pennant. It'll be another 40 years before they win their next."

People laughed at first, but look at the calendar. The 40th anniversary of that last pennant is upon us, and what else besides "the Looie Curse" can explain the near-misses, close calls and ill fortune the Sox have experienced since '59? Who, for example, could conceive of 10 straight losses to the Yankees in the first half of the '64 season, at the end of which the White Sox were one game behind New York? How else does one explain the '67 Sox, a half-game out with five games left, losing all five—to 10th place Kansas City and eighth-place Washington?

What other explanation can there be for what happened in 1972, when defending AL home run champion Bill Melton was joined by the exciting slugger Dick Allen? Melton went down the final week of June with a herniated disc and was lost for the season, one that ended with the Sox just five games behind the eventual world champion Oakland A's. And what about the next year? With Melton healthy, Allen again terrorizing the league, new centerfielder Ken Henderson hitting .311 and the Sox up 5 1/2 games on Oakland entering the final weekend of May, Henderson tore up his knee May 25 and Allen broke his leg three weeks later.

What besides "the curse" could cause respected hitters like Carlton Fisk, Harold Baines and Greg Luzinski to combine to bat .146 (7 for 48) in the 1983 AL playoff series with Baltimore? And can there be any other explanation for the 1994 season, when perhaps the finest all-around Sox team in our lifetime seemed poised for an overdue trip to the World Series, only to have the players and owners wreck it all with a season-ending strike?

Ah, but the curse will soon be lifted, and in the meantime, rather than dwell on past disappointments, this book means to bring back the one year since 1919 that the White Sox were American League pennant-winners and there actually was a World Series played on Chicago's South Side. It was a year when new houses sold for under $20,000, when $10,000 was considered a fine annual salary, when there were five TV channels available in Chicago to go with 16 AM radio stations and 17 FM stations.

It was a time when steel mills on Chicago's Far South Side employed thousands, when the stockyards on the South Side were, as Billy Pierce likes to say, "in full bloom," and when the Prudential Building was Chicago's tallest. It was a time when Richard J. Daley was just beginning his second term as Chicago's mayor, a time when everyone's hero, "Ike"—Dwight D. Eisenhower—was nearing the end of his second term as president. It was a time when we worried about the latest rantings of Soviet Russia's leader, Nikita S. Khrushchev, and when Chinese Communists were regarded with nervous suspicion rather than invited to White House coffee klatches.

It was a time in professional sports when there were eight teams each in the American and National Leagues, when there were just six teams in the National Hockey League, 12 in the National Football

League and eight in the National Basketball Association. The Yankees ruled baseball, the Montreal Canadiens hockey, the Baltimore Colts football and the Boston Celtics basketball. Chicago was the NHL's westernmost outpost, Minneapolis—home of the Lakers—the NBA's "far west" locale. Big-league baseball was only a year old on the West Coast, the Dodgers having fled Brooklyn for L.A. and the Giants having departed New York for San Francisco for the 1958 season.

It was, in short, a quite different time. The White Sox, too, were quite different. They had no such sluggers as Frank Thomas and Albert Belle. The '59 Sox's leading longball hitter was catcher Sherman Lollar, who was coming off career highs in home runs (20) and runs batted in (84). On the other hand, the '59 Sox opened that season with a pitching staff considered the best in the game, with All-Star-caliber starters Early Wynn, Billy Pierce and Dick Donovan leading the way, and a defense that was the envy of every other big-league club, with Lollar behind the plate, future Hall-of-Famers Aparicio and Nellie Fox at short and second and the ballhawking Jim Landis in center field. They were baseball's fastest team, with burners such as Aparicio, Landis, Jim Rivera and Bubba Phillips and several others with good speed—Fox, Al Smith, Sammy Esposito and the rookie hopeful, Johnny Callison.

The White Sox of 1959, unlike the White Sox of the '90s, were built, then, on pitching, speed and defense, as was the case all through the '50s. The Sox had finished fourth in 1951 and third in '52 through '56 before climbing to second under new manager Al Lopez in '57 and '58. They were still trying to catch Casey Stengel's Yankees, with their assortment of sluggers—Mickey Mantle, Yogi Berra, Bill Skowron, Elston Howard, et al.—and excellent pitchers—Whitey Ford, Bob Turley, Art Ditmar, Ryne Duren and the like. And most observers believed the Sox simply didn't have enough strength to do it.

Among those observers was the club's new president, Bill Veeck, who had come back to his hometown of Chicago to again operate a major-league baseball team, something he hadn't done since he sold the Cleveland Indians late in 1949—unless one chooses to classify the St. Louis Browns, whom Veeck owned during 1951-53, as a major-league baseball team. Veeck hardly was convinced the '59 White Sox were of championship caliber, particularly in the power category. "As the 1959 season began," he wrote in his autobiography, "we were, it seemed to me, far better equipped to battle McGraw's Giants than Stengel's Yankees."

As the 1959 season unfolded, that assessment was proven correct. The White Sox, as Veeck had feared, struggled for runs. However, so did their opponents. The Sox played 50 games that were decided by one run. They won 35 of them. "When I think of that season," Veeck wrote, "I think of a squibbling hit and everybody running... A typical White Sox rally consisted of two bloopers, an error, a passed ball, a couple of bases on balls and, as a final crusher, a hit batsman. Never did a team make less use of the lively ball."

Veeck was exaggerating a bit, perhaps, but it is true that the White Sox finished sixth that season in the eight-team American League in runs scored, sixth in batting average and last in home runs (with 97, lowest total in the majors). It is also true that they allowed the fewest runs and finished first in fielding, earned-run average, triples and stolen bases (their 113 being the highest total in baseball since the Dodgers' 117 in 1949).

In the pages ahead is the story of how the White Sox progressed through the 1959 season, month by month, from a team counting, with fingers crossed, on untested rookies to a team rolling confidently to the pennant. All the memorable moments are relived, from Nellie Fox's game-winning, 14th-inning home run on Opening Day in Detroit to Harry "Suitcase" Simpson's game-winning grand slam against the Yankees in late June to the four-game series sweep August 28-30 at second-place Cleveland to the pennant-clincher September 22 at the same site—and the air-raid sirens in Chicago that greeted the good news from the shore of Lake Erie. The failed June 15 trading-deadline attempts to land Cleveland's Minnie Minoso or Washington's Roy Sievers—attempts that unfortunately did bear fruit during the off-season—and the background of the August acquisition of Ted Kluszewski are detailed. So is the last World Series to be played in Chicago and the sudden, unexpected dealing away of the team's brightest farm-system products: Callison, Norm Cash, John Romano and Earl Battey.

So settle back in your easy chair, put on some Paul Anka or Frankie Avalon or Bobby Darin and take yourself back to the days of Ozzie and Harriet, Sgt. Bilko, Topper and Rin Tin Tin—and of Nellie and Looie, Staley and Lown, Smitty and Klu ...and sirens too. To 1959, the summer of the Sox.

SKETCHES

The 1959 White Sox:
A Quick Who's Who

(Players appearing in regular-season games; does not include September roster additions Joe Stanka, Gary Peters, Camilo Carreon, J.C. Martin and Joe Hicks)

(by uniform number)

1 JIM LANDIS, *Centerfielder*

Before '59: Brilliant defensively but a bust with the bat as a rookie in 1957, had come into his own as an all-around player in '58, having hit .277 with 15 home runs and 64 RBIs with 23 doubles and 7 triples and 19 stolen bases, taking over the No. 3 hole in the lineup.

During '59: Got off to a slow start and was hitting only .250 in mid-July before turning it on for stretch drive to finish at .272, but with only 5 homers. Stole 20 bases and saved many games with great catches. Hit .292 in World Series.

After '59: Won five Gold Gloves; named to the All-Star team in 1962 after hitting .283 with 22 homers, 85 RBIs in '61. Dealt to Kansas City after '64 season, ended career in '67 with career batting average of .247 but on-base percentage of .346. Lives in Napa, California. Son Craig was first-round pick of San Francisco Giants in 1977, played for Giants and Braves.

2 NELLIE FOX, *Second Baseman*

Before '59: Sparkplug of the White Sox since first big season, 1951, when he came out of nowhere to hit .313 with 32 doubles and 12 triples. Having compiled .297 career average and been on the All-Star team eight straight seasons, was coming off a .300 season in '58 and had won first of three Gold Glove awards (award was begun in '57). Since coming to the Sox on October 19, 1949 from the Philadelphia A's for backup catcher Joe Tipton, had led American League in hits four times, had hit .300 or better five times and had played in 513 straight games—and 789 of the last 790.

During '59: At age 31, again sparked the team with his usual hustle and fire and hit in the high .300s through May. Hit only .260 from July 25 on, but the Sox wouldn't have been where they were without him. Again an All-Star starter, wound up hitting .306 and was named AL Most Valuable Player. Hit .375 in the World Series.

After '59: Never hit .300 again but remained Sox regular second baseman until his trade to Houston for minor-league pitchers Jim Golden and Danny Murphy in December 1963. Became Joe Morgan's mentor with the Astros. Finished with a lifetime average of .288. Died of cancer in 1975. He was finally voted into the Hall of Fame in 1997.

3 LOU SKIZAS, *Outfielder*

Before '59: Highly regarded Yankee farmhand from Crane Tech High School on Chicago's West Side had broken in with the Yanks in '56 but was traded shortly after the season began to Kansas City A's, for whom he hit .314. After tailing off in subsequent years with A's and Detroit, he was drafted by the Sox from the Tigers' Triple-A Charleston club in December '58.

During '59: Got into eight games and was just 1-for-13 (.077) when traded with pitcher Don Rudolph to Cincinnati for outfielder Del Ennis on May 1. Never played in majors again. Finished season at Triple-A Havana.

After '59: After a couple of years in the minors, taught and coached at the University of Illinois. Lives in Champaign, Illinois.

3 DEL ENNIS, *Outfielder*

Before '59: One of the National League's top sluggers during 1946-57 but, at age 33, was coming off a rare bad year (3 homers, 47 RBIs, .261).

During '59: After opening season with Reds, was traded to Sox on May 1 and hit well for a few weeks, moving above .300 mark on mid-May road trip during which Sox took AL lead. But 2-for-21 skid hastened departure from everyday lineup. Released on June 15 with a .219 average.

After '59: Retired from baseball, finishing with a career .284 average and 288 home runs. Died in 1996.

2

3 JIM McANANY, *Outfielder*

Before '59: Signed by the Sox's superb scouting tandem of Hollis Thurston and Doc Bennett during freshman year ('55) at Southern Cal, he made a name for himself by hitting .400 for Colorado Springs in '58.

During '59: Began year at Triple-A Indianapolis and was hitting .315 when called up by the Sox on June 27 at the age of 22. He made an immediate impact with his hitting and fielding, he saw his batting average climb to .396 in mid-July before finishing at .276.

After '59: With reacquisition of Minnie Minoso, lost regular job and was optioned to Triple-A San Diego shortly after '60 season began and hit just .228 in 92 games. Taken by Los Angeles Angels in expansion draft but ended up with the Cubs' Triple-A Houston club in '61 (.318) before being brought up to Wrigley Field. For Cubs, was 3-for-10 in '61 and 0-for-6 in '62, all as pinch-hitter, and made final out of Warren Spahn's 300th victory. Owns insurance agency and lives in Culver City, California.

4 RON JACKSON, *First Baseman*

Before '59: Signed for big bonus in 1954 out of Western Michigan University, 6'7" slugger spent '54 and '55 with the Sox under terms of old bonus rule. Hit well in minors in '56 and '57 but not so well in '58 with the Sox (.233).

During '59: Farmed out in May despite single, double and homer in seven at-bats, went on to hit .286 at Indianapolis with 30 homers, 99 RBIs.

After '59: Traded to Boston for lefty Frank Baumann only weeks after World Series, started '60 season as Red Sox first baseman. After hitting .266 in 10 games was assigned again to the American Association, where he hit .290 in '60 and then .265 with 25 home runs in '61 before retiring and entering insurance business. Lives in Kalamazoo, Michigan.

5 BUBBA PHILLIPS, *Third Baseman*

Before '59: Originally with Detroit, came to Sox after 1955 season for pitcher Virgil Trucks. Converted from outfield by new manager Al Lopez in spring training of '57, hit .270 that year and .273 in '58, when he missed two months with a broken foot.

During '59: Hit at a .300 clip through May, finished at .264 with 27 doubles, five homers and 40 RBIs and in a platoon with left-handed-hitting Billy Goodman. Also filled in capably in center field when needed. Was 3-for-10 in three World Series games.

After '59: Was part of seven-player deal with Cleveland in December '59 that brought Minnie Minoso back to the Sox. Best year was '61, when he hit .264 with 18 homers and 72 RBIs for Indians. Retired to hometown of Hattiesburg, Mississippi, after 1964 season at age 34. Died in 1993.

6 BILLY GOODMAN, *Third Baseman*

Before '59: Singles hitter carried .305 lifetime average that included batting title in 1950, when he hit .354 in his third full season in majors. Hit .299 in '58, first year with Sox. Came to Chicago in December 1957 deal that also brought pitcher Ray Moore and outfielder Tito Francona from Orioles for outfielder Larry Doby, lefty Jack Harshman and two minor-leaguers.

During '59: At age 34, was bothered by illness in season's early months and, still weakened, was only hitting in the .190s by end of July. Regained old form to finish at .250. Hit .231 in World Series.

After '59: Played in just 71 games next two years with Sox before finishing career in '62 at Houston with lifetime .300 average. Died in 1984.

7 JIM RIVERA, *Outfielder*

Before '59: Known for his speed, hustle, circus catches and head-first slides, had been a fan favorite since coming to the Sox from St. Louis Browns in July 1952. Regular until '58, typical season was 12 homers, 60 RBIs, .255 average and 20-25 stolen bases.

During '59: At 37, he got into only 80 games with just 177 at-bats, missing three weeks with a cracked rib suffered while making a diving catch, but still managed to hit key homer in pennant-clinching game September 22 in Cleveland. Was 0-for-11 in World Series but made game-saving catch in Game 5.

After '59: Batted just 17 times in '60 and wound up with Kansas City A's in '61. Finished playing career hitting .259 in Pacific Coast League in '63 with Seattle, for whom he had starred in 1951. Owned and operated restaurant in Crooked Lake, Indiana, for several years before retiring to Ft. Wayne, Indiana.

8 RAY BOONE, *First Baseman*

Before '59: Had enjoyed a 10-year career, best years coming with Detroit, where he led AL in RBIs in 1955 with 116. Sought for many years by Sox, finally came to Chicago on June 15, 1958 with pitcher Bob Shaw for pitcher Bill Fischer and ourfielder Tito Francona. Finished '58 at age 35 with .242 average and 13 home runs.

During '59: Got into nine games with Sox (.238) before being traded on May 3 to Kansas City for Harry "Suitcase" Simpson. Was sold to Milwaukee Braves for stretch drive.

After '59: Finished in '60 with Red Sox, for whom he still scouts. Son Bob, former Royals manager, held big-league record for games caught; grandsons Bret (Braves) and Aaron (Reds) play in majors.

8 HARRY SIMPSON, *Outfielder/First Baseman*

Before '59: "Suitcase" had spent seven years in AL with Cleveland, Kansas City and New York, hitting .300 in '55 and .293 with 21 homers, 11 triples and 105 RBIs in '56. Played in '57 World Series with Yankees, dealt back to Kansas City in '58 and hit .255 at age 32.

During '59: Came to Sox on May 3 for Ray Boone and, though getting only 14 hits in 75 at-bats (.187), four of his hits came with bases loaded to win games, including grand slam off the Yankees' Bob Turley on June 27. Dealt to Pirates August 25 in waiver deal that brought Ted Kluszewski to Sox.

After '59: Was back with Sox in spring training in '60 but was sent to Triple-A San Diego when Sox cut down to 28-man Opening Day roster limit. Hit .222 there in 95 games, then .303 with 24 homers and 105 RBIs in '61 for same club. After a 19-homer, .279 year at Indianapolis in '62, played several years in Mexican League. Died in 1979.

8 TED KLUSZEWSKI, *First Baseman*

Before '59: Was one of National League's feared sluggers during the '50s, hitting, in successive years ('53-'56), 40, 49, 47 and 35 homers for Reds with 108, 141, 113 and 102 RBIs. Batted .320, .316, .326, .314 and .302 in '52 through '56. Cut off uniform sleeves to expose bulging biceps. Back injuries caused lessening of playing time after 1956.

During '59: After hitting .262 in 60 games for Pirates, came to Sox on August 25. Provided immediate boost in morale and hit .297 rest of season, then hit .391 in World Series with three homers and 10 RBIs, a record for a six-game Series.

5

After '59: Opening Day first baseman for Sox in '60 before being reduced to pinch-batting duties by Roy Sievers' hot hitting. Still ended up at .293 with 39 RBIs on his 53 hits. Lost in expansion draft to Angels, for whom he hit 15 homers in '61 to finish career with 279. Later was batting coach for Cincinnati's "Big Red Machine" and owned restaurant in Cincinnati. Died in 1988.

9 JOHNNY CALLISON, *Outfielder*

Before '59: Signed out of high school in June 1957 by Thurston-Bennett scouting duo, hit .340 for Bakersfield, his hometown team in the California League. Moved up to Triple-A Indianapolis for '58, hit .283 with league-leading 29 homers, then hit .297 in 18-game September trial with Sox—at age 19.

During '59: Handed left-field job in spring training but, weakened by late-April illness, lost weight and strength and, hitting in the .160s, was optioned to Indianapolis June 27 to make room for Jim McAnany. Hit .299 with 10 homers at Indianapolis, was recalled in September and hit grand slam at Detroit on season's final Saturday. Finished at .173, then was traded to Phillies in December for third baseman Gene Freese.

After '59: Came into his own in '62, hitting .300 with 23 homers, 10 triples and 83 RBIs, then settled in as one of NL's top outfielders for several years. Peak year '64, when he hit 31 homers and won All-Star Game with pinch homer in ninth. Lives in Glenside, Pennsylvania.

10 SHERMAN LOLLAR, *Catcher*

Before '59: Had appeared in three All-Star Games while establishing himself as league's No. 2 catcher behind Yankees' Yogi Berra but had outplayed Berra in '58, hitting .273 while posting career highs in homers (20) and RBIs (84). Had been with Sox since November 1951 trade with St. Louis Browns.

During '59: Led club with 22 homers and 84 RBIs, again named to All-Star team. Hit memorable home run off Minnie Minoso's glove to win opener of four-game weekend series in Cleveland August 28-30. Was among team leaders and, at age 35, welcomed occasional break from catching to play some first base.

After '59: Declined rapidly in '60 and lost starting job in '61 to rookie Camilo Carreon. Remained with Sox until retiring after '63 season, then coached for Baltimore Orioles and Oakland A's. Died of cancer in 1977.

11 LUIS APARICIO, *Shortstop*

Before '59: Signed by then-GM Frank Lane out of Venezuela in winter of 1953-54, played in '54 at Waterloo and in '55 at Memphis, where he fielded brilliantly and stole 48 bases. AL Rookie of the Year in '56 for Sox, who, to create an opening for him, had traded his country-man, shortstop Chico Carrasquel, to Cleveland in deal for Larry Doby. In first three seasons had established himself as majors' most sensational fielding shortstop and had led AL in steals each year, with a high of 29 in '58. All-Star Game starter in '58.

During '59: Let loose on base paths for first time, tied Sox record with then unheard-of total of 56 stolen bases to ignite club's "Go-Go" running game. Had career-best 98 runs scored. Led AL shortstops in assists, putouts, chances per game and fielding percentage. Hit .308 in World Series.

After '59: Led AL in steals next five years (with 51, 53, 31, 40 and 57). Traded to Baltimore after '62 season with Al Smith for Hoyt Wilhelm, Pete Ward, Ron Hansen and Dave Nicholson, helped Orioles win 1966 pennant and World Series, hitting .276 in regular season and again leading AL shortstops in fielding. Traded back to Sox after '67 season, hit .264, .280 and a career-high .313 next three years. Traded to Boston after '70 season at age 36 for Mike Andrews and Luis Alvarado, ended career in '73 with nine Gold Gloves and as all-time leader in games played at shortstop. Voted into Hall of Fame in 1984. Lives in Maracaibo, Venezuela, where he has been successful in insurance and oil businesses.

14 SAMMY ESPOSITO, *Infielder*

Before '59: Starred in football, basketball and baseball at Fenger High School on Chicago's Far South Side, started as a sophomore at guard on Indiana University's basketball team in '51-52 season before signing with Sox in the summer of '52. Teammate of Luis Aparicio at Memphis in '55, both came to Sox as rookies in '56.

During '59: Continued in role as club's No.1 utility man but hit career-low .167 in 69 games, down from .247 in 98 in '58. Got into two World Series games.

After '59: Was with Sox through April '63, finished career that year with Kansas City A's as roommate of rookie Ken Harrelson. Was head baseball coach and assistant basketball coach for many years at North Carolina State, where he recently retired as associate athletic director. Lives in Raleigh, N.C.

15 DON RUDOLPH, *Pitcher*

Before '59: Lefty had been in Sox system since 1954 and had had brief trials in '57 and '58. Was better known as husband of stripper Patti Waggin.

During '59: Made Opening Day roster as reliever and got the save in the opener at Detroit. After three more relief outings, was traded to Cincinnati in Del Ennis deal. Was in five games for Reds before being farmed out.

After '59: Led Pacific Coast League with 2.42 ERA (12-10 record) for Seattle in '60, then went 18-9 with 3.54 for Indianapolis (American Association) in '61, earning return to majors in '62, when he was 8-10, 3.62 for Washington. Ended career after two more years with Senators. Died in trucking accident in 1968.

15 KEN McBRIDE, *Pitcher*

Before '59: Had spent five years in Red Sox system, going 48-36.

During '59: Acquired from Boston before season as forerunner to Jackson-Baumann deal, was 11-5 at Indianapolis when Sox brought him up August 1, just days before he turned 24. Made debut August 4 at Baltimore as starter, leaving in seventh inning of game Sox eventually lost 3-2. Pitched in 11 games with 0-1 record and 3.18 ERA in 22 2/3 innings. Didn't appear in World Series.

After '59: Went 11-14 with 3.23 ERA at Triple-A San Diego in 1960 (and 0-1, 3.86 in five games with Sox) before going to Angels in expansion draft. Was 12-15 with 3.65 ERA for Angels in '61, then 11-5, 3.50 and 13-12, 3.26 next two years for same club, earning All-Star honors. Retired after '65 season. Lives in Cleveland.

16 AL SMITH, *Outfielder*

Before '59: Hit .281 for Cleveland in '54, his first full year in big leagues, and homered in World Series before hitting .306 with 22 homers and a league-leading 123 runs scored in '55. Was coming off two down years ('57 with Indians and '58 with Sox, who got him from Cleveland with Early Wynn for Minnie Minoso and Fred Hatfield in December '57). Playing on bad left ankle, hit .252 for Sox in '58 with only 12 homers, and drew boos from Sox fans angered by the trade of Minoso.

During '59: Got off to slow start, hitting below .200 by May 1; came alive in July, hitting six home runs that month that either tied or won games. Homered ahead of Jim Rivera's home run in pennant-

8

clincher at Cleveland. Still, finished at just .237 with 17 homers and 55 RBIs. Hit .250 in World Series.

After '59: Came all the way back in '60, hitting .315, then hit 28 homers with 93 RBIs in '61. Traded with Luis Aparicio to Orioles, retired after '64 season. Worked for Chicago Park District for many years. Still lives in Chicago.

17 EARL TORGESON, *First Baseman*

Before '59: Had been with Boston Braves and Phillies in National League, starting in 1947, and had hit .389 in 1948 World Series. Sox got him from Detroit for Dave Philley in June 1957, and he'd hit .295 the rest of season, platooning with Walt Dropo. In '58, had hit .266 but with 10 homers in just 188 at-bats, going 9-for-24 as pinch-hitter (.375).

During '59: At age 35, took over for rookie Norm Cash as regular before April was over and hit just .220 in 127 games but drove in 45 runs in 277 at-bats. Most memorable hit was his home run in 17th inning that beat Baltimore June 4 at Comiskey Park. Having lost starting job to Ted Kluszewski, was 0-for-1 in World Series.

After '59: Sox's No.1 pinch-hitter in '60, hitting .293 (12-for-41) in that role. Closed career in '61 with Yankees. Died in 1990.

18 BARRY LATMAN, *Pitcher*

Before '59: Like USC freshman teammate Jim McAnany, signed in 1955 with Sox and went to Waterloo, where he went 18-5 at age 19. Moved on to Memphis and Indianapolis before going 3-0 with 0.75 ERA in 13-game, 48-inning trial with Sox in 1958.

During '59: Was in 37 games, 21 as a starter, compiling 8-5 record with 3.75 ERA and two shutouts. Victory over Indians August 30 on two days' rest completed decisive four-game series sweep in Cleveland. Did not appear in World Series, while Fairfax (L.A.) High School teammate Larry Sherry ended up being Series MVP.

After '59: Traded day before '60 opener to Cleveland for Herb Score. Named to All-Star team in '61, when he was 13-5 for Indians. Also pitched for Angels and Astros. Retired after '67 season. Construction consultant in southern California. Lives in Playa del Rey, California.

19 BILLY PIERCE, *Pitcher*

Before '59: Since coming to Sox on November 10, 1948 for catcher Aaron Robinson, had won 148 games and lost 121, including seasons of 20-9 in '56 and 20-12 in '57. Led AL in strikeouts in '53 (adding seven shutouts), in ERA in '55 (1.97) and in complete games in '56, '57 and '58. All-Star Game starter in '53, '55 and '56. Was coming off 17-11, 2.68 season in '58 that included near-perfect game June 27, when Senators' Ed FitzGerald, the game's 27th batter, broke up no-hitter with pinch bloop double with two out in ninth.

During '59: Hampered by sore hip, had rare off year, going 14-15 with 3.62 ERA in 32 starts. Did beat Yankees 4-3 on July 28 to put Sox in first place to stay. Then was snubbed by Al Lopez in World Series, appearing only in relief, working four scoreless innings over three games.

After '59: At 33, was staff's top winner with 14 in '60, but after 10-9 mark in '61 was traded to Giants in six-player deal that brought knuckleballer Eddie Fisher to Chicago. With San Francisco, was 8-0 at Candlestick Park in '62 and 16-6 overall for NL champs and beat Whitey Ford in one World Series start and lost 3-2 in his other one, finishing with 1.89 Series ERA. Ended career after '64 season with 211-169 mark and 3.27 ERA, plus 1,999 strikeouts. Driving force behind Chicago Baseball Cancer Charities Inc. Lives in Lemont, Illinois.

20 JOHN ROMANO, *Catcher*

Before '59: Native of Hoboken, New Jersey, made late-season debut in 1954 at Dubuque in Sox farm system, hitting .355 in 27 games; then, at Waterloo in '55, set Three-I League record with 38 homers and hit .321. Was coming off All-Star season in '58 at Indianapolis, where he'd hit .291 with 25 homers and 89 RBIs.

During '59: Supplanted Earl Battey as No. 2 catcher and, as season progressed, often started against lefties, with Sherm Lollar playing first base. Starred as pinch-hitter, going AL-best 8-for-13 (.615). Overall, hit .294 with five homers and 25 RBIs in 126 at-bats. Hitless in lone World Series at-bat.

After'59: Dealt to Cleveland in Minnie Minoso trade, became All-Star catcher, reaching highs of .299 in '61 and 25 homers in '62. Returned to Sox with lefty Tommy John and outfielder Tommie Agee in January 1965 deal with Indians and A's, totaled 33 homers in two years before being sent to St. Louis Cardinals for outfielder Walter Williams in December '66. Retired after '67 season and worked as cost estimator for Bergen County, New Jersey, before retiring in 1998. Lives in Upper Saddle River, New Jersey.

21 GERRY STALEY, *Pitcher*

Before '59: Had won 111 games in big-league career that began in 1947 with Cardinals. Won 19, 17 and 18 games in successive years ('51-'53) for St. Louis. Spent '55 with Reds before September purchase by Yankees, from whom Sox bought him on May 29, 1956. Sinkerball specialist had posted ERAs of 2.06 and 3.18 in 97 games over '57 and '58 seasons.

During '59: Had greatest year at age 38, appearing in league-high 67 games, posting 2.24 ERA with 8-5 record and 14 saves. Two memorable games: July 18 in New York, when he threw one pitch, a double-play ball by Hector Lopez to end 2-1 victory over Yankees; September 22 in Cleveland, when again he needed just one pitch, a double-play ball by Vic Power with bases loaded, to end Sox's pennant-clinching 4-2 triumph. Was 0-1 with 2.16 ERA in four World Series games.

After '59: Began '60 season sensationally before tailing off in September, still finished 13-8 with 2.42 ERA in 64 games. After 0-3, 5.00 start through 16 games in '61, was traded in June to Kansas City in eight-player deal that netted Sox Ray Herbert. Sold to Detroit for stretch drive that August, retired that winter and became parks director in Vancouver, Washington, where he still lives.

22 DICK DONOVAN, *Pitcher*

Before '59: Had been staff mainstay since 1955, when, as 27-year-old rookie, went 15-9 with five shutouts despite missing three weeks in the wake of an emergency appendectomy July 31 that may have cost the Sox the pennant. Was 12-10 in '56, then 16-6 with 2.77 ERA, walking just 45 in 221 innings, in '57. Had started 3-10 in '58 before finishing with 15-14 record and 3.01 ERA.

During '59: Like Pierce, had off year, going 9-10 with 3.66 ERA, limited by some arm problems in July to just under 180 innings pitched. Threw crucial 2-0, five-hit shutout at Cleveland August 29. In World Series, started and lost 3-1 to Don Drysdale in Game 3, then saved 1-0 Game 5 victory with clutch pitching in eighth and ninth innings.

After '59: Lost rotation spot with poor beginning in '60, ended 6-1 but with 5.60 ERA. Went to new Washington club in expansion draft, led AL in '61 with 2.40 ERA, then went 20-10 for Cleveland in '62 with league-high five shutouts, walking 47 in 250 2/3 innings. Retired in '65 with 122-99 career record and 3.67 ERA. Worked as stock broker and in real estate. Died in 1997.

24 EARLY WYNN, *Pitcher*

Before '59: Had compiled 249-203 lifetime record, mostly with Cleveland Indians, for whom he had won 20 or more games four different years (1951, '52, '54, '56). Came to Chicago with Al Smith in Minnie Minoso deal of December '57, went 14-16 with 4.12 ERA but led AL in strikeouts at age 38 and was winning pitcher in All-Star Game, his fourth All-Star appearance.

During '59: Considered to be on decline, instead had one of his best years, going 22-10 with 3.17 ERA and five shutouts. Also had big year with bat, hitting .244 with 2 homers, one of which beat Boston's Tom Brewer 1-0 on May 1. Looked up to by young and old on ball-club for his fearlessness and competiveness. Served notice early that he'd be up to task by beating first-place Cleveland twice within two weeks (April 26, May 10). Started and was winning pitcher in pennant-clincher September 22 at Cleveland. Won Game 1 of World Series 11-0 but was KO'd in third inning of Game 4 and in fourth inning of Game 6.

After '59: Slipped to 13-12 in '60 but had decent ERA (3.49) and led AL with four shutouts. Was 8-2 in July '61 when sidelined for year with shoulder and elbow ailments. Was 7-15 in'62, losing final three bids for 300th victory. Released by Sox, caught on with Indians, for whom he won No. 300 in '63, then retired to serve as pitching coach. Worked as color man on Sox radio broadcasts in early '80s. Hall of Fame 1971. Lives in Nokomis, Florida.

25 RODOLFO ARIAS, *Pitcher*

Before '59: Little (5-10, 165) Cuban lefty had been in Sox system since 1953, when he struck out 247 in 219 innings at Madisonville in the Class D Kitty (Kentucky-Illinois-Tennessee) League. Teammate of Luis Aparicio and Earl Battey at Waterloo in '54. In '58 at Havana (Triple-A International League), had gone 7-7 with 3.80 ERA and had thrown a no-hitter.

During '59: At age 28, won job as lefty reliever and stayed with club all season. Finished 2-0 with 4.09 ERA in 34 games covering only 44 innings. Did not appear in World Series.

After '59: Cut before Opening Day, spent '60 at San Diego (3-1, 3.91) and Miami (7-9, 3.57) in Orioles' chain, then went to Reds'

Jersey City farm in '61 (8-9, 3.38). Split '62 between San Diego and Columbus (five games each) before retiring. Lives in Miami.

26 EARL BATTEY, *Catcher*

Before '59: Another Hollis Thurston find, signed upon graduation from Los Angeles' Jordan High in June 1953. He, and not teammate Luis Aparicio, was the Three-I League Rookie of the Year in 1954, when he hit .292 in 129 games. Made big-league debut at age 20 on September 10, 1955, catching final inning of Sox's critical 9-8, 10-inning victory at Yankee Stadium. Opened '56 and '57 seasons with Sox but was farmed out both years. Was with club entire '58 season, hitting .226 in 68 games but showing power with 8 homers in 168 at-bats.

During '59: Got into only 26 games, batted just 64 times, hitting .219. Did not play in World Series.

After '59: Traded to Washington with minor-leaguer Don Mincher in April 1960 for Roy Sievers, blossomed as everyday player, his leadership and defense helping his new club (soon to become the Minnesota Twins) develop into contender. Hit .270, .302, .280, .285, .272 and .297 next six years, last of which was Twins' pennant season. Best year was '63 (26 homers, 84 RBIs, .285). Retired after '67 season. Coaches baseball at Forest High School in Ocala, Florida, where he lives.

27 TURK LOWN, *Pitcher*

Before '59: Drafted by Cubs from Brooklyn Dodgers' system after 1950 season and spent '51-'53 in Chicago, posting 16-27 record. After success with Los Angeles (PCL) in '54 and '55, was sold back to Cubs, for whom he appeared in 61 and 67 games in '56 and '57, saving a total of 25 games. Traded to Reds in May 1958, then came to Sox a month later in waiver deal for Walt Dropo and got into 27 games, with 3-3 record and 3.95 ERA. Hard-throwing righthander struck out Mickey Mantle and Ted Williams first time he faced them.

During '59: At age 35, appeared in 60 games and was 9-2 with 2.89 ERA and led league with 15 saves, teaming with roommate Gerry Staley to form baseball's top bullpen duo. Made three World Series appearances, all scoreless.

After '59: Had three more solid years in Sox bullpen, then retired after '62 season. Lives in Pueblo, Colorado.

28 CLAUDE RAYMOND, *Pitcher*

Before '59: Righthanded reliever pitched in Milwaukee Braves' system, from which Sox drafted him in December 1958. Best year had been at Jacksonville in '57, where he was 12-6 with 2.50 ERA and 140 strikeouts in 133 innings in Class A South Atlantic League.

During '59: Made club out of spring training but after getting into three games (0-0, 9.00 ERA in four innings) was returned to Braves' Wichita farm just days before his 22nd birthday.

After '59: Became dependable reliever for Braves, Astros and finally Expos in his home province of Quebec. Had strikeout-walk ratios of 40-15 (in '62), 56-22 ('64), 79-16 ('65) and 73-25 ('66) and career-high 23 saves in '70. Has been on Expos' TV-radio team for more than 25 years. Lives in St. Luc, Quebec.

29 RAY MOORE, *Pitcher*

Before '59: Had lifetime 43-40 record and 3.93 ERA with three clubs (Dodgers, Orioles and Sox) over five seasons. Came to Sox from Baltimore in December 1957 deal with Billy Goodman and Tito Francona. Plans had called for Moore to be Sox's closer, but he ended up starting 20 games and beating world-champion Yankees three times, two of them shutouts. Overall, posted 9-7 record with 3.81 ERA.

During '59: Began season in rotation, but early-season failures combined with success of young Bob Shaw landed him in bullpen. Was 3-6 with 4.12 ERA in 29 games but, in emergency start August 24 at Comiskey Park, beat Yankees 4-2. Pitched one inning in World Series.

After '59: Winning pitcher in relief on Opening Day 1960, made 13 more appearances before being sold to Washington, where he became Senators' top reliever, saving 13 games. Saved 14 more for Twins in '61. Retired in '63. Died in 1995.

32 DON MUELLER, *Outfielder*

Before '59: New York Giants' regular rightfielder 1950 through '57, a Nellie Fox-type hitter who seldom struck out and hit lots of singles and doubles; posted averages of .333, .342 and .306 in '53 through '55, leading NL with 212 hits in Giants' world championship year of '54. Sold to Sox in spring training of '58, when emergence of young Giant outfielders Leon Wagner, Felipe Alou and Willie Kirkland made him expendable. Had hit .253 in 70 games for Sox in '58 but was 9-for-26 (.346) as pinch-hitter.

During '59: Had two hits in four at-bats, all as pinch-hitter, when he was released in early May.

After '59: Retired after release by Sox, ending career at age 32 with lifetime .296 average. Lives in Maryland Heights, Missouri.

32 LARRY DOBY, *Outfielder*

Before '59: First black player in American League, broke league's color barrier July 5, 1947 with Cleveland Indians. Went on to lead AL in homers twice ('52, '54, with 32 each time) and RBIs once (126 in '54). Drove in 100 or more runs five times. Traded to Sox in October '55, hit .268 in 1956 with 24 homers and 102 RBIs. Fell off to 14, 79, .288 in '57 before being traded to Baltimore. Orioles dealt him to Cleveland before Opening Day '58, and he hit .283 with 13 homers as part-timer for Indians.

During '59: Opened season as Detroit's leftfielder but soon lost starting job and was hitting .218 when sold to Sox May 13. For Sox, was 14-for-58 (.241) with 0 homers and 9 RBIs. Sent to Triple-A San Diego August 1 to make room for pitcher Ken McBride, broke ankle while sliding and missed chance to be activated September 1 for stretch drive.

After '59: Was in Sox camp in '60 but retired when he was released. Later was hitting instructor for Cleveland and Montreal before joining Sox in same capacity in 1977. Named to replace the fired Bob Lemon as Sox manager in June 1978 by Bill Veeck, the man who first signed him, and team went 37-50 rest of season, his only one as a manager. Voted into Hall of Fame, 1998. Still works for Major League Properties Inc. Lives in Montclair, N.J.

35 BOB SHAW, *Pitcher*

Before '59: After five years in Detroit system, was traded to Sox on June 15, 1958 and, in 29 games for Sox, including three starts, was 4-2 with a 4.64 ERA.

During '59: After allowing three earned runs in 14 relief jobs covering 24 1/3 innings, was given chance to start May 13 in Boston and responded with five-hit shutout, winning spot in rotation. Ended up 18-6 with 2.69 ERA and three shutouts. Among biggest wins: 2-1 over Yankees July 18 in New York; 5-0 over Yanks August 23 in Chicago; 7-3 over Indians in opener of August 28-30 series in Cleveland; and 1-0 over Detroit and Jim Bunning September 18 at Chicago, cutting magic number to 2. Lost Game 2 of World Series but was winner of 1-0 thriller in Game 5.

After '59: Dropped to 13-13, 4.06 ERA in '60, then was traded in June 1961 to Kansas City. Was 15-9 with 2.80 ERA for Milwaukee Braves in '62, and 16-9, 2.64 in '65 with Giants. Last year was '67, when he was a combined 3-11 for Mets and Cubs. Returned to Sox for spring training in '68 but was released. Worked as pitching coach in Dodger system, then for Milwaukee Brewers. Authored a book on the art of pitching. Lives in Jupiter, Florida, where he is in real estate development and also runs a business that installs synthetic-turf golf courses.

38 NORM CASH, *First Baseman*

Before '59: A 13th-round draft pick by the Bears out of Sul Ross College in Texas after 1954 season but instead signed with Sox on May 20, 1955. Played at Waterloo in '55 with Messrs. Romano, Latman, McAnany et al., and hit .290 with 17 homers, then hit .334 with 23 homers and 96 RBIs for same club in '56. Spent all of '57 and part of '58 in military service, hitting .247 in 29 games at Indianapolis in '58. Then hit .290 with seven homers in 30 games in Venezuelan winter league.

During '59: Won Sox's first-base job late in spring training, hitting .417 with three homers—all in last week of exhibitions. Hit two homers first week of season but tailed off and lost starting job, finishing at .240 and 4 homers but .378 on-base percentage. Was 0-for-4 as pinch-hitter in World Series. Traded to Cleveland in Minoso deal that December.

After '59: Dealt to Detroit before Opening Day 1960, spent rest of career with Tigers, hitting 373 more home runs, belting 30 or more five times. Was AL batting champ in '61 when he hit .361 with 41 homers and 132 RBIs. Hit .385 with homer in '68 World Series. Finished 17-year career with .271 lifetime batting average and .377 on-base percentage. Died in 1986.

42 AL LOPEZ, *Manager*

Before '59: Had set all-time record for games caught (1,918) in 18-year career with Dodgers, Braves, Pirates and Indians before turning to managing in 1948 at Indianapolis, Cleveland's top farm. Took over as Cleveland manager in '51 and never finished lower than second, beating out Yankees for '54 pennant with club that won 111 games (in 154-game schedule). Resigned at Cleveland after '56 season, named Sox manager that November. His '57 and '58 Sox teams had finished second to Yankees.

During '59: His team won 35 of 50 one-run games en route to franchise's first pennant since 1919.

After '59: Sox fell to third, then fourth and fifth before three successive second-place finishes ('63-'65), when Sox won 94, 98 and 95 games. Retired after '65 season but returned to replace Eddie Stanky briefly in '68 and for first 17 games of '69 season. Overall winning percentage .581. Hall of Fame 1977. Still lives in hometown of Tampa, Florida.

MARCH

New Owners, Old Problems

Charles A. "Chuck" Comiskey II was an angry young man. In fact, he had been an angry young man all winter long. The 33-year-old native of the Chicago suburb of Hinsdale, Illinois, since late 1955 the nominal front-office chief of the Chicago White Sox, was angry with his sister, Dorothy Comiskey Rigney, who had sold her 54 percent interest in the ballclub to a fellow native of Hinsdale, one Bill Veeck. Thus he was angry, too, with Bill Veeck, whom he was attempting to stop—via rather hopeless litigation—from taking formal control of the team founded by his grandfather at the turn of the century.

Finally, he was still angry at his baseball team, which had opened the 1958 season in a stupor, had played under .500 ball until early August, and had finally limped home at 82-72, a distant second behind the perennial American League champion New York Yankees. The sad showing on the field had been reflected at the turnstiles: The White Sox had drawn only 797,451 fans to Comiskey Park, by far their lowest figure since the long-forgotten dark days of 1950, the year before the Sox had climbed out of the second division to begin their string of what would become 17 consecutive winning seasons.

Most of the anger, however, stemmed from the very idea that Chuck's sister would have the audacity to sell her shares, and thus controlling interest in the ballclub, to an outsider and let the team pass out of the Comiskey family's hands. The actual sale of the club was completed on March 10, 1959, and Comiskey, formerly the wheeler-dealer, was suddenly reduced to the role of a mere minority stockholder, owner of 46 percent of the ballclub, still having the ear of his trusted manager, Al Lopez, but no longer the man running things.

"We all felt a little bad for Chuck," remembered Billy Pierce, the left-handed pitcher who had toiled for Comiskey since 1949, "because he was kind of our age. And there was some closeness there."

And, noted Sammy Esposito, the Chicago-born utility infielder who had signed with the Sox out of Indiana University in 1952: "Chuck was like one of the guys. You'd see him at spring training, go out and have a beer, go get a meal with him. He was very congenial, friendly, and was part of the ballclub. I always got the feeling he would've loved to have been one of the ballplayers. He loved the game, grew up in it. He was marvelous. We were very fortunate to have played under him for all those years."

It is possible that, had it not been for the disappointing 1958 performance of those young men who so enjoyed playing for Comiskey, he still would have been the man running the show as spring training opened in Tampa. The alarming drop in attendance caused by the '58 Sox's lackluster play surely provided Dorothy Comiskey Rigney as much of an impetus to look for a buyer as did her growing weariness with her younger brother's bent for filing lawsuit after lawsuit designed to wrest away control of the club.

"See, I thought in '57 we were gonna win—actually, we should've won it," said Comiskey, remembering how his team had held a six-game lead over the Yankees that June. "Well, anyway, we didn't. So I'm optimistic going into the '58 season. So we go out, and the chemistry, the whole attitude, it wasn't there.

"Everybody was flat. So I was angry. That's the fall I cut everybody 10 percent. Fox, Pierce, all of them. Ten percent. And I had talked with Senor Lopez, and he told me he wanted them all in camp the next spring, on time and signed. When I mailed out the contracts, I told them that Mr. Lopez wanted them all in camp on time, contracts signed, that we felt we could win the pennant. And that if they performed in 1959 like we felt they could perform, they would be rewarded in 1960.

"Well, they grumbled a little, but everyone sent back their contracts signed. Except Donovan."

Dick Donovan, the outstanding right-hander from Quincy, Massachusetts, had gone 16-6 with a 2.77 earned-run average in 1957 but started out '58 by losing 10 of his first 13 decisions. He rallied to finish 15-14 with a 3.01 ERA, which, in his mind, didn't merit a 10 percent paycut. Not only that, he had gotten married during the off-season and thus, if anything, was counting on a salary increase.

"We went back and forth on the phone I don't know how many times," said Comiskey, "and so finally we were about $6,000 apart. I had decided in my own mind I'd split the difference, go up $3,000 from my figure. But he wasn't going to budge from his figure. Well, we wanted everyone in camp and signed. So I told my secretary to make out a contract with no figure filled in, and I'd sign it. And she screamed. 'You can't do that!' 'Why not?' 'He's liable to write in $100,000.' That was huge money in those days. I said, 'No, I trust Dick. You go ahead and send it out.'

"Well, I hear nothing from Dick. Finally, we go to Tampa, first day for pitchers and catchers to report, and here comes Donovan toward me. 'You screwed me,' he says to me. 'Now Dick, how can you say that to me, a good Christian? How did I screw you?' He just says, 'You screwed me,' and he hands me an envelope. 'Here's the contract.' I say, 'Thanks, Dick,' and I put it in my pocket. And he looks at me, incredulously, figuring I wanted to know immediately what figure he had written down. And I just walk away. So, later, I pull out the contract, and you know what? He had split the difference, too. He had written in the figure I was going to give him."

Having all the players signed and in camp didn't solve all the White Sox's problems, however, such as sorting out the new ownership setup, figuring out who was going to play first base and third base—an annual White Sox spring ritual—and trying to find someone besides Sherm Lollar capable of hitting the long ball on a regular, or even semiregular, basis. (Lack of power always had been a problem, but particularly so since the trades of Minnie Minoso to Cleveland and Larry Doby to Baltimore in December '57).

First was the matter of the front office. As March began, other teams' executives still were unclear as to whom they were to speak should they wish to talk trade with the White Sox. On the other hand, Comiskey, fellow club vice president John Rigney (Chuck's brother-in-law) and Veeck weren't talking much to each other. Veeck was talking, naturally, to his old friend and associate Hank Greenberg, who had joined him in his purchase of the Sox. But Greenberg and Al Lopez, who'd had a strained relationship in Cleveland and had parted company three years earlier, still were not on the best of terms. And Greenberg, like Veeck, wasn't making much headway with Comiskey in his attempts to work out an amicable agreement on how the club would operate or as to Comiskey's role in the new operation.

"I didn't really have that much of an ax to grind with Bill," Comiskey claimed. "I knew Mr. Allyn (Arthur C. Allyn Sr., father of the future Sox owners, Arthur Jr. and John) from Cleveland and St.

Louis. He was the money man behind all of Bill's operations. And I knew two or three other of Bill's associates. Newt Frye, for one. And Doug Casey, Mr. Allyn's partner, was a very good friend of mine. Older, but they were around the baseball scene. I had dinner with them a lot. Good people. The only one I really had trouble with in that whole situation was Greenberg. I would've made a deal, after Bill bought my sister's stock, but we could never get down to the nut-cracking.

"See, what they really needed, to get the better tax write-offs, was 80 percent of the stock. And then I would've retained 20 percent, with the right to buy back my (other) shares at a later time. In the meantime, we would've been able to set up the depreciation on the ballpark, the players, etc., etc. I was willing to do that. I mean, it would've benefited me too. But every time we'd come down to the 11th hour, Greenberg would come up with another idea and throw a monkey wrench into the whole thing. Unbelievable."

So that problem remained unsolved, as did the others—third base, first base and long-ball hitting. As the month moved along, the word coming back to Chicago from Tampa via the four Chicago papers—the *Tribune*, the *Daily News*, the *Sun-Times* and the *American*—was that Lopez was again figuring on Bubba Phillips and aging Billy Goodman as a third-base platoon; that graybeards Ray Boone and Earl Torgeson and even the former bonus baby, 6-foot-7-inch Ron Jackson, all figured in the first-base picture; and that long-ball support for Lollar most likely would have to come from two rookies up from Indianapolis— leftfielder Johnny Callison, who turned 20 on the 12th of the month, and backup catcher John "Honey" Romano, 24. And how often did rookies make a big impact on the White Sox?

As a result of the business as usual coming out of Tampa, folks back in Chicago weren't paying too much attention to what was happening on Florida's Gulf Coast. Their interest was devoted more to the race for mayor between the incumbent, Richard J. Daley, and his Republican challenger, Timothy P. Sheehan, who predicted that labor racketeering, gambling and other crime would rouse the citizens and cause them to vote Daley out of office in April. The sports headlines were being made by the Chicago Cardinals, who traded star running back Ollie Matson to the Los Angeles Rams for seven players and two high draft choices, and by the Blackhawks, who, led by the brilliant youngster Bobby Hull and the veteran Eddie Litzenberger, were preparing to take on the world champion Montreal Canadiens in the Stanley Cup playoffs.

And the hottest sports rumor was that coach Ray Meyer was going to leave DePaul to fill the vacancy left at Wisconsin by the retiring Bud Foster.

In other news that March, comedian Lou Costello died of a heart attack at age 53, and former heavyweight champion Joe Louis got married—for the fourth time. American Airlines announced the nation's first jet service from Chicago to San Francisco would begin March 22 and that the trip would take just 4 hours 10 minutes, 2 1/2 hours faster than any other airline. President Eisenhower signed the bill, paving the way for Hawaii to become the 50th state, and in far-off Tibet, Chinese Communist soldiers put down a rebellion led by supporters of the Dalai Lama. Also, the new Cuban leader, Fidel Castro, declared with a straight face that elections in his country would have to be delayed for two years to give opposition parties time to develop their policies and platforms.

In the book stores that month, the top sellers were *Dr. Zhivago*, *Lolita*, *The Ugly American* and *Exodus*, all of which later would become rather successful movies. In the record shops, the hot hits included "Come Softly to Me" by the Fleetwoods, "The Happy Organ" by Dave "Baby" Cortez, "It's Late" by Ozzie and Harriet Nelson's youngest son, Ricky, and Brook Benton's "It's Just a Matter of Time."

In Florida, it was just a matter of time before the Chicago writers began poking a bit of fun at the White Sox's ineffective offense. On the 27th of the month, the *American's* Warren Brown, after pointing out that Callison and Romano had both homered in the team's third exhibition game on March 9 but that no Sox player had hit anything even remotely resembling a home run since, wrote in his column of a clinic put on by the Sox for an assemblage of Tampa youths before a game with Detroit. Wrote Brown: "Nelson Fox, Luis Aparicio, Jim Landis, John Callison, Jim Rivera, Earl Battey and Ron Jackson all participated in demonstrations of how double plays are made, how baserunner leads are taken, how a cutoff play is made, and so on. There was no hitting demonstration, program chairman Ed Short being smart enough to know that if the kids in the stands wanted to see hitting, they'd wait till the Tigers arrived."

With almost all of his off-season having been spent in various Cook County courtrooms, Comiskey hadn't had much time to address the team's hitting problems. Indeed, the only new non-pitching addition was Lou Skizas, an outfielder from Chicago's West Side who, after showing initial promise with the Yankees and Kansas City Athletics, had plummeted all the way to Detroit's Charleston farm. His .163 average there impressed no one, save Comiskey, who promptly drafted him, perhaps because Skizas' dad ran a restaurant frequented by Sox fans at 35th Street and Racine Avenue, just a few blocks west of Comiskey Park.

Thus, the club's only real hope for added everyday offense was Callison, who had enjoyed a terrific September with the Sox after leading the American Association in '58 with 29 home runs—while hitting .283 and driving in 93 runs—at age 19. At age 18, after signing with the Sox out of high school—for $3,000 by the exceptionally productive scouting team of "Sloppy" Thurston and "Doc" Bennett—he had gone to work immediately for his hometown Bakersfield team in the Class C California League. There, in a league dominated by another future All-Star outfielder, Vada Pinson, he hit .340 with 17 homers, 61 RBIs and 31 stolen bases—in just 86 games. Justifiably excited, the Sox invited him to spring training in March '58 and decided to use him as the main focus of a promotional film depicting the development of White Sox farmhands as they advanced to the big leagues. The film, when completed, would be shown not only to prospective Sox signees and their parents but also to potential season-ticket buyers.

"Actually," Callison recalled, "they started it in the winter of '57-'58, in California. And they never paid me anything, no. They told me they'd give me a couple hundred dollars, to just step in the batting cage, take some swings. And they ended up making the whole movie about me, and didn't pay me nothin'. But I was just a kid from Bakersfield. What the hell did I know? But anyway, they went on and on, filming, followed me all over the place the next season with Indianapolis. What'd I get out of it? I got a film. And yeah, I still have it. It's in color. Well, it started out in color. But it's so old, it's now black and white."

Truth be told, there was not much colorful, either, about Callison's showing in the exhibition games that spring. Through March 15, he was only 3-for-22, one of the hits that homer in Game 3. "I was trying to hit home runs," he remembered. "I thought I was a home run hitter. So I kept overswinging, kept striking out, silly stuff." Yet Lopez stayed with him, letting him play every exhibition game and naming him his Opening Day leftfielder, convinced the 5'10", 175-pounder was a star in the making.

Remembered Lopez, 38 springs later, "John was a hell of a good-looking prospect. He had a good, live bat. He could run good. He was just a kid. I didn't how good he was gonna be. But I thought he had a good chance to be a real good ballplayer."

Lopez wasn't alone. Scouts from other clubs were also high on Callison. Their consensus report, from the March 1959 issue of *Baseball Digest*, went as follows: "Fine all-around ability. Fields well, has good arm, runs well, hits to all fields with power. Can be pitched to because of lack of experience, but should overcome that. Not quite ready for majors"—Lopez apparently disagreed with that part— "but best prospect seen all season (1958)."

Not surprisingly, then, Callison was the runaway preseason pick to win the American League Rookie of the Year award in two separate writers' polls (Ron Fairly of the Dodgers and a Phillies second baseman named George "Sparky" Anderson were the choices in the NL), and his teammates couldn't help being impressed the previous September, when he'd hit .297 with four doubles, two triples and a homer and 12 RBIs in just 18 games. "He had great tools," Sammy Esposito remembered. "It was just a matter of putting it all together. He was like a miniature Mickey Mantle type. Good power, built good, ran good, threw well above average."

But he wasn't hitting that March, so the quest for added offense resumed. It did so quietly at first, Lopez huddling with manager Mayo Smith and GM Gabe Paul of the Cincinnati Reds, the Sox's co-tenants at Tampa's Al Lopez Field, to discuss a possible exchange of veteran outfielders, the Sox's Don Mueller for the Reds' Del Ennis. Ennis had dropped from 24 homers and 105 RBIs in 1957 to three and 47 in 1958, the kind of White Sox-type power numbers that perhaps had caught Lopez's eye. Then, talks became a bit more open when Billy Jurges, Washington coach and also the Senators' top trade consultant, stopped in on March 26 for a visit with Lopez that lasted almost an entire evening. Jurges told reporters that Washington slugger Roy Sievers, who had hit 42 and 39 home runs the previous two seasons, was the man the Sox wanted, and the Senators were mulling over a list of players from which they would choose as many as five—among them supposedly Esposito, Earl Battey, Bubba Phillips, Ray Moore and Jim Rivera. "Lopez knows what he wants, and I'm sure Cookie and Mr. Griffith know what they'd take from the Sox," said Jurges, referring to Senators manager Cookie Lavagetto and owner Calvin Griffith. "It's just a question of them getting together."

Of course, the two clubs had been trying to get together on a Sievers deal since the winter of 1955-56, or as Warren Brown noted, "since the days of Marty Marion, back at a time when Lopez and Hank Greenberg were buddy-buddy at Cleveland and Lou Skizas hadn't yet been discovered." Years later Comiskey revealed, "Go back to '56. I packaged Lollar in a deal for Sievers. There were other names, too, but those two would've been the headliners in the trade. But I could never get 'Griff' to agree on it."

Lopez had no reason to believe that pattern would change, so he already had decided he would step up his running game. He had realized that, in 1958, Luis Aparicio had stolen 29 bases and been caught only six times, and that Jim Landis had been successful on 19 of 26 steal attempts. If opposing catchers weren't going to be able to throw them out, then why not, thought Lopez, simply have Aparicio and Landis try to run more often? So he decided to turn them loose on the bases. By so doing, his team would steal more bases and, by disrupting opposing pitchers and defenses, steal more ballgames, too.

Recalled Landis, "He came to Looie and me in spring training and told us we had the green light—'unless.' Which was definitely different than in '58 and the year before that. In other words, we had the green light unless the coach told us no. But that didn't happen too often in '59."

"I had gotten used to only stealing when the ballclub needed it," remembered Aparicio. "The reason he let me go (in '59) was because the percentages were in favor of the ballclub. I didn't steal for my own record. I stole because that was what we had to do to score runs. Sherman was the biggest RBI man on the club, and he only had 80 something that year."

"The way I played it," confirmed Lopez, "I put Aparicio and Landis on their own and let them steal. Get a jump and steal. Sometimes, with Aparicio on, we'd have to put the take sign on for Fox. Nellie was an aggressive hitter, liked to hit everything. We'd have to put the take sign on to give Aparicio a chance to steal. But for the other guys, we wouldn't put the take sign on. Looie was stealing, and if the guy swung and got a base hit, Looie would go to third. Or, if the guy hit a ground ball, we'd at least be out of the double play.

"But with Aparicio, the percentage, with no outs, is to let him steal. Now you have him at second with no outs, and now Nellie can hit, pull the ball, bunt, get him over to third. And a sacrifice fly or something like that, and you've got the run."

So this was how it was going to be. The White Sox would steal and scratch for runs, perhaps get the long ball now and then from Lollar and, hopefully, Callison, and then depend on the defense—Lollar, Aparicio, Fox and Landis provided the best in baseball up the middle— and the pitching to hold the opposition. Lopez had no real concerns about his pitching. Pierce and Donovan both had finished strong in '58, combining for 32 victories between them. And though Wynn had struggled somewhat (14-16, 4.12) in '58, his first year in Chicago, he'd led the league in strikeouts at age 38 and now, in spring camp, he was the staff's most effective pitcher. Expected to take over as the No. 4 starter was 22-year-old righthander Barry Latman, brilliant (3-0, 0.75 over 48 innings) in the final two months of the '58 season. "Barry was a big, strong kid," said Lopez. "Could throw real hard." But Latman's father had died in mid-March, and the pitcher missed a week while he attended to funeral and other family matters back home in Los Angeles. So Lopez began paying extra notice to the fine spring work of another young righthander, Bob Shaw, tentatively scheduled for bullpen duty with Ray Moore, rookie lefties Don Rudolph and Rodolfo Arias and the two veteran late-inning men, Gerry Staley and Turk Lown. And Lopez wasn't the only one noticing Shaw.

"In camp that spring," remembered Jack Kuenster, longtime editor of *Baseball Digest* and then a baseball beat writer for the *Chicago Daily News*, "I used to see Nellie Fox standing out there at second base with his arms folded, just watching when Bob Shaw was on the mound, warming up. He'd watch and watch and watch. And I asked him one time what he was doing out there, and he said he was just watching to see how Shaw's ball was sinking. That sinking fastball. So Fox knew then that Shaw was going to be a big man."

Shaw merely was hoping for the opportunity to show he could be a big man. He had pitched winter ball in Cuba for a second straight year and was ahead of many of the pitchers in camp because of it.

"I beat Puerto Rico—Juan Pizarro and Roberto Clemente and those guys—2-0 for Cuba in the final game of the Caribbean Series, and I was Most Valuable Player in the series," Shaw said. "That was in the winter of '57-58, when I was still with Detroit. Then I went back and pitched the next winter in Cuba. I didn't have quite the success I'd had the previous winter, but things were different."

In fact, the differences were, well, revolutionary.

"I was pitching right during the revolution," he recalled. "I was there in Havana when Castro came into town, you bet. January 1st. So things were different. They had guns, people were shooting at each other. Oh, yeah. I mean, it was a different ballgame. I remember

January 1st. I thought there were firecrackers going off, but those weren't firecrackers. They were shooting the guards at the Havana prison. I mean, we were kinda hiding. I was sleeping in the bathtub because there was a lot of gunfire and hand grenades and everything going off. And then we kept thinking it was gonna get better, and it didn't. Finally, it did calm down.

"And at the ballpark, the Cuban guerrillas, they would be in the dugout or on top of it, with guns. I remember I was pitching one game and a couple shots rang out, and I ran and dove into the dugout, and it was a concrete dugout. So it was somewhat distracting.

"But I'd had such a good winter the year before, it was going to be hard to duplicate it. I pitched well, just not as well. But it certainly was good preparation for spring training."

This spring training, despite five straight rainouts in mid-March and the disappointing turnouts at Tampa—factors that caused Comiskey, Veeck & Co. to explore the possibility of moving their camp site to Sarasota—was going a long way toward establishing in the minds of Sox players the feeling that something special might lie ahead. Recalled Jack Kuenster: "The players themselves knew early that they had a good chance, that this could be their year. In spring training, via the grapevine, the word was that the Yankee pitching staff was in trouble, that their pitchers were hurting. And it proved out."

Indeed, rumors were flying that the Yankees were offering Washington five players—apparently all deals made with the Senators required an expenditure of five players—for pitcher Pedro Ramos, the hard-throwing Cuban righthander. Yankee manager Casey Stengel moved to silence the rumors: "A lot of people are havin' me make deals with Washington or somebody. I ain't so sure that's what I want to do, because sometimes you wonder about lettin' stuff you have get away for somethin' maybe you don't really need as bad as some people think you do." Even so, the thought that Yankee pitchers were not themselves— Cy Young Award winner Bob Turley's fastball was missing in action, Johnny Kucks was awful and Don Larsen and Tom Sturdivant were nursing sore arms—cheered one and all in the Sox spring camp, even Billy Pierce, who had been in Sox spring camps since 1949 and must have started wondering at some point whether he was doomed to a career of finishing second to the Yankees.

"We always thought, 'This could be the year,'" he said, "because with a few changes two or three years there, we could've won something. Key ballgames that we lost—mostly to the Yankees, but some to other clubs too—and then bingo, we'd lose two, three more in a row. If we'd won that one key ballgame, it's a different world. So we always thought we had a shot at it, because the Yankees weren't winning it by 20 games."

The feeling that the Yankees certainly would not do so this year was spreading through the entire Sox entourage, and Al Lopez, who had preached every March that the Yankees could be had, took special note of the improved sense of urgency, though overlooking the unimproved power hitting. Remembered Chuck Comiskey: "Lopez said to me, four weeks into spring training, 'I don't know what you did to these guys, but they all have a real good attitude. Their approach to the game is different, as opposed to last spring.' Now, whether it was, 'Let's stick Comiskey—then we'll really nail him to the cross next year,' or they looked in the mirror, like we all did, and realized we all could have done more in '58, I don't know. But Lopez said it, even before we left Tampa, 'We're gonna win it this year. The attitude's great, and I think we have the horses to do it. They really want to win. There's a really good attitude here.' Now, he'd been around enough ballclubs to know attitude."

Newcomer Lou Skizas noticed the attitude, too, and he noticed the respect accorded Lopez. He became almost an instant admirer of his newest team. Recalled Skizas, almost four decades later: "I played against the White Sox three years (with the Yankees, A's and Tigers), and I'd always wondered what kept that ballclub together, 'cause on paper they didn't look that good, but they'd always find a way to beat you. But then, when I got to spring training with them in '59, I saw what they had. They had a bunch of gutsy guys. That ballclub was probably the 'hustlingest' ballclub I ever saw. Before the game, watch your shoes and watch your jock strap, 'cause you never know where they're gonna end up, OK? Because the practical jokers are every place. But once the game starts, let me tell ya: You had Rivera, who'd be in the Hall of Fame if he could hit a baseball. I mean, he was absolutely spectacular. These guys today should see the way he played, hustling, diving all over the place. You had Fox. You couldn't get him out of the lineup, for heaven's sake. He'd break three bones and he'd show up ready to play the next day.

"You had Looie, Lollar, that great pitching staff. And I'll tell you what: Lopez was a no-nonsense guy. I never saw the kind of respect given to one man as I did with him. He was the Senor from Tampa, from Ybor City. He would absolutely take no shit. And I'll tell you something else. I was with the Yankees for a while and I went to spring training with them two or three years, and Stengel never had the respect from his players that Lopez had from his. No way.

"Yeah, the clubs I was with admired the White Sox for their heart, their enthusiasm and their fight. You had to do that, because they would never, ever beat themselves. You had a bunch of professionals—Donovan, Pierce, Wynn. You had the bullpen with Staley and Lown. Those guys were hard-core professionals. They knew how to pitch. And behind them, I mean, you never saw that kind of hustle. You don't see it today and you didn't see it back in those days. The White Sox were just absolutely exciting to watch."

Skizas was hoping he'd have the chance to watch them all season and perhaps contribute as a righthanded hitter off the bench. Hopeful, too, were his backers at the Austin Market on West Madison Street, Skizas' fellow West Siders who, Warren Brown wrote, "have never forgiven Stengel for letting Skizas go and keeping Mickey Mantle." It turned out that "the Nervous Greek," as Lou was called, was dealt away before the season was a month old, not knowing what he would be missing.

"I knew they had a good ballclub," he said, "but I didn't think they could beat the Yankees."

Neither, as March neared its end, did the great Red Sox leftfielder, Ted Williams, who intoned, "The White Sox can't be much, not if they have to put so much emphasis on Callison. How can you put so much emphasis on a rookie who hit only .283 at Indianapolis?"

Williams' negative comment couldn't suppress the positive vibes the White Sox were feeling, however, and when Pierce threw seven superb innings to beat the St. Louis Cardinals on March 31 in Tampa, the Sox had won their fourth straight. And even though Johnny Callison still wasn't hitting, and though Al Lopez still hadn't found a regular first baseman, an air of confidence was building.

On that same day, the Dow Jones Industrial Average closed at 602.65, down almost four points. But, at least in the players' eyes, the Chicago White Sox's stock was on the rise.

APRIL

Indications in Detroit

April arrived on a Wednesday with the news that Chicagoland barbers, certainly no fools, had voted 998-695 to raise the price of a haircut from $1.75 to $2. Mickey Rooney was in his final week at the Chez Paree, Sarah Vaughan was performing at Mister Kelly's and, at The Regal on the South Side, Lionel Hampton was headlining, with The Flamingos, Slappy White and Dee Clark also on the bill.

Providing a clue as to how negligible an impact the National Basketball Association had at the time on Chicago-area sports fans, the *Tribune* covered the NBA draft with a six-inch story on Page 3 of the April 2 sports section. The Philadelphia Warriors selected Kansas All-American Wilt Chamberlain with the first pick, and other notable selections included Bob Boozer by the Cincinnati Royals, Bailey Howell by the Detroit Pistons and Tom Hawkins by the Minneapolis Lakers.

In Tampa, meanwhile, the clock was ticking down the White Sox's final hours at Al Lopez Field. GM Gabe Paul of the Reds remarked that "Tampa is not big enough for both" his club and the Sox. But when only 2,464 people showed up to watch the Reds and Sox play on "Appreciation Night" April 2, Paul likely had cause to wonder if perhaps Tampa was even big enough for one team. The Sox, though, were more than happy to leave Tampa to the Reds, and two days later Bill Veeck and Chuck Comiskey announced the signing of a five-year contract making Sarasota, Florida, effective in 1960, the team's new spring-training base. Five years became 38 until, in 1998, the club moved its spring operations to Tucson. Al Lopez Field, named for Tampa's most famous sports son, was not blessed with similar longevity.

"They tore it down a few years ago, you know. I outlasted my field," Al Lopez chuckled in the spring of 1997.

In the spring of 1959, Lopez wasn't chuckling when newspaper people wrote that he had no first baseman. No doubt that annoyed him, but so did the fact that what was being written was essentially true. As the month began, neither veterans Ray Boone nor Earl Torgeson nor 25-year-old Ron Jackson had seized the opening. Jackson, in fact, had gone 3-for-29 in the spring games. "We thought he was gonna be a hell of a ballplayer," remembered Lopez, "and he never developed the way he should've. Big, tall kid. He could hit the ball a mile. He hit one in Denver—I think they're still looking for the ball." Actually, it was found, an estimated 542 feet from home plate that day in April '58 when Jackson's blast had helped the Sox beat St. Louis and helped him wrap up a starting job. A year later, though, Jackson was becoming a forgotten man, and a new camp sensation was about to make heads turn.

Norman Dalton Cash, age 24, from Justiceburg, Texas, had spent most of March playing outfield in morning "B" games, contests conducted in near privacy. He had to be thinking he, like Jackson, was becoming a forgotten man. Signed by the White Sox in May 1955 out of Sul Ross College in Texas after also receiving an offer from the Chicago Bears, the onetime football star had gone to Waterloo, Iowa, and hit .290 with 17 homers in 92 games. For the same club in 1956, the lefthanded hitter had belted 23 home runs and batted .334. Then he had gone into the Army, in effect costing him the '57 and '58 seasons. However, he had pleased the Sox, or so he thought, by playing winter ball with Luis Aparicio's Rapinos team in Venezuela, where he had hit .290 with seven homers in just 30 games. He had arrived in Tampa confident he would have the opportunity to make an impression. As camp wound down, however, he could have been forgiven for wondering if he had made the correct career choice. True, he had been only a 13th-round pick of the Bears, but in those days, when the NFL consisted of just 12 teams, a 13th-round pick was equivalent to a fifth- or sixth-rounder today.

"Papa Bear Halas gave me a call one day after we had signed Norm Cash," Chuck Comiskey recalled. "Irene Kerwin, the girl on the board, said, 'You have a call from Mr. Halas.' 'George, how are ya?' He says, 'Charlie, what are you doing?' 'What do you mean, what am I doing?' 'You signed one of my football players.' 'What do you mean?' 'Cash. That kid out of Texas. My people down there'—Halas always had "my people" everywhere— 'tell me he really wanted to play football. He's a good running back. I was really looking forward to having him come into camp.' I said, 'Well, we like his bat a little bit, George. Our scouts say he can really pop those wrists when he swings that bat.'

"I'll tell you a compliment paid Norm Cash by a pretty good hitter himself, Rogers Hornsby. Rog went down to spring training a couple of years to help our kids with their batting. He saw Cash the first time in the spring of '56, and that's all he would talk about around the coffee shop that spring: 'That's the best set of wrists I've seen on a kid in years. He is really quick. He's got a couple little things he needs to work on, but you just don't find wrists like that anymore. He can cock that bat and he can wait on that pitch until the last second. He's quick enough to get that bat around.'"

Now, three springs later, things were about to fall into place for Cash. On April 1, after getting only four "A" game at-bats all spring, he was given a chance by the still-searching Lopez to play an entire game at a new position, first base. He responded with two hits and a run batted in against the Milwaukee Braves. Two days later, against the Cardinals, he had a single and a triple, making him 5-for-11. Lopez was noticing. "I'll use him a lot in the remaining exhibition games," he told reporters. "So far his inexperience at first base hasn't hurt us, and if he keeps hitting I won't be afraid to gamble with him."

Cash kept hitting. There was a homer against the Pirates on April 4, the Sox's final game in Tampa, followed by a 400-foot triple, another homer and four RBIs in a victory over the Senators April 6 in Charlotte, N.C. That gave him eight hits—including two doubles, two triples and two homers—in 17 "A" at-bats. Said Lopez: "Cash is definitely in the running now to open the season at first for us."

The next afternoon, Cash won the Opening Day first baseman's job by hitting another home run plus a single against Cincinnati's Triple-A farm team in Nashville to raise his average to .500. And even though he went hitless, as did most of his teammates, the next day in Indianapolis against Reds rookie lefty Jim O' Toole, a 21-year-old from the South Side of Chicago, Cash nonetheless finished the exhibition season with a .417 average and a team-high three home runs. On the plane that night to Detroit, Lopez made it official: Cash would bat fifth and play first base in the season-opener Friday at Briggs Stadium against the Tigers' Jim Bunning.

That news capped a noteworthy few days, not only for Cash. That Monday, the Republicans had announced that they had selected Chicago as the site for their 1960 national convention. Monday evening, David Niven ("Separate Tables") and Susan Hayward ("I Want to Live") were honored as Best Actor and Best Actress at the Academy

Awards, and there were nine Oscars for "Gigi," including the one for Best Picture. On Tuesday, Mayor Daley had captured 71 percent of the vote to win re-election over Republican congressman Timothy P. Sheehan, and "Rio Bravo," starring John Wayne, Dean Martin and Angie Dickinson, made its Midwest premiere at the Chicago Theatre. Thursday had brought word of the death of Frank Lloyd Wright at age 89, and on that same day seven test pilots were selected for Project Mercury, NASA's program designed to send a man into space and bring him back. The chosen seven: Scott Carpenter, Leroy "Gordy" Cooper, John Glenn, Virgil "Gus" Grissom, Wally Schirra, Alan Shepard and Don "Deke" Slayton.

But for the White Sox, the highlight of this week was to be Friday's opener, when they would begin to attempt to show the baseball experts the error of their ways. Oh, columnist David Condon, as was his custom, picked the Sox to win the pennant, as did his young *Chicago Tribune* colleague, beat writer Richard Dozer, who noted the Sox had played .588 ball after June 13 the year before, a better percentage than any team in baseball over that same period. But these two were alone in their optimistic assessment. Warren Brown of The *American* put them down for second place, noting, "I don't suppose they ever will get over the blind staggers that seize them every time the Yankees are in sight." The *Daily News'* John Carmichael and Jack Kuenster both picked them for third, behind the Yankees and Tigers, who had traded with Washington for a new left side of the infield (third baseman Eddie Yost and shortstop Rocky Bridges) and with Cleveland for pitching help (Don Mossi and Ray Narleski) and for an outfielder (Larry Doby) who always had hit well in Briggs Stadium.

At the *Sun-Times*, sports editor Dick Hackenberg not only had the Yankees and Tigers finishing ahead of the Sox, but the Cleveland Indians as well, the Tribe having been strengthened by GM Frank Lane's deals with Detroit for second baseman Billy Martin and with Boston for centerfielder Jimmy Piersall. The same paper's Gene Kessler and Edgar Munzel picked the Sox second to the Yankees, and Jerome Holtzman (then known as "Jerry") had them third, behind New York and Detroit. Nationally, the picture was pretty much the same: *The Sporting News'* annual poll of baseball writers—this time 226 of them —foresaw a Yankees runaway, with Detroit second and the White Sox third. Only five voters picked the Sox to win. (In the National League poll, the Milwaukee Braves were the overwhelming choice, with the eventual champion, Los Angeles, the pick for fifth. Only two writers picked the Dodgers to finish first). Finally, J.G. Taylor Spink, editor of *The Sporting News*, weighed in with his selections: Yankees and White Sox, 1-2.

As for Yankee manager Casey Stengel, he had no doubt his team was going to win its fifth straight pennant, even though Yogi Berra had hit .119 in the spring exhibitions, Hank Bauer .146 and Mickey Mantle .238 and despite the fact Berra and Mantle were nursing sore arms and Bill Skowron was in the hospital with a strained back. Casey talked of how he could platoon lefthanded-hitting outfielders Norm Siebern and Enos Slaughter with righthanded hitters Elston Howard and Bauer, mentioned he could flip-flop Andy Carey and lefty Jerry Lumpe at third and do the same with Tony Kubek and Bobby Richardson at short. Then, in summation, Stengel proclaimed to New York beat writer Joe Trimble: "I've got this league by the ass." All Al Lopez would say in response was: "I know we're better than last year. And I don't think we're gonna get off to the same slow start we had last year. So the Yankees better not get too overconfident."

First, however, there was the matter of the Tigers and Opening Day on Friday, April 10. Despite a gametime temperature of 37 degrees, a crowd of 38,322 fans—some, it soon became apparent, well fortified with alcohol—turned out to see if the Tigers were as improved as most everyone in the media seemed to believe. "It was freezing," recalled the *Daily News'* Jack Kuenster. "I even wrote down the temperature on my score sheet—it was 33 degrees when the game ended. And Bill Veeck, I remember, was there in an open sport shirt, and we were freezing up in the press box. They had a heater going up there, too. It didn't help."

Nonetheless, the game went on, with Jim Bunning and Billy Pierce dueling into the fifth, when the White Sox scored twice on Jim Landis' home run and the Tigers scored three to go ahead 4-3. That's how the score stood until the top of the seventh, when, with two out and no-body on, ex-Yankee Tom Morgan walked Johnny Callison, allowed a single to Bubba Phillips and then walked Earl Torgeson, who was hit-ting for Pierce's replacement, Turk Lown. Lopez sent up Billy Goodman to bat for Luis Aparicio, and Goodman hit a soft liner to the left of the Tigers' new leftfielder, Larry Doby. Doby moved over, reached up and dropped the ball for an error. All three runners scored, making it 6-4 Chicago, and when Nellie Fox followed with a single off Ray Narleski to score Goodman, it was 7-4 and the crowd, already a bit unruly, became more so. Altogether, play was halted four times by fans entering the playing field. But there was more.

Recalled Callison, the 20-year-old leftfielder playing in his first major-league opener: "People were throwing shit at me in the outfield. I had an empty fifth of whiskey come flyin' over my head. Just missed me. And somebody got me in the head with a marble. I was a little shaky out there anyway. I didn't need that. And there was one guy climbing up the foul pole. I'm thinking, 'What the hell is this? They don't do this in Bakersfield.'"

They did it in Detroit. Bill Veeck complained that there was no visible park security to speak of, and while that may have been true, he also could have complained that one member of his bullpen crew, Ray Moore, was providing no visible relief to speak of. With two out in the eighth, Moore walked Doby and Rocky Bridges, then served up a game-tying pinch home run to Charlie "Paw Paw" Maxwell, the popular Michigan native who had suddenly lost his starting left-field job to the newly arrived Doby. The stalemate was to continue into the 14th inning, although the Tigers had their chances, particularly in the 10th, when they loaded the bases with none out against Gerry Staley, the sixth Sox pitcher of the afternoon. But, in a preview of what was to come this weekend and throughout the season, Staley first dispatched a formidable pinch-hitter, Gus Zernial—36 but still dangerous—via a forceout at the plate. Then he got Eddie Yost to bounce one back to the mound to begin a pitcher-to-home-to-first double play. In the 12th, Callison, who had failed to get a hit all day, chipped in by gunning down a runner at second base with a perfect throw from the left-field corner.

So it went until two were out in the Sox 14th. Don Mossi had worked a scoreless 11th, 12th and 13th, effortlessly mowing down chilled Chicago batters. Up now was Sammy Esposito, who had taken over at short for Aparicio in the seventh. "Sure I remember," he said, laughing. "It was snowing, it was about 20 degrees or so. I think everybody on both teams was hoping somebody would just win and get it over with, no matter who won, it was so miserable out there. I remember I was lucky. My thumb was so cold on my throwing hand that when I got a couple ground balls over there at short, I couldn't feel the ball. I don't know how the hell I got it over to first."

Now, batting in the 14th, Esposito lined a ball to left for what his manager believed should have been a two-base hit but became just a single. "Lopez thought I should've gotten a double on it," said Esposito, "because to get to second base in a tie ballgame in extra innings is very big. But I was so darned cold, it was tough to loosen up, really." In the dugout, despite the cold, Lopez was hot, because he knew the next hitter, Nellie Fox, was more likely to get a single than an extra-base hit, especially against a tough lefty like Mossi. Esposito, had he been at second base instead of first, could score easily on a single. But just then, Lopez's thoughts were interrupted by the crack of the bat. Fox, who already had collected three singles and a double, drilled an inside fastball down the right-field line, toward the corner, where the sign read 325. The ball just made it into the stands, and the White Sox, on Fox's first home run since September 19, 1957, had a 9-7 lead.

Related Jack Kuenster, years later: "In batting practice—and I was down there at the batting cage when this happened—Fox hit one into the lower right-field seats, just inside the foul pole, for a home run. And the players really gave him the needle. And I'll always remember Nellie saying, 'Don't worry—you'll see more of those.' He was giving it right back to them. So sure enough, he hit a home run to win the game."

And when Gerry Staley got the first two outs in the Detroit half of the 14th and lefty Don Rudolph retired lefthanded pinch-hitter Neil Chrisley for the third out, off the hook were Al Smith, who had struck out four times; Ray Moore, whose gopher ball had let Detroit back into the game; and, finally, Sammy Esposito.

"Lopez did call me in after the game," Esposito remembered. "He was so happy we'd won the game, but I think if we'd have lost, he'd have fined me. He let me know that I should have been at second base on that ball."

Saturday brought a smaller crowd but, thankfully, a slightly bigger temperature: 39. Fittingly, the Sox starter was 39-year-old Early Wynn, already the winner of 249 games in his career. "Ol' Gus" set off in quest of No. 250 and quickly ran into some difficulty, as the Tigers loaded the bases with nobody out in the second inning. Then came another one of those early-season indicators that 1959 might be a different year for the White Sox. Wynn proceeded to strike out, in order, Detroit pitcher Paul Foytack, Eddie Yost and the eventual 1959 American League batting champion, Harvey Kuenn. Meanwhile, the Sox had scored in the first inning in what would become typical '59 fashion. With two outs, Jim Landis walked and then took off for second base as Foytack delivered to Sherm Lollar. Lollar blooped a single to center, and Landis didn't stop sprinting until he had crossed home plate with the game's first run. Later came Chicago runs in quite unusual fashion: Luis Aparicio homered with two out in the seventh off Ray Narleski to break a 3-3 tie, and Lollar, who already had homered once this afternoon, did it again in the eighth, also off Narleski, and now the score was 5-3. Wynn made it stand up, retiring the final 10 Tigers in order.

The next day, Norm Cash, who had singled twice in the opener, hit the first of his 377 career home runs, a two-run shot into the upper deck in right-center off Frank Lary, in a three-run first inning. Later came a triple by Landis and a single by Lollar to put the Sox ahead to stay in the seventh, followed by another stolen run in the eighth, when two errors, a Landis steal and a sacrifice fly by Al Smith made it 5-3 Chicago. But again the key was the escape act performed by the pitchers, this time rookie lefty Rodolfo Arias and second-year righthander Bob Shaw. First Arias entered in the seventh after Detroit had filled the bases with one out against starter Dick Donovan. The little Cuban calmly retired lefty-swinging Gail Harris on a called third strike, then got Gus Zernial, again pinch-hitting, on a pop fly to Smith in right. Then, with one out in the eighth, Turk Lown walked two Tigers and Don Rudolph walked one. Enter Shaw, who needed just one pitch, a sinking fastball, to make the danger disappear. Eddie Yost grounded the ball to Bubba Phillips, who stepped on third for one out and fired to Cash at first to complete the double play. Shaw closed things out with a scoreless ninth, and the White Sox headed home to Chicago in first place with a 3-0 record and with their manager actually saying the "P" word.

"Why shouldn't I talk pennant?" Al Lopez said to reporters after the team's charter landed at Midway Airport on the city's Southwest Side. "This is the fast start we've been looking for. Beating a club as good as Detroit three in a row can do wonders for a club like ours. We got off to a lousy start last season and the Yankees had an unbelievable one. In the last half of the season, we outplayed every other team in the league. With the kind of start we got in Detroit, this could be our year."

That's what Bill Veeck, in his apartment at the Sherry Hotel on South Shore Drive, was hoping, despite his continuing belief that the Sox needed another bat or two. Failing that, he planned to make it a fun year, anyway. Already he had promised several surprises for the home opener, Tuesday, April 14, but one of them, Fidel Castro, the new Cuban leader, had begged off an invitation to throw the ceremonial first pitch. So when the ageless Veeck favorite, Satchel Paige, asked for and received his release from the Triple-A Miami Marlins that Monday, the rumors began that one of Veeck's surprises would be the delivery, likely in dramatic fashion, of the 53-year-old former Negro leagues pitching star who had helped Veeck's Indians win the pennant in 1948. The only problem was that Lopez didn't want Paige around, and Veeck respected his manager's wishes. Wrote Veeck: "I felt Satch would help us. I knew he'd help us at the gate. But Al wants only the players who catch every plane and meet every roll call, and Satch wasn't a particularly good bet to catch the next streetcar."

Added Lopez, almost 40 years later: "Bill was like a godfather to Satchel. He loved Satchel. In 1956, when I was managing at Cleveland and Hank Greenberg was the general manager, Bill was running the club at Miami. And he had Satchel down there. And he used to call Greenberg up in Cleveland and say, 'Hank, tell Al to take Satchel up. He'll help him.' And I told Hank, 'I don't have any doubt at all that Satchel could help me. He can pitch. But I can't put up with that stuff where he'll show up whenever he feels like it. You gotta think about the morale on the club.'

"I don't have one thing in the world against Satchel Paige. I liked him, and I admired him because he was a hell of a pitcher. But I didn't want him on the club. And I give Bill Veeck credit for not asking me to take him in Chicago. Never once did he ask me to take him in Chicago. He knew I didn't want him and he was nice enough to never ask me if I'd take him. And I appreciated that, because I know he'd have loved to have him on his team again.

"See, Bill had talked to John Rigney about Satchel even before he got the Sox. We were at the winter meetings (in December 1958), going over players, and John Rigney brought up Satchel Paige. And I said, 'John, what do you want with Satchel Paige?' He didn't know that I'd turned him down a couple years before. John says, 'Well, I think he could help us, and he could help our attendance.' 'Well, I think he can pitch, John, but I think he'd hurt us more with the morale of the club. I don't think it's right to have a guy who comes when he feels like it.' And John said, 'Well, if you don't want him, Al, we won't take him.'"

Still, apparently there was always that concern in the back of Lopez's mind that Paige might indeed suddenly turn up in a Sox uniform. "We had been talking about sending Callison back down for a while, to get his feet back on the ground," said Chuck Comiskey, recalling a conversation he'd had with Lopez that May. "And Al said to me, 'Charlie, until there's a player ready to replace him, I will not leave an opening on the roster, because I won't have Paige on my ballclub. I don't trust Bill.' Now, he knew Bill. He said, 'I don't trust him. He'll bring Paige in by helicopter, put him down in the middle of the field and all that. I don't go for that bullshit. I don't want that. So I won't give you an opening on the roster.'"

Despite the rumors, then, the home opener went on without the delivery of Satchel Paige. Instead, the rather disappointing crowd of 19,303 was treated to Veeck, wooden leg and all, marching to the mound to throw the first pitch to an unexpected batterymate, Chuck Comiskey, in a somewhat disingenuous attempt to display to one and all that peace had arrived in the White Sox family. Then came the National Anthem, during which the fireworks crew Veeck had hired mistakenly launched bombs from behind the left-field wall toward the playing field instead of away from it. That sent players scurrying for cover and Veeck hustling out onto the left-field ramp to let the crew below know they were done for the day—and, as far as he was concerned, forever. Perhaps unbeknownst to Veeck and the fireworks people, earlier that day an Atlas ICBM had blown up almost upon lift-off at Cape Canaveral, scattering debris all over the launch area. Thus, it was not a good day for rockets.

It was, however, a good day for the White Sox, as Billy Pierce, who hadn't earned his first 1958 win until May 16, outdueled Kansas City's young Ralph Terry 2-0 in just 1 hour 55 minutes. The Sox scored their runs in the fifth, when Johnny Callison, 0-for-12 up to that point, opened the inning by beating out a bunt for his first '59 hit. Bubba Phillips followed with a double off the wall in left, sending Callison to third. Pierce walked to load the bases, and Luis Aparicio smashed a single past third baseman Hal Smith to score Callison and Phillips. And that was it, except for the announcement during the seventh inning that all liquid refreshment for the remainder of the game was on the house. The roar that greeted that news rivaled the one that followed Aparicio's decisive hit. What mattered most, though, was that the Sox had needed only four games to gain their fourth victory this season, whereas they had needed 13 to do so in 1958.

The inevitable defeat came the next day, when 22-year-old Barry Latman, who had missed time in spring training to return home to Los Angeles for the funeral of his father, was subjected to a third-inning knockout by the Athletics. The big blow was a grand slam by the Kansas City pitcher, Bob Grim. That made it 8-0 in the third, and Latman's next pitch nailed Joe DeMaestri above the left ear. "What do you mean, 'nail' somebody?" Latman said, in mock protest, almost four decades later. "That would be awful. You're not supposed to throw at people." DeMaestri, who had tripled in two runs his previous at-bat, was carried off on a stretcher. Latman was escorted off by Al Lopez, his 1959 debut over after just 2 2/3 innings. Afterwards, with Kansas City having held on for a 10-8 victory, a reporter asked Latman, "Wasn't your fastball moving?" The pitcher's droll reply: "It was moving, all right—to right field, to center field, to left field."

It was suggested to Latman, years later, that his poor first outing could have been partially blamed on the fact he had been set back in his conditioning by his March absence. "Who knows? I can't use that as an excuse," he said. "All I know is my dad died in the middle of spring training and I was gone for a week. He hadn't been sick. He just had a heart attack, and that was it. He was 48. They called me up and said he was gone."

The White Sox were glad to see the A's leave town after another loss in the series finale, this one administered by longtime Sox nemesis Ned Garver, who was now 24-15 lifetime against Chicago after his five-hit, 6-0 decision over Early Wynn. The next day, the stock market hit an all-time high as the Dow Jones Industrial Average went to 624.06, and Norm Cash hit his second homer in a week off Frank Lary, this a three-run blast, as the Sox won 6-5, keeping the Tigers winless through their first six games. After Detroit's Billy Hoeft beat Ray Moore on Saturday, Lopez penciled in Jim Rivera to play left field in place of the struggling Johnny Callison for Sunday's game. Rivera's pinch double two days before had beaten Detroit, and now he was getting his first start of the year. But Sunday brought temperatures near 40, and Veeck decided to cancel the game. Moaned Rivera in the clubhouse: "First day I get in the lineup, and they call it off." Chirped Lou Skizas in reply: "That's why they called it off."

Skizas was enjoying life with his hometown team and his road roommate, fellow Chicagoan Sammy Esposito. "There were always laughs," Skizas said, chuckling in recollection. "You had Rivera, you had Esposito. Sammy was a good-looking guy, good with the ladies. Jim was shy, and didn't look so good. Sammy and I had a lot of fun. Both Chicago guys, him from the South Side, me from the West Side. Both kinda cool and groovy, coming from the parks and the streets and the alleys of Chicago. We just blended real nicely."

Remembered Esposito: "Skizas—and Bob Shaw, too—were our two brain surgeons. Those guys were *too* intelligent. They were ahead of their time academically. You know, in the old days, to a lot of us, school wasn't as important as it is today. Those two guys were students. They read a lot. And Lou was really way out in left field. Good guy, though."

As the White Sox opened a two-game series Tuesday, April 21, in Kansas City, the guy out in left field again was Johnny Callison, even though he was 1-for-21 for a none-too-robust .048 batting average. "I didn't hit shit, I know that," said Callison, looking back. "It surprised me, yeah. I always thought I'd hit. But I was just overmatched for a while there." Even so, Lopez stuck with him. "Al was neat. He was really good to me. He was tougher on the veteran players than he was on us younger guys. I used to screw up, and he always had a seat right next to him in the dugout. And one of the coaches would come down to me and say, 'Al wants to see ya.' You know, 'Oh shit. What's gonna happen?' But no, he'd sit you down and say, 'You're doing this wrong, you did this. Here's what you do to correct it.' Which stuck with me. Of course, he'd say, 'Now don't do it again.' You know, a little threat at the end."

That night, Callison walked twice and cracked his first home run of the year. Unfortunately, Nellie Fox made two errors at second base, Al Smith made one in right field—and misplayed two other balls—and Bob Grim beat the Sox for the second time in six days, 8-3, on four hits. The next afternoon, Bill Veeck tried again to land Roy Sievers from Washington. Again, Cal Griffith said no. And that evening, as if to let their boss know they didn't need Sievers, the Sox went out and scored 20 runs. Of course, they got 11 of them in one inning, the seventh, with the aid of just one hit, an RBI single by Callison. Kansas City pitchers served up 10 walks in the inning, with three errors and a hit batsman thrown in. More important was that the Sox, trailing 6-1 to Ned Garver after two innings, had rallied to take a 7-6 lead after six—Fox leading the way with a double, three singles and five RBIs— and that Bob Shaw, relieving Early Wynn in the second, threw three-hit, shutout ball the rest of the way for his first win of the year.

Now it was on to Cleveland for a four-game weekend series with the first-place Indians, who were off to a 9-1 start. That became a 10-1 start when the Sox (6-5), having gotten a homer from Ray Boone and two steals each from Luis Aparicio and Jim Rivera to build a 4-1 lead for Dick Donovan entering the seventh, literally threw away the game. A two-out bases-loaded pinch single by ex-Sox Tito Francona off Turk Lown had tied the game 4-4 in the seventh, and Rodolfo Arias, again with the bases loaded in the eighth, uncorked a wild pitch and the go-ahead run was home. The Tribe went on to win 6-4, but thereafter, the weekend belonged to the White Sox. Saturday's game, which included a two-run homer by Callison and another game-tying pinch single by Francona, turned on three ninth-inning Cleveland errors, which gave the Sox two runs for a 5-5 tie. Then, with two on and one out, Earl Torgeson batted for Lown and crushed one over the wire fence in right-center for three runs and the victory.

At the start of Sunday's double-header, the temperature was 40, and that number dropped as the afternoon wore on, causing several of the sportswriters to depart the unheated press box for the warmth of the clubhouse, where the radio broadcast served as their eyes and ears. Despite the cold, the Sox were anything but. First Early Wynn and Gerry Staley (four innings of shutout relief) stopped the Indians 6-5, thanks to a six-run fourth inning keyed by Wynn's two-run double. And in Game 2, Billy Pierce went the distance to beat Gary Bell 5-2 and had a two-run double of his own, plus a triple over the head of centerfielder Jimmy Piersall to set up a two-run ninth. Meanwhile, in New York, the Yankees were getting swept by the Orioles. So suddenly, the White Sox (9-5) were just a game back of the Indians, and the mighty Yankees (6-7) had dropped into the second division.

The weekend was not without its reversals, however. Seven members of the club—Callison, Torgeson, Donovan, Billy Goodman, Don Mueller, Earl Battey and manager Al Lopez—complained of flu-like symptoms Monday in Chicago. Hardest hit was Callison, who seemingly was just beginning to come out of his slump. Now he was confined to bed with a 103-degree temperature and more than just the usual case of flu. "I got the Asiatic flu," he said. "Remember how that was going around? Well, I caught it that weekend in Cleveland. And I lost about 15 pounds, and I only weighed 175 to start with. That was my peak. You lose weight when you're in top condition, it's tough. I really got weak."

It would take him weeks to fully recover, and by that time he was in Indianapolis. In the meantime, his replacement, Jim Rivera, would go down as well. It happened on Thursday night, April 30, at home against the Yankees before a decent crowd of 26,944. New York had won the series opener the day before when the Sox—still missing their top three lefthanded-hitting bench men (Torgeson, Goodman and Mueller)—stranded 11 runners and lost 5-2 on a cold, windy afternoon to Bob Turley as the Yankees got homers from Mickey Mantle, Bill Skowron and Hank Bauer. But on Thursday night, the conditions and results were far better. Bill Veeck staged his first "Lucky Seat" giveaway of the year, and the people fortunate—or unfortunate—enough to be in seats with special coupons attached thereto became the recipients of whatever goodies Veeck had happened to dig up for the occasion. One startled fan received 1,000 kosher hot dogs, another 1,000 cupcakes, another 1,000 cigars, and so on.

The between-innings frivolity in the stands couldn't take away from the tautness of the game on the field, another of the many terrific duels between the league's finest lefties, Billy Pierce and Whitey Ford. The two battled into the 10th, tied 3-3, when Yogi Berra, with a man on second and two out, ripped a low liner to left. Rivera raced in, dived headlong and caught the ball. In all those years of headfirst slides and diving catches, "Jungle Jim" never had suffered a serious injury. His good fortune had just ended, although, as he came jogging off the field, he didn't realize it.

"When I made the catch," he remembered, "I didn't think nothin' of it. I didn't do nothin' but get up, throw the ball in, and the inning was over. I didn't feel it until I got up to the plate. Ryne Duren had come in to pitch for them. And when I swung, man, my ribs just hurt like hell. And I didn't want to come out. 'Cause, you know how you are: You say, 'To hell with it. I'll play.' So anyway, I struck out, and I came back to the dugout, and they said, 'What's wrong?' And I said, 'I don't feel so good.' So they took me to the hospital for X-rays."

Meanwhile, Duren, the Yankee relief ace, wasn't doing too well, either. In the Sox 11th, he loaded the bases with three walks, only the last of which—to Billy Goodman with two out—was intentional. That brought up Al Smith, favorite target of the Comiskey Park boo-birds since he had arrived on Opening Day 1958 as replacement for the beloved Minnie Minoso and proceeded to have his second straight poor season. At the moment, he was 0-for-4 on the night, 0-for-7 for the series and hitting all of .173. As Smith stepped into the box, the boos came cascading down. Years later, he said the booing fans had never bothered him. "As long as they didn't come out on the field, I didn't mind. See, Minoso was run, run, run. I wasn't like that. I'd catch the ball, but I'd catch it my way. I was slow at it—I'd run when I got ready. That was the type of ballplayer I was. They thought I wasn't hustling."

They knew he wasn't hitting. But Smith was about to come through with the first of many decisive hits he would deliver in this remarkable season. On a 2-2 pitch from Duren, he swung and drove the ball deep into the gap in right-center for the game-winning hit.

With one swing, Smith had turned the boos into cheers, at least for the time being, and, on April 30, had provided Pierce with his third 1959 win. Pierce's third 1958 win had come on *May* 30. On the downside, trainer Eddie Froelich had received the results of Rivera's X-rays from nearby Mercy Hospital. The verdict: Jungle Jim had suffered a cracked rib and would be out at least three weeks. So the Sox had finished the month with a 10-6 record and with two lefthanded-hitting outfielders, Callison and Rivera, unable to perform.

Thus it was not without a good deal of interest that Bill Veeck and Hank Greenberg took notice of that evening's news from Kansas City: Harry "Suitcase" Simpson, a much-traveled lefthanded-hitting out-fielder signed years earlier by Veeck and Greenberg when they were in Cleveland and when Simpson was with the Philadelphia Stars of the Negro National League, had hit a pinch home run off Baltimore's Billy Loes in the last of the ninth to give the A's a 4-3 victory. Veeck made a mental note: Call Kansas City GM Parke Carroll first thing in the morning.

MAY

Ol' Gus, and Veeck's Wrecks, Too

Newspapers this month kept a vigil over John Foster Dulles, the former secretary of state who had been forced to resign in April because of cancer and who now was failing fast. There was more trouble for the U.S. in the arms race, too. Another Atlas ICBM blew up one minute after launch on May 18, just five hours after a Navy Polaris test rocket fizzled in flight when the second stage failed to fire. Radios, however, blared music that helped keep things upbeat. Johnny Horton, in "The Battle of New Orleans," sang of how Andrew Jackson's men had chased the British "on down the Mississippi to the Gulf of Mexico," Bobby Darin wished for a "Dream Lover" so he no longer would have to dream alone, and Lloyd Price praised the woman of his dreams for having plenty of "Personality."

If there was one key player on this White Sox club who was a dominating personality, it would have to be one Early Wynn, born January 6, 1920, in Hartford, Alabama. He had been pitching in the American League since 1939 and, before coming to the White Sox with Al Smith from Cleveland for Minnie Minoso in December 1957, he had won 20 games or more on four different occasions. Casey Stengel had long since paid him the ultimate compliment, telling writer Roger Kahn: "If there was one ballgame that I had to have and I could pitch anybody in our league, it would be the big, mean feller that pitches for Cleveland and which is named—wait, I got it—Wynn."

Jim Landis had found out about Wynn during spring training 1958, as the Sox barnstormed their way north with the St. Louis Cardinals. One day, Wynn was pitching to the Cards' Joe Cunningham, later a White Sox teammate. Cunningham took a vicious swing and missed. Smith, playing in left field, called over to Landis in center: "Watch the next pitch." Wynn wound up and nailed Cunningham in the back, simply because he was angry at him for taking such a big cut. And this was just an exhibition game. "I said,

'My God!'" Landis recalled. It hadn't surprised Smith in the least. He had played with Wynn since 1953. "Yeah, big swings would get him mad, and you'd better not hit one back up the middle, either. Even in batting practice. Sometimes they'd have the starting pitchers throw some batting practice. And I'd tell these guys, 'If you hit one back at him, or a line drive over his head, get the hell out of that cage,'cause the next one he throws he's gonna throw right at your legs.' His son, Joe Early, came out and took batting practice against him one day. And he hit one back through the middle, and I said, 'Hey, better come on out of there—your daddy's gonna throw at ya.' And he tried to get out of the batting cage, but he wasn't fast enough. Early drilled him right in the side. It didn't make any difference to Early."

Later in that 1958 season, Landis learned more about the guy they called "Ol' Gus." "I don't remember what I did, but I screwed up, and he lost the ballgame, a tough ballgame. And he comes over to me in the clubhouse and says, 'You're gonna go out to eat with me tonight.' 'OK, fine.' You know, you're not gonna say no to Early. But the point was, hey, it's over, there's more games to come."

"I remember Early's first year with us," added Sammy Esposito. "I had started the game and somebody pinch-hit for me, and I was up in the clubhouse. I took a shower and then I was watching the game on TV. And Early got knocked out. He came up there, and I was just relaxing, sitting up there watching the game. And he used to tear up clubhouses. He picked up a chair and threw it against the wall. Then he looked at me with that look of his. So I picked up a chair and threw it against the wall. Then he said, 'Well, that's better. Let's have a cold one together.'"

Often Wynn needed more cold ones to offset the kind of cuisine he especially enjoyed. "Wynn," remembered Chuck Comiskey, "used to eat spicy food, Mexican stuff, before it was really popular—enchiladas, tacos—and then wash it down with a couple bottles of beer."

Wynn's reunion with Al Lopez, his manager in Cleveland, had come about quite by surprise. Lopez, Comiskey and John Rigney had just made a deal with Baltimore at the December '57 winter meetings, unloading two of Lopez's least favorite players, Larry Doby and Jack Harshman, for Billy Goodman, Ray Moore and Tito Francona. Frank Lane, the new Cleveland GM, stopped by to congratulate the Sox braintrust on a good deal and then suggested the Sox trade him Minnie Minoso, the man he had acquired from the Indians way back in 1951, when he was the Chicago general manager. Lopez asked, "Who would you give us for Minnie, Frank?" And that's when Lane offered Wynn and Smith. That, in Lopez's judgment, was too good an offer to refuse.

Remembered Comiskey: "The reason Al wanted to get Early Wynn was, he said, 'I need a guy with a really mature head on this staff. Pierce and Donovan are just a notch away from being really good American League pitchers.' Now Pierce had been around a long time (and had won 20 games in '56 and '57 and started three All-Star Games). But Al said, 'Wynn will instill this toughness. He'll show them how to be tough.' Now, we never expected him to have the year he had in '59. Never in a thousand years. But he got caught up in it. Everybody got caught up in it. And he did help the staff. When a Donovan or a Shaw, in particular, came in off the field, they would sit next to Wynn. And Wynn would say, 'OK, you got this guy this way so far. You're getting into the later innings now. How you gonna work on him?' So he was like a coach on the bench."

"Wynn," agreed Bob Shaw, "was a big influence on my pitching, on my attitude and my approach. And it was all positive. It was toughness: Don't give in to the hitter. And it's a business. So I think without question he was a good influence on me, 'cause I kinda took to it. I didn't mind being a little mean once in a while, having to move the hitter back. A lot of guys just don't want to get into some kind of confrontation with a hitter, 'cause in those days, us pitchers had to hit. But Early was tough. Very tough-minded, very competitive. Was very strong mentally. Worked hard. He was ready to pitch. The rest of the club, too, respected him as a person and for his ability and for his toughness. He'd go out there to beat your rear end. You knew he was gonna come after you."

On the night of May 1, at Comiskey Park, Early Wynn came after the Boston Red Sox in a manner that suggested that 1959, for him, was going to be a year to relish. He struck out 14 Red Sox and allowed just one hit—a first-inning single by Pete Runnels just to the left of Luis Aparicio, seconds after Wynn had moved Looie over a couple of steps to his right. And then, with the game scoreless in the last of the eighth, Wynn, a switch-hitter batting lefthanded against Tom Brewer, hit an opposite-field home run into the first row for the game's only run. "That home run," he said that night, "just proves my argument that the ball is getting livelier all the time."

Yet, if the ball was livelier, Bill Veeck was wondering to himself up in the Bards Room after the game, why was Wynn the only guy on his ballclub who could hit the ball out of the park? The Yankees had plenty of people like that. So did the Indians, who had just beaten New York on a two-out, three-run pinch homer in the 10th by the red-hot Tito Francona. Veeck picked up the phone and called Cincinnati General Manager Gabe Paul and completed his first deal as boss of the White Sox. It was a deal the two clubs had been talking about, off and on, for more than a month. To Chicago came veteran outfielder Del Ennis, whom Veeck had first seen 15 years earlier in the Class C Inter-State League. Ennis was five weeks away from turning 34 but, Veeck figured, was still capable of adding to his career home run total, which now stood at 286.

To the Reds went a disappointed Lou Skizas ("I'd been hoping to stay there, with those guys—and it was home, too") and the lefty reliever Don Rudolph—plus his wife, the exotic dancer with the stage name of Patti Waggin. Patti's fame had, ahem, far outstripped that of her husband, who hadn't accomplished a great deal in three different trials with the White Sox. Her earnings were greater, too, than Don's: She was making $750 a week while her husband was making the big-league minimum, $7,500 a year. He had first seen her in Colorado Springs in 1954, when he was a Sox farmhand and she was working her way through college as a stripper billed as "The Coed with the Educated Torso." They married in 1955 and were inseparable thereafter, save when Rudolph's team went on the road—which is when Patti went on the road as well. When Rudolph's team was at home, so was Patti. And during his off-season, Don served as his wife's press agent.

"Don was a very, very close friend of mine," said Barry Latman, a teammate of Rudolph's for two years at Indianapolis. "And Patti was really a very nice girl. And we'd play pepper. She'd come to the ballpark early and we'd play pepper, out on the field. When she wasn't working, she'd be one of the guys."

Sadly though, because of her husband's expendability and the Sox's need for a hitter, she no longer would be one of the guys in Chicago. Said Veeck: "Alas, the wrong Rudolph had the great curves."

Ennis reported in time for the next afternoon's game with the Red Sox, was placed in the No. 4 spot in the lineup and played left field. He was hitless until the eighth, when he doubled and scored the Sox's second run in a 5-4 defeat, which wound up just a few minutes before Willie Shoemaker rode Tomy Lee to victory in the 85th Kentucky Derby. Heartened by Ennis' presence and convinced he would provide a lift—and mindful that Jim Rivera was out for three weeks and that his two young lefthanded power-hitting hopefuls, Norm Cash and Johnny

Callison, were hitting .167 and .133, respectively—Veeck decided to obtain a veteran lefthanded hitter. Before Sunday's game with Baltimore, he got in touch with Kansas City's Parke Carroll and finalized a straight swap of Ray Boone for Harry Simpson, who thus far had batted only 10 times and had collected two hits—one of them that game-winning homer three nights earlier.

Simpson, delighted to leave the lowly A's, flew to Chicago and moved in with his brother Frank at 5620 S. Wabash. Boone, on the other hand, almost killed the deal by threatening to retire from baseball before Veeck helped talk him out of it.

As for that afternoon's game, rookie catcher John Romano's pinch home run off lefty Billy "Digger" O'Dell in the eighth had tied the score 2-2, and Al Lopez had turned the pitching over to Turk Lown, the former Cub. Lown promptly served up home run balls to the two least likely long-ball candidates in the Baltimore lineup—second baseman Billy Gardner, who had hit three homers in 1958, and ex-Sox shortstop Chico Carrasquel, who had hit four. After the 4-2 loss, there was both rejoicing—albeit muted—and anger in the Sox dressing room.

Romano, who had batted only seven times all season and whose home run was his first in the major leagues, was quietly exulting when someone tapped him on the shoulder. He was wanted upstairs in the club's offices.

"Chuck Comiskey had always treated me like a kid brother," Romano began. "Wanna know something? I'll never forget him. He told me in spring training that year, 'John, you show me you can play in the big leagues, and I'll give you a bonus.' That time I hit my first home run, a guy in our clubhouse said Chuck wanted to see me. I went upstairs, and Chuck said to me, 'Well, John, I told you if you showed me you could play up here, I'd give you a bonus. Give me a figure.' You know, me, I'm a young kid. I've got no money at all. I'm ready to say two hundred. I said, 'Chuck, no sense asking me how much I want. Look, you've treated me so well, whatever you give me, I feel it's great.' He said, 'You got yourself 15 hundred, John.'"

The mood was slightly different downstairs. In the wake of those two ninth-inning home runs, Lown's ERA had risen to 6.24, and Lopez's temperature was rising as well. "Lown's best pitch is his fastball, but he insisted on throwing curveballs to Baltimore hitters," fumed the Senor. "The curves he threw to Gardner and Carrasquel hung, and they hit 'em out of the park."

Some 38 years later, Lopez's disdain for Lown's throwing anything but his fastball was still fresh in the pitcher's mind. "Lopez had a phobia about my curveball and my slider," Lown said. "As far as he was concerned, when I was out there, it was 'Throw the fastball,' and that was all. The only time he wanted me to throw anything else was when he gave the sign. Which wasn't often. And it worked. I guess he thought I had a better fastball than Bob Feller. But how could I argue with him? All the while I was with him, I had good years, so it worked out just fine.

"But I remember one game against Cleveland. Vic Power was up. Good hitter. And Sherm (Lollar) called for a slider. And as you know, Lopez wanted me to throw the fastball. So Sherm comes out and says, 'Now, make sure it's outside—make sure it's outside.' And I throw it, and it's right down the middle. And he hit a line drive right at the third baseman. And the inning was over, and boy, I walked off that mound with my head held high—and then I caught holy hell for throwing that slider. Another time I threw a slider, and a guy hit a home run, and before I turned around Lopez was on the mound. He chewed me up and down. And then, Sherm says to himself, 'I better go and find out what's goin' on.' And he comes walking out, and Lopez says, 'You damn fool, you're worse than Lown for calling it.'"

Lopez's distress was to increase in the week ahead. The Washington Senators came into town and slugged their way to 8-3 and 6-4 victories behind the home run hitting of rookie Bob Allison, Harmon Killebrew and Jim Lemon. That made it four straight Chicago defeats. Only Nellie Fox, leading the league at .389, was doing much hitting, and only Billy Pierce and Early Wynn (both 3-2) among the starters and Gerry Staley (2.30 ERA) and Bob Shaw (1.27) among the relievers were doing much pitching. When the first-place Cleveland Indians took the Friday night opener of a four-game weekend series 3-1 on Cal McLish's five-hit pitching and Rocky Colavito's two-run homer off Dick Donovan, the Sox were 11-11, having blown the benefits of their 4-0 start. Sherm Lollar was hitting .237, Bubba Phillips .213, Al Smith .205, Jim Landis .193, Norm Cash .191 and Johnny Callison .118. Even the newcomer Simpson was 0-for-6 since putting on a Chicago uniform.

But then came a streak that helped reinforce among the players the feeling that they could make a race of it in 1959. It began on May 9. In Washington, Fidel Castro assured newspaper editors that the Cuban rebels were not communists. The laughs in Chicago, meanwhile, were provided by Mike Nichols and Elaine May, performing at the Medinah

Temple. Carol Channing was headlining at the Empire Room of the Palmer House, and the must-see movies downtown were "Al Capone," starring Rod Steiger, at the Cinestage and "Some Like It Hot," with the sizzling Marilyn Monroe plus Jack Lemmon and Tony Curtis at the United Artists Theatre. At 35th and Shields that afternoon, the White Sox took advantage of Herb Score's wildness and beat the Indians 9-5. In a double-header the next day, the Sox stole five bases—three by Luis Aparicio—Phillips went 5-for-8 and Smith 4-for-7 and Del Ennis hit a home run. Billy Pierce went 11 innings again to beat Cleveland 5-4 and Early Wynn shut out his former club 5-0 before 28,293—including almost 4,000 mothers who got in free on Mother's Day merely by showing a photo of any of their offspring. The first inning of Game 2 was vintage '59 White Sox: Aparicio grounded a hit to center and raced to second for a leg double when centerfielder Jimmy Piersall was a tad slow in getting to the ball. Nellie Fox then singled to score Looie with the only run needed by Wynn, who was now 6-0 against the Indians since they had traded him.

It was on to Boston for the beginning of a 13-game, 13-day trip that would include an 1,100-mile flight from Baltimore to Kansas City. The Sox were 14-11 and 1 1/2 games out of the lead when they arrived at Fenway Park on Tuesday, May 12. That day, Eddie Fisher arrived at a Las Vegas courthouse with Elizabeth Taylor on his arm and divorced Debbie Reynolds, got a wedding license in the same building and then went off and married Liz—all in two hours' time. And in San Francisco, comedian Jonathan Winters was being held for observation in a hospital psychiatric ward after police found him threatening to jump from the rigging of an old-time sailing vessel on display in the Embarcadero.

That night in Boston, Nellie Fox's hitting streak was snapped at 16, but, after 4 hours 23 minutes, the White Sox beat the Red Sox 4-3 on Al Smith's home run in the 12th. Del Ennis and Jim Landis each had three hits, Landis threw out the potential go-ahead run at the plate in the seventh and Turk Lown, firing fastballs, pitched three scoreless innings in relief of Dick Donovan. The next afternoon, Al Lopez handed the ball to young Bob Shaw, who had been outstanding in 14 relief appearances covering 24-plus innings. Close to 40 years later, Lopez admitted, "We didn't expect anything from him. We didn't know much about the kid. We'd gotten him from Detroit the year before. But you've got to give them a chance to pitch. They'll show you whether they can pitch or not. You gotta kind of nurse them along a little bit, try to keep 'em out of trouble if you can. Give them the confidence. The big thing is confidence. Once Bob Shaw got confidence, he became a good pitcher."

He acquired a good bit of it that afternoon, shutting out the Red Sox 5-0 on five singles and zero walks. "I think as you pitch well, you start to get confidence, the feeling that, 'I belong,' that, 'Hey, I can do the job up here,'" said Shaw, recalling his feelings that day. "And then, needless to say, once I pitched the shutout against Boston, now definitely you're feeling even better. And then they put you in the rotation, and now you really feel good."

Indeed, after this outing, Lopez announced that Shaw, whose ERA had shriveled to 0.82, was his No. 4 starter and that he would go again four days hence, in Washington. There was another announcement, this one from Chicago, where Bill Veeck issued the word that he had acquired 34-year-old Larry Doby—another over-the-hill longball hitter to go with Del Ennis and Harry Simpson—from Detroit for $20,000. Veeck, who had brought Doby to the major leagues in 1947 as the first black player in the American League, was delighted. Lopez was not. Weary of Doby's penchant for strikeouts and brooding, Lopez had already traded Doby away twice, once from Cleveland to the White Sox and then from the Sox to Baltimore. As for Doby, being reunited with Veeck far outweighed the prospect of again playing for a manager with whom he seldom had seen eye to eye.

"Coming back with Bill was always a pleasure," said Doby, who 28 years later would again rejoin Veeck and the Sox as batting instructor and, later, as manager. "I always had great respect for him and admired him as a person, and certainly there was never any questioning his integrity. So wherever Bill went, if I got the opportunity to be with him, it would be fine with me. But I had no problem with Al Lopez. He spoke his mind about certain things, and I spoke my mind about certain things. And I think that, whether right or wrong, a man is entitled to his opinion. So I never questioned his opinion. And certainly he gave me an opinion, and I gave him an opinion. Now, whether he accepted it or not or whether he questioned it or not, I don't know."

But if Lopez wasn't tremendously pleased to welcome Doby back to the Sox, several of the players were, including former Cleveland teammates Simpson, Early Wynn and Al Smith, as well as Sammy Esposito, who when Doby was dealt to the Orioles had traded in his No. 48 uniform jersey for Doby's old No. 14.

"I offered to give Larry his No. 14 back," Esposito recalled, "but he said to go ahead and keep it. He was fine about it. He didn't care. Larry and I were very good friends. He was a very intelligent person, ahead of his times. Had great vision. We got along great."

Unfortunately, Doby and Lopez did not. But the way his ballclub was performing, Lopez was not going to let the Doby reacquisition spoil his mood. And when Doby reported the next day—and took uniform No. 32, available because of the recent release of Don Mueller—Lopez was all smiles: The Sox had stepped out of character and pounded out 19 hits —including homers from Jim Landis, Earl Torgeson and Del Ennis, who had raised his average to .344—and routed Boston 14-6. The Sox had won six straight and were a half-game out of first. Next stop, New York, for games Friday night and Saturday with the struggling Yankees. Bob Shaw wasn't the only confident member of the Chicago traveling party.

"After we had completed that series with the Red Sox," the *Daily News'* Jack Kuenster recalled, "we were riding the bus out to Logan Airport, and I was sitting next to Al Smith. And he told me, 'We're gonna win the pennant.' I had a pretty good relationship with the ballplayers. I could talk to them like I talked to anybody else. And I said, 'Oh, cut it out. All you guys do is hit singles.' And he said, 'Don't you worry about it. We're gonna win it with singles, speed, pitching and defense.'"

Decades had passed, but Smith remembered the conversation. "That's right. That's what I told him. We had good defense and we had good pitching. And I felt that, with the pitchers we had—Wynn, Pierce, Donovan, Shaw—they could hold 'em to two or three runs. And I always felt if we went into the late innings and we needed one run to win, we could do it, especially if Aparicio was coming up. Because that was the year Aparicio ended up stealing 56 bases. So with me, that feeling started early in the season."

The feeling was spreading that weekend. First, Aparicio stole two bases and Billy Pierce beat Whitey Ford 6-0, striking out seven, for his 33rd career shutout, lowering his ERA to 2.90. And then, with Bob Turley leading 3-2 on Saturday with two out and nobody on in the ninth, Yankee centerfielder Mickey Mantle misplayed Nellie Fox's drive into a three-base error. Jim Landis followed with a walk and Sherm Lollar with a game-tying hit. In the 11th, Del Ennis singled home Fox with the go-ahead run, and Turk Lown, who had escaped a bases-loaded jam in the 10th, retired the Yankees in order, striking out Mantle to end the game. The winning streak was at eight, and while the Sox were still a half-game behind Cleveland, they had shoved the Yankees into seventh place.

"I do remember," said Lown, "that we had a positive attitude that year when we played the Yankees. And I think it built up from those first few games we played 'em. We beat 'em early a couple of games, and it ballooned up, and bingo ..."

Even the floundering rookie, Johnny Callison (.119), was enjoying the ride. True, he had lost his job to Ennis, and his roommate, Norm Cash (.188), had lost his to Earl Torgeson. But this was his first trip to New York, and he was being treated like a regular. "Fox and Pierce, they just took me under their wing," Callison said. "They were great to me. I'll never forget, we went out to Yankee Stadium on the subway. They called me 'Rookie John.' They said, 'Rookie John, come on with us.' And I had to hold Pierce's coat tails on that subway. I was scared to death. 'Where the hell am I?'"

Cash, meanwhile, had a different question. Like, where was his cash? "Norm got robbed that first trip into New York," Callison reported. "He'd come in one night, hung his pants up, woke up the next day, found the pants on the floor. The door was open just a crack. 'What happened?' 'Oh shit. Somebody robbed me.'"

Cash's money wasn't the only thing stolen that weekend. Aparicio stole three more bases in Sunday's double-header split in Washington (Pedro Ramos stopped the Sox streak in Game 1, the Senators beating Dick Donovan for the first time since July 31, 1956, before Bob Shaw won the nightcap). Earl Torgeson and even Sherm Lollar each stole a base in the second game as well. Aparicio's thefts gave him 13 on the season. "Sometimes I call for a pitchout, and even then I can't get him," Yankee catcher Yogi Berra had complained to New York sportswriter Dick Young the day before. "I can tell when Aparicio is going, but what good does it do? He still steals it." Looie stole another one the next night when Early Wynn, aided by Lollar's fifth homer and Al Smith's second, stopped the Senators 9-2 on five hits for his sixth victory and his fifth in his last six starts. That made it 10 wins in 11 games for the White Sox, who went into first place by a half-game over Cleveland, a 3-0 loser at Baltimore. "There's a long way to go," Al Lopez told the writers, "but believe me, we feel we are capable of staying up here."

Lopez had kept his team up there by playing the same lineup throughout the road trip: Aparicio SS, Fox 2B, Landis CF, Lollar C,

Ennis LF, Torgeson 1B, Smith RF, Phillips 3B and the pitcher. There was some question as to whether such a lineup could provide enough steady offense for a club with pennant aspirations, and the first "See I told you so's" were voiced the next night in Baltimore, when Billy O'Dell and 20-year-old reliever Jerry Walker held the Sox to one run and six hits as the Orioles won 2-1. Yet one run would have been enough to win that game too if it hadn't been for one of the freakiest plays in a long line of oddities that seemed to victimize the White Sox in Memorial Stadium, the ballpark Sox broadcaster Bob Elson referred to as "the chamber of horrors."

With two out and Billy Gardner on first base in the second inning, O'Dell, hitting right-handed, sliced a Billy Pierce fastball down the right-field line. The ball hit the foul line—the only one in the majors made of wood—and hit it in such a way that it bounced over the head of the oncharging, and stunned, Al Smith. The ball rolled along the cinder warning track toward the right-field corner, 309 feet from the plate, and by the time it was retrieved and relayed home, O'Dell had slid in with the strangest home run ever witnessed by Lopez and Pierce and just about everyone else at Memorial Stadium that night.

"That," remembered Lopez, "was the damnedest thing I ever saw."

Recalled Pierce: "The ball hit that thing and it really bounced. How often could that have happened? It had to hit in the middle so it would bounce high enough, and yet go kinda sideways too. One of those things. A few years later, when I was traded to San Francisco, O'Dell was already there with the Giants. And he kidded me in the clubhouse: 'Oh, yeah, I remember the night I ripped that home run off of Billy.' Made it sound like he really belted it."

When Larry Doby, in a pinch-hitting role, belted one to straight-away center with two out in the ninth, it looked for a moment as if the Sox had tied the game. Instead, the ball hit off the wall, just below the 410-foot sign, for a double, and Walker struck out another pinch-hitter, Billy Goodman, on three pitches to end the game and Chicago's stay in first place. But the gloom in the visitors' clubhouse that night was gone by the time the Sox arrived for the next evening's game. That afternoon in New York, the Tigers had pounded the Yankees 13-6, dropping the world champions into last place—the lowest the Yanks had been that late into a season since 1940. "They ain't changed baseball any this year so that you can win with no hittin', pitchin' or fieldin', even if you are wearin' a Yankee uniform," moaned Casey Stengel, obviously concerned. Said Pierce: "I think May is too early to worry about your own club and how it's doing, but you look at the standings and see the Yankees down at the bottom—that gave everybody an extra shot. I don't think there's any question about that."

Thus inspired, the White Sox, getting a four-hitter from Dick Donovan and four hits (but no steals) from Luis Aparicio, beat the Orioles 5-2. The key blow came in the eighth, when Harry "Suitcase" Simpson, 0-for-8 to that point with the Sox, stroked a bases-loaded pinch single to left off Billy Loes—whom he had beaten with a ninth-inning home run in April at Kansas City—to stretch the lead from one run to three. The ballclub, in a festive mood befitting a team near the end of what so far had been an 8-2 road trip, spent much of that Thursday, May 21, an off day, flying to Kansas City. Bob Shaw, the next evening's scheduled starter, interrupted his card game with Sammy Esposito to flag down a stewardess as she passed by his seat. "Is there any significance," he asked her, "in all those flames around the wing?" The woman gasped, Shaw's straight face could remain straight no longer, and he and his teammates had their laughs at her expense. Clearly, this club was far from tight.

The same could not be said for Friday night's game. Again Shaw was tough, but so was the home team's Bob Grim, who, as a Yankee, had at one time held a 7-0 career mark against the White Sox. The Sox, though, managed to take a 2-1 lead into the last of the ninth before the A's rallied, helped along by a dropped flyball in right field by Jim Rivera, just off the injured list. When Shaw walked pinch-hitter Kent Hadley with two outs to fill the bases, Al Lopez brought in Turk Lown to face Dick Williams. Lown, on the road trip, had allowed just one run across eight innings. Still, had there been one out instead of two, the call would've gone out for Gerry Staley, the sinkerballer. "Lopez," recalled Jack Kuenster, "always said he had the perfect bullpen combination, even though they were both righthanders—Staley with the sinkerball to get the double play, and Lown with the fastball to get the strikeout."

He didn't get the strikeout this time. Instead, Williams lined a fastball into center field. The A's, it appeared, would win the game 3-2. But Jim Landis, getting his usual terrific jump, came racing in, dived for the ball and caught it to save Shaw's fourth victory. "I always felt a little cocky about the knack I had of getting a jump on the ball," said Landis, many years later. "There are some things you work on, and there are other things that are just there—and that was one of them."

Now the Sox had won 12 of 14 and were 9-2 on the trip. But then they hit a slight bump in the road, losing the final two games in Kansas

City 16-0 and 8-6 as the pitching (first Wynn and then Pierce suffered early KO's) and defense (there were misplays by Al Smith in right and Larry Doby, filling in for Earl Torgeson, at first) suffered a temporary collapse. Hector Lopez was the big gun for the A's, going 5-for-8 with eight RBIs. Meanwhile, "Veeck's Wrecks"—the veterans Doby, Del Ennis and Harry Simpson—were struggling instead of leading. Doby was 0-for-8 in the two games and was batting .197 on the season, Simpson (.158 overall) was 1-for-9 in a Sox uniform and Ennis was fighting an 0-for-19 slump that had dropped his batting average to .230.

Still, the overall White Sox picture was bright that Sunday evening as the team returned to Chicago, one game out and ready to meet the first-place Indians that Tuesday night at Comiskey Park. Nellie Fox was hitting .363, Bubba Phillips .300 and Luis Aparicio .298. The only bad news was in the papers. John Foster Dulles was dead of cancer at age 71, 39 days after his resignation, and foreign ministers from around the world descended uponWashington, D.C., for memorial services. And in Chicago, Susan Hansen, 25, a divorced mother of three, was found beaten to death in her Hyde Park home. Her ex-husband, Duncan, 28, a teacher at Calumet High School, was being held for questioning. The next day, Monday, May 25, he was charged with murder. The case would hold the public's attention all summer and into October.

But then, too, so would the White Sox. And the first tangible indication of that came Tuesday night, when 40,018 people paid their way into Comiskey Park to help cap off what had been a rather significant day. In Springfield, the Illinois Senate voted to raise the state sales tax a half-cent to 3 cents. In Pompano Beach, Fla., former White Sox great Ed Walsh, winner of 40 games in 1908, died of cancer at age 78. In Milwaukee, Pittsburgh Pirates lefty Harvey Haddix was perfect for 12 innings before losing the perfect game, the no-hitter and the ball-game to the Braves in the 13th. And in New York, the last-place Yankees announced yet another of their deals with Kansas City, their in-league farm team (this was the 14th, involving 52 players, in the last four years). This time, the Yankees landed the hard-hitting Hector Lopez, fresh off his weekend of destroying White Sox pitching, and right-hander Ralph Terry, rapidly developing into an outstanding young pitcher. All the Yankees had to give up was infielder Jerry Lumpe (.222 with two RBIs) and sore-armed pitchers Tom Sturdivant (0-2, 4.97 ERA in 25 1/3 innings) and Johnny Kucks (0-1, 8.64 ERA in 16 2/3). When Cleveland GM Frank Lane, who had been offering actual quality for Lopez, heard of the deal, his reaction—the part the newspapers judged printable, anyway—was: "A damned outrage—another Yankee-Kansas City crime."

When he cooled down sufficiently, Lane took a cab from the Indians' hotel to Comiskey Park, where he sat down for dinner with Bill Veeck in the Bards Room. Still needing a third baseman, Lane tried to talk Veeck out of Billy Goodman. Veeck in turn suggested a bigger trade, one designed to bring Minnie Minoso back to the South Side. It would be more than six months before that deal would come to fruition. For now, though, the two repaired to the press box to watch that evening's first-place showdown. The festivities began with the landing, in short center field, of a helicopter, from which emerged not Satchel Paige but four midget "Martians," one of them Eddie Gaedel, among Veeck's more famous hires. The foursome surrounded the dim-inutive Luis Aparicio and Nellie Fox, whom they apparently mistook for two of their own and with whom they tried to depart before being convinced that the Sox had greater need of them. That was the most excitement for the home fans until the postgame fireworks spectacular, because, in between, the Sox did nothing against lefty Don Ferrarese, who not only shut out Chicago 3-0 (with relief help from Jim Perry) but also hit three doubles off Dick Donovan, two of them driving in runs. Said Al Lopez, only half-joking: "I was glad they took him out. He was liable to come up to bat again."

The fans, however, found no humor in the proceedings. Wrote Warren Brown: "The booing of the disgruntled crowd ... was directed mostly at Al Smith (0-for-3), though there was some vocal volume left when another old favorite, Larry Doby, batted for Dick Donovan in the seventh, this against Perry, and struck out." Brightening, though, Brown noted that there would be another night game on Thursday, this one a makeup contest against Detroit. "There will be," he wrote, "more fireworks, maybe more midgets. Maybe another helicopter, out of which Satchel Paige will appear."

But Brown was getting ahead of himself. First there was Wednesday afternoon's game with Cleveland, and this was more like it. The much-maligned Doby broke a 1-1 tie in the sixth with an RBI single off Gary Bell, and Earl Torgeson followed with a home run. Johnny Callison, like Doby getting a rare start, went hitless but made a terrific leaping catch at the left-field wall to take extra bases away from Jim Baxes, and Early Wynn cast his usual amazing spell on his former teammates: 8 1/3 innings, five hits, one run, seven strikeouts. When Gerry Staley got the final two outs of the 5-1 victory, the Sox were again one game back of the Tribe. And when Thursday night's game was rained out, they were a half-game behind, because Cleveland had lost to Kansas City.

The drive to the top petered out over the final three days of the month. First Don Mossi and then Frank Lary beat the White Sox in the first two games of the Detroit series, and with Jim Bunning set to pitch the third one—Game 2 of the Memorial Day double-header—the outlook was as dreary as the weather: The nightcap was delayed 1 hour 29 minutes by rain. Sure enough, Bunning led 3-0 in the seventh before Harry Simpson tripled as a pinch-hitter and scored on Luis Aparicio's infield out. In the eighth, reliever Tom Morgan wild-pitched a run home. And, in the ninth, Nellie Fox doubled home the tying run and John Romano, rewarded with a start behind the plate after going 4-for-4 as a pinch-hitter, singled home the winning run. The remnants of the crowd of 23,621 went home happy, perhaps unaware that Rodger Ward had won the Indianapolis 500 with a record average speed of 135.857 mph, but mulling the possibility that the kid, Johnny Callison (3-for-7 on the day), might be coming out of it and that maybe Larry Doby (4-for-8, with two sensational sliding catches in right field) might not be through after all. And how about that goofy Veeck, giving out, to individual lucky-seat winners, 22,000 fig bars, 1,000 cans of chow mein noodles, 50,000 assorted screws, 1,000 cartons of orange juice and 10,000 cupcakes. The cupcake winner was a woman, and the winnings were delivered to her home.

"Do you have any idea," wrote Veeck, "how much room 10,000 cupcakes take up? We told the supplier, 'Just keep on moving them in.' He filled the kitchen and the hall and moved out to the back porch, and he was still unloading cupcakes."

The month ended with a loss to those former cupcakes, the Kansas City A's, who in 1959 were making life miserable for the White Sox and, oddly enough, Early Wynn, who otherwise was enjoying a splendid season and an outstanding month. This day—Sunday, May 31—the visitors from Missouri made merry at Ol' Gus' expense, knocking him out with a five-run second inning and going on to win 9-1 behind Ned Garver. Now Wynn was 7-1 against the rest of the league but 0-3 against Kansas City. And the Sox, 25-19 overall, were 3-6 against Kansas City.

Ah, but they were still just a game out of first place. And the Yankees were still in last. Could there finally be a miracle on 35th Street?

JUNE

Have Suitcase, Will Travel

As always, there was the bad news. Over the just completed Memorial Day holiday weekend, a record 310 people had been killed on the nation's highways. Rumors were flying that the Chinese Communists were about to test their first nuclear weapon, and Soviet Foreign Minister Andrei Gromyko was insisting that Russian troops, already ominous with their presence in East Berlin, be stationed in West Berlin as well.

The good news, for Chicagoland's younger set anyway, was that June had arrived, that school would soon be out and that Riverview, the famed amusement park on the North Side, was open once again. Riverview, where, promised the aptly nicknamed TV personality Dick "Two Ton" Baker, you could "laugh your troubles away." Riverview, with its frighteningly entertaining set of roller coasters—The Flying Turns, The Silver Flash, The Blue Streak, The Greyhound and, most thrilling of all, The Bobs.

The White Sox, figuratively, spent the entire month of June at Riverview. They didn't realize it when June began, but they were in for a roller-coaster month, one in which they were not to win more than three games in a row. All month, they were up and down, the biggest dip a five-game losing streak in mid-June that dropped them for one day into the second division. Mostly, though, they won and lost in fits and starts, as some players wondered why Bill Veeck was saying all those unflattering things about them in the Saturday Evening Post and as others worried they were about to be traded to Cleveland or Washington or Baltimore or some other destination during Veeck's quest for a power hitter or two. In short, this was a somewhat unsettling month.

It began with the Sox in the final days of a two-week homestand while comedian Red Skelton (at the Chez Paree), trumpeter Al Hirt (at the Empire Room) and singer Judy Garland (at the Opera House—tickets from $2.20 to $8.90) were just arriving in town for one-week stays. After yet another loss to Kansas City, which was 21-21 on the year, in fourth place and 7-3 thus far against Chicago, the Sox flailed away in futility the next night, Tuesday, June 2, at the fluttering knuckleball of Hoyt Wilhelm. The 36-year-old career reliever, whom Orioles manager Paul Richards had converted into a starter, owned a won-lost record of 8-0 after this evening's 3-2 victory over Bob Shaw. Wilhelm was bothered only by a swarm of tiny insects that visited him during the bottom of the first inning.

"It's the strangest thing that ever happened to me in a game," Wilhelm related afterward. "There was a cloud of gnats over the mound so thick that they were flying into my mouth. I couldn't breathe, and I couldn't see the plate. I never should've thrown a pitch until they cleared away, but I went ahead and walked (Nellie) Fox. After I threw two balls to (Earl) Torgeson, I had to quit."

He resumed pitching 16 minutes later, after a series of attempts to get rid of the gnats. Trainers, umpires and grounds crew members tried towels, torches and insecticides to make the pests perish, all to no avail. Finally Veeck summoned the fireworks crew from the center-field bullpen, and a launch site was hastily erected at the mound. Kah-boom! All it took was one bomb, and the gnats were blown to kingdom come. Wilhelm returned and was undisturbed the rest of the way. After the game, Veeck, eyes twinkling, came clean.

"Since I will probably be accused of having something to do with those bugs," he said, "I might as well say right now that I have had them in a bottle and have been training them for several years for just such an occasion."

Billy Pierce took the occasion of the next afternoon's game to get personal revenge on the Orioles' Billy O'Dell, defeating the Baltimore lefty 6-1 as Pierce's roommate, Nellie Fox, tripled in two runs and Larry Doby tripled in another. That ended a skid of eight Chicago losses in 10 games, and yet, even with all those defeats, the Sox were still just .003 out of first place, the league-leading Cleveland Indians having played similarly putrid baseball for the last week and a half.

The next afternoon, the Sox moved into first place with another of the kind of victories that tend to convince a team and its fans that this is their year. It started at 1:30 and ended 17 innings and 4 hours 37 minutes later, when Earl Torgeson, who had entered in the seventh inning as a pinch-batter for the suddenly feeble-hitting Jim Landis, stepped up to face Orioles rookie Jerry Walker with the score tied 5-5. Among the reasons the game had not ended much, much earlier were Barry Latman's 4 2/3 hitless innings in relief of Dick Donovan, who left in the third, trailing 4-2; Doby's two RBI singles, the second of which tied the game in the eighth to send it into overtime; five innings of relief from Bob Shaw, pitching on less than two days' rest; and Willie Miranda's throwing error in the 13th, allowing Torgeson to score the tying run after Albie Pearson's base hit off Shaw in the top half had put Baltimore ahead.

There were two outs and none on when Torgeson swung at Walker's 1-1 pitch, a fastball, in the 17th and drove it into the right-field lower deck to win the game—at 6:07 p.m. "I remember distinctly there were two outs," Shaw said, decades later, "because I remember saying, 'Oh geez, I gotta go out there again.' Because I'd already pitched five innings (after pitching into the ninth two nights before). But he popped it. And, boy, normally, you jump up. But I was so tired, and it was a real hot day. I just sat there and said, 'Dear Lord, am I ever glad he hit it.'"

Forgotten in the jubilation that followed Torgeson's blast was that Doby, 10-for-31 with seven RBIs since being inserted into the regular lineup eight days before, was headed for Mercy Hospital, the result of a play at home plate that afternoon. "I hurt my back—I hurt it sliding," he remembered. "And they sent me to the hospital and I was in traction for about a week." So Doby, riding high and driving in runs for a spell, however brief, suddenly was on his back, an early victim of the White Sox's roller-coaster June. No problem. Into the breach, the very next night, stepped Doby's former Cleveland teammate, Harry Simpson.

The Sox were tied 2-2 with the Boston Red Sox in front of a Friday night crowd of 32,321, a knowledgeable bunch that figured a little noise might serve to unnerve Boston reliever Murray Wall, who had entered to pitch the eighth inning. The fans were correct. Torgeson responded to the staccato clapping with a leadoff single. Al Smith placed a bunt halfway between home plate and the pitcher's mound, and Wall grabbed the ball and fired to second, trying to get Torgeson. He was too late, and everyone was safe. A little noise was replaced by a lot, especially when Wall fired a wild pitch to Jim Landis, who had finally ended an 0-for-27 slump—which had placed him on the trading block—with a single his last time up. Now came an intentional walk to fill the bases for Gerry Staley, who had replaced starter Early Wynn in the Boston half of the inning. Al Lopez sent Simpson up to hit for Staley, and Red Sox manager Pinky Higgins countered that move by bringing in lefty Leo Kiely to face Simpson. "Suitcase" lined Kiely's 2-2 delivery up the alley in right-center to the wall for a bases-clearing double and a 5-2 White Sox victory. Twice now, Simpson had come through for the Sox with bases-loaded pinch hits, good for five runs. He was in essence scoffing at one of the sport's givens: With the bases loaded, count on the White Sox to come up empty.

They even came up empty in that Sunday's between-games cow-milking contest, an idea Bill Veeck had hatched in his desire to celebrate National Dairy Week. Roused from the Sox clubhouse to compete against Boston's Pete Runnels, Jim Busby and Gary Geiger were Nellie Fox, Early Wynn and Ray Moore. The latter was a farmer, all right, but a tobacco farmer, not, it quickly became apparent, a dairy farmer. The Red Sox team badly defeated the Chicago threesome, which was hampered by the fact that Fox's cow three times kicked over Nellie's pail. Veeck, watching the proceedings with the crowd of 25,844, feared a more poorly aimed kick.

"The cow kept kicking, and Nellie kept trying," Veeck noted in his autobiography, "and I started writing mental headlines: 'Fox In Hospital In Critical Condition As Result Of Veeck Gag.' Nellie's cow lost no milk that day, and I lost no more than three buckets of blood."

Veeck admitted at times his concern that stunts like this one may have slightly annoyed the no-nonsense Senor Lopez, but Lopez says the concern was unnecessary. "No, I always went along with Bill," he chuckled. "We got along real well. Bill and I were good friends."

Added Bob Shaw: "My opinion is that it didn't bother Al. You know, if you want to milk cows, fine, we're going into the clubhouse, gonna have a sandwich, take it easy for a bit. I don't think it bothered him. I know it didn't bother me. The players got kind of a kick out of it."

Fortunately, in this case, Fox did not.

Sox players, amused by Veeck's promotions, were beginning to warm up to him as their new boss. "I think he had that knack for making ballplayers feel good," said Shaw. "Like you'd do a good job, he'd send you to Marshall Field's and get you a $50 sport shirt. I remember he gave me $50 once and told me to go to Marshall Field's and get a new sport shirt, and I got five 10-dollar shirts. And he did not like that. He was very upset. He said, 'I told you to get one shirt for $50.' But my dad being a schoolteacher, and with my background,

I was a little more frugal.

"I can remember one time I happened to win a big ballgame, and he sent me to Spencer's to get a new suit made for $300. And in those days, a $300 suit was really, really something. It was really a beautiful suit. So he would do some of those things. And that was really nice. As we all know, we didn't get paid a whole lot then."

Remembered Earl Battey: "I didn't play much, but Bill was always good to me. When I did get a chance to play and made some sort of contribution, he always said, 'Well, go down here and see this guy and pick yourself out a couple pairs of pants or shoes.'"

What the players did not appreciate about Veeck was his willingness to openly disparage the club's pitty-pat offense and, in his mind, the Sox's utter incapability of winning the pennant. As the Sox left Chicago Monday, June 8, for a two-week sojourn along the Eastern seaboard, Veeck went public in a *Saturday Evening Post* profile: "We can't win with our present personnel. The Yankees still have too much class. We have to buy or trade for two long-ball hitters to be a real contender." Indeed the Yankees had won nine of their last 11, including three out of four over the weekend in Cleveland, and were only three games behind the first-place Sox, but Veeck's players didn't agree with their boss' approach. Said one, in the visitors' clubhouse in Washington: "What is he trying to prove?"

It wasn't so much what Veeck was trying to prove as much as what he was trying to trade. While he remained back in Chicago working the phones, his No. 1 aide, Hank Greenberg, was with the White Sox in Washington, huddling with Senators owner Calvin Griffith before driving over to Baltimore to meet with Orioles field manager Paul Richards and Cleveland General Mananger Frank Lane, whose club was in town for a three-game series. (Veeck's other erstwhile "lieutenants," Chuck Comiskey and John Rigney, were not in on the negotiations. Rigney had resigned his duties with the club, and Comiskey was still attempting to litigate his way back into control via yet another lawsuit, which had drawn this reaction from Veeck: "Let's just say this won't bring us any closer together." Eventually, Veeck moved to smooth things over by raising Comiskey's salary from $28,000 to $35,000 and promoting him from vice president to, as Veeck wrote, "the more imposing position of executive vice president so that he would be able to hold up his head at class reunions.")

To Griffith, Veeck and Greenberg proposed giving Earl Battey, Al Smith and two or three others as well as a hefty lump of cash for Roy

Sievers plus a spare Senator or two. To Richards, they offered Smith in a deal for another outfielder, Bob Nieman, who had batted .325 with 16 homers the year before, was on his way to a .292, 21-homer season and had hit well as a member of the White Sox in 1955-56. To Lane, they offered a variety of players, supposedly including Jim Landis and Bubba Phillips, for a package of Indians, chief among them Minnie Minoso, the exiled Comiskey Park hero. For some reason, Greenberg was also intent on landing from Cleveland one Carroll Hardy, a former University of Colorado baseball and football star who was drafted in 1955 by the San Francisco 49ers as a defensive back and punter but ended up on offense and caught 12 passes for four touchdowns, one a 79-yarder from Y.A. Tittle. (After that season, Greenberg, who had signed Hardy as an outfielder two years before for the Indians, convinced him to concentrate on baseball. Hardy should have concentrated on football: In parts of eight big-league seasons, he hit .225 with 17 home runs.)

For their part, the Orioles, Senators and Indians, posturing in the newspapers, feigned disinterest in the White Sox offers, Griffith mentioning that "Sievers is just too valuable for me to trade," and Lane declaring, "Sure, Bill and Hank can have Minoso, but not for nothing. This isn't Christmas." Even so, Lane motored over from Baltimore to watch one of the Sox-Senator games that week, and Griffith looked on intently as Al Lopez obligingly employed all of Veeck's trading pawns, including the infrequently used Battey, in the Washington series.

"The ballplayers all used to say if you went into a town and you hadn't been playing and all of a sudden you're in the lineup, 'Yeah, there's a trade brewing—they're showcasing you,'" said Battey, who did wind up with the Senators the next spring. "But I wasn't aware of the trade talks. I found out later on, though, from someone in the Washington organization, that there was a trade offer in which John Romano was supposed to go to Washington. But the Senators weren't interested in him because they didn't need another power hitter. They needed a good defensive catcher."

All the while, Lopez quietly was hoping nothing would come of the discussions. He certainly did not want to give up on Battey, the 24-year-old catcher whom he was grooming to replace Sherm Lollar and whose throwing arm and receiving he loved, or on Smith, a player he liked and admired and who had produced for him when both were in Cleveland. "Smitty would have won the MVP award in '55 if we had held on and won that pennant—he did everything for us that year,"

Lopez said, referring to Smith's .306 batting average, 22 home runs and league-leading 123 runs scored. Nor did Lopez share Veeck's and Greenberg's lack of enthusiasm for Landis, whom Lopez had played regularly the year before even when he was hitting .180 in June and who ended up at .277 with 15 homers—in his first full big-league season.

At the moment, though, Lopez was trying to nurse both Landis and Smith through tough times. Both were hitting in the mid-.220s, which, when added to Johnny Callison's .179, gave the Opening Day outfield an aggregate batting average of about .200 to go with a total of seven home runs. The offensive vacuum in the Chicago outfield hit home with Sox fans when Cleveland rightfielder Rocky Colavito hit four home runs to lead the Indians past the Orioles 11-8 on Wednesday night, June 10. And it really hit home with Chuck Comiskey when he checked the listing of league leaders in the papers and saw Detroit right-fielder Al Kaline hitting .344 with 12 homers and 38 runs batted in— the same RBI total as the trio of Smith, Landis and Callison combined. Nearly 40 years later, Comiskey sat in a booth of a suburban Chicago restaurant and issued what amounted to a self-deprecating personal apology to White Sox fans.

"It was in June 1953," said Comiskey, beginning to tell his sad tale from the era of the bonus babies, players who, if they signed with a club for more than $4,000, had to remain on the big-league roster for two years before they could be farmed out for minor-league experience. "We had signed (pitcher) Gus Keriazakos to a big bonus, and we had (infielder) Jimmy Baumer on our list (as a bonus player) too, so we were kinda playing with 23 players. Anyway, Harry Postove, one of our scouts, had talked about this kid Kaline out East, in Baltimore. So comes the time he's gonna sign, and we have a couple more men, including Johnny Rigney, our farm director then, go out there. They look at the kid, and he's about 150-155 pounds, but they all come back and say, 'He's got the tools,' etc.

"See, there were three clubs we thought were really zeroed in on him—the Phillies, the Tigers and the White Sox. Johnny McHale (Sr.) was with the Tigers at the time as their farm director, and he told me later, 'We had kinda given up, 'cause we thought he was going to the White Sox. So we just kinda backed off of him. But then our scout called us back and said Kaline might be available, that he didn't think the White Sox were gonna make a strong effort to sign him.'

"Well, anyway, we knew if we signed him we were gonna have to put him on the roster, and the reports were, 'He's not gonna be able to hit major-league pitching right now, he's just not that quick or that strong yet.' So Frank Lane (then the Sox GM) and I are sitting there wondering, 'What should we do?' Postove is calling both Lane and me at our homes: 'Frank, Charlie, don't lose this kid! I really like him.' So we'd gotten ourselves into a box. We had a couple bonus players already, so we said, 'Well, it's not big money (Kaline ended up signing for just $18,000), but it *is* money.' So we backed off. And it's a kid we could've had."

Well, maybe and maybe not, said Kaline, 44 years after the fact. "I knew the White Sox were following me; I knew Harry Postove was watching me all the time. What I didn't know was the extent of their interest. But I had looked at Detroit's minor-league system and the team they had at the time—they finished last in '52—and no one had had any really good years." He also had looked at the contending Sox and their outfield at the time: veterans Minnie Minoso, Jim Rivera and Sam Mele. "Being a bonus player," he said, "I didn't want to sit around for two years and waste my skills and not play. I could've gotten more money from one of the other teams, but I thought I'd have a chance to play in Detroit. So that's the main reason I signed with them. I wanted a chance to play."

Now, in June '59, Al Smith and Jim Landis wanted a chance to stay. On June 10, Smith tripled in two runs in the first inning and Early Wynn went on to five-hit the Senators 4-1 for his eighth win. The next night, Landis broke a 1-1 tie with a two-run double in the ninth to enable Billy Pierce, who allowed only one hit, to beat the Senators and Camilo Pascual 3-1. Luck remained with the Sox the next evening in Baltimore, when the elements washed out a likely loss to the all-but-unhittable, and still unbeaten, Hoyt Wilhelm. A 6-4 defeat Saturday—uneventful but for a three-run homer by Nellie Fox (his first home run since Opening Day) and another scoreless, four-inning relief job by Barry Latman—was followed by a 9-6, 3-2 sweep of the Orioles on Sunday, June 14. In Game 1, Wynn (9-4) went 4-for-5 with two doubles, Earl Battey was 3-for-5 with a triple, Larry Doby returned to the lineup with a two-run single and Fox, hitting .342, was 3-for-4 with four RBIs to lift his club-leading total to 35. In Game 2, the Sox again beat Billy O'Dell, this time for Dick Donovan, as John Romano singled in the tying run in the ninth and Smith singled in the game-winner in the 10th, giving the Sox a 7-1 record in extra innings.

The Sox boarded their charter to New York, where Billy Casper, 27, had just won the U.S.Open at Winged Foot for a record check of $12,000 and where—more important to the Chicagoans—the Yankees had dropped the afternoon's double-header to the Tigers, 9-5 and 12-6, before 50,183. The Sox could breathe a bit easier now that the Yankees were five games back, tied for fifth with their cousins from Kansas City. But Chicago's hold on first place was tenuous, what with Cleveland just a half-game back, Detroit two out and Baltimore just three behind. And the players, with a day off before starting their three-game series with the Yankees, still had to sweat out the trading deadline, which was midnight Monday. It was not a day off for the writers. Sox public-relations man Eddie Short, revealed the *American's* Warren Brown, on Monday morning had warned the four Chicago newsmen following the club "not to stray too far. Big news, he said, was impending."

As it happened, there was no big news. Bill Veeck had a feeling such might be the case from the tone of his conversations with Cleveland's Frank Lane the day before, when Lane's Indians were beating the Senators a pair in Washington. The two had been talking seriously, twice a day, about a Minnie Minoso deal for the last two weeks. Now, as Veeck sought to hammer out the final details, Minoso chose that afternoon to have a double-header players only dream about. Minnie had two singles, a double, a home run and four RBIs in the opener, then added a grand slam and a sacrifice fly in the second game. Veeck later told the *Chicago Daily News'* Bill Furlong: "We thought we had a deal all worked out—it was four for four. I called Lane Sunday during the double-header—it was when Minnie had hit his first homer—and Frank was getting less enthusiastic about the deal. By the time Minnie had driven in nine runs, Frank was completely unenthusiastic."

The next day in Boston, with the trading deadline just hours away, Minoso—who had been told of the trade talks by Lane and was more than willing to return to Chicago—buried the deal with a three-run homer that buried the Red Sox 4-1 and moved the Indians into first place, percentage points ahead of the White Sox. Minnie, in the last seven games, had hit .387 with four homers and 15 RBIs to raise his batting average to .303. Still, Veeck would not give up. He called Lane seven times on the 15th, twice in the morning and then at 4 p.m., 4:30, 7:30, 10:30 and finally just before the midnight deadline. Each time, Lane said no.

So Veeck had shifted gears. In a bid for Roy Sievers, he called Calvin Griffith in Washington at 3:30 p.m., 5 and 11. Griffith remained unmoved. Finally, at 11:55 p.m., Veeck gave it his last shot: Al Smith, Earl Battey, Billy Goodman, Jim Rivera, Ray Moore and $250,000 for Sievers, catcher Clint Courtney and pitcher Russ Kemmerer. Griffith thought it over and decided not to do it. Said Veeck: "I'm probably the only guy in the world daffy enough to make such an offer, and Cal must be the only guy daffy enough to turn it down." Veeck was genuinely shocked that Griffith, who certainly needed the money, could say no to the deal. "This is a player," he told Furlong, referring to Sievers, "who is 32 years old, has a history of a bad shoulder and who has been out this year because of an arm injury. He's hitting .230 and he's got four home runs."

With those stats, Sievers seemingly would have fit right in with the Sox, but Veeck was confident the big righthanded hitter would hit his stride with a change of scenery—which he did the next year, when the Sox finally did acquire him. But Al Lopez was glad the 1959 Sievers proposal fell through. Said Al, several years later while sunning himself by his backyard pool in Tampa: "I wouldn't have given the money for him, let alone the players."

And so, the only move Veeck was able to make on what he had vowed would be a memorable June 15 was the release of Del Ennis, whose average had dipped to .219, to make room for Norm Cash, whose national serviceman's exemption had expired and who now counted against the 25-man roster. The lack of action was a letdown for Veeck, who later that week told the *Chicago Tribune's* Richard Dozer: "I'd have bet everything I had at even money that we were going to make both those deals." They did not, and Lopez, the happier for it, sighed in relief and began planning for the Yankee series.

Noting that manager Casey Stengel had scheduled three right-handed starters—Art Ditmar, Bob Turley and rookie Jim Bronstad—Lopez said he was going to return his first-year would-be lefthanded sluggers, Cash and Johnny Callison, to the lineup to perhaps take advantage of the short right-field porch in Yankee Stadium. Also, Lopez said, Larry Doby would be playing in right field for the time being against righthanded pitchers and as long as, Warren Brown added in the *American*, "he isn't troubled by any of the various ailments that are habitual with him."

But on a night that TV's Superman, George Reeves, 45, shot himself in the head, Ethel Barrymore passed away at age 79 and Chicago's Mayor Daley was stunned by the death of his father, Michael, at age 78, Lopez's plans were dying as well. Ditmar beat Billy Pierce 5-1 and, while Cash celebrated his permanent roster spot with two hits, Callison was hitless and Doby went 0-for-4 with two strikeouts and misplayed Hector Lopez's fly ball into a double during New York's pivotal three-run sixth inning. The next afternoon, Doby called Jim Landis off Mickey Mantle's fly to right-center but dropped the ball for a run-producing three-base error, and the Yankees were on their way to a 7-3 romp, highlighted by Mantle's third-tier blast off Ray Moore. Thus ended Doby's days as a starting outfielder. Wrote Brown:

"After being assured by Doby that he was ready to play, Lopez intended to station him in right field for all three games. After all, Al is acutely aware that Doby is back with the White Sox only because of his sponsorship by the 54 percent owner of the club (Veeck). But the Doby of 1959 ... is not even a reasonable facsimile, much as Veeck wishes him to be, of the Doby who was an energetic and fine ballplayer at Cleveland in what now must seem even to Veeck as the long ago. After another dismal showing Wednesday ... Lopez reached the conclusion that Veeck himself hardly could insist on Doby's being kept in the lineup."

Joining Doby on the bench for the June 18 series finale were Callison and Cash, their spots taken by Jim Rivera (right field), Al Smith (left) and Earl Torgeson (first base). The lineup changes brought no change in the outcome: The Yankees won 5-4 in the 10th when Mickey Mantle crushed a Gerry Staley sinker, one that didn't sink quite enough, into the bleachers in right. The Yankees had battered the White Sox around for three days, much as heavyweight champ Floyd Patterson and challenger Ingemar Johansson were battering sparring partners around in preparation for their title fight one week hence at Yankee Stadium. Their stay in New York was a total loss for the Sox as a team and almost the same for Cash. A robbery victim during his first trip to Gotham, the rookie had taken special precautions when handed his paycheck at the Roosevelt Hotel by traveling secretary Bernie Snyderworth.

"He stuck his paycheck inside his pillowcase," remembered his roommate, Callison, "and then he forgot all about it until we were on the bus, riding out to the ballpark. So he had to go back to the hotel, and he looked through all those pillowcases. And he found it. I mean, we weren't making any money. There was a lot of panicking going on."

The players weren't admitting it, but there was a bit of panic setting in with regard to the Yankees. The Sox were glad to escape from the Bronx just 1 1/2 games behind Cleveland, but there were the Yankees, left for dead by some observers a month before but now just 3 1/2 out of the lead and closing fast. And when Whitey Ford beat Cleveland's Gary Bell 3-2 on Friday night in New York and the Yanks routed Herb Score 10-2 the next day as Bill Skowron homered twice and drove in half the New York runs, the Yankees, it seemed to everyone, were on their way to yet another pennant.

"I remember that the Yankees had gotten off to a bad start," said Sammy Esposito, "and we just kept waiting for them to jell. It was just like when you were playing them. If you were ahead, you knew they were gonna catch you, and if they were behind, they knew they were gonna catch you. It was that kind of feeling in those days, because they were so good. So finally, in June, they made a run. And we said, 'Here they come.' And all of a sudden, they leveled off again."

The Indians helped by sweeping the Sunday, June 21, double-header 5-4 and 4-2 before 68,680 at Yankee Stadium while Billy Pierce was ending the White Sox's losing streak at five by defeating the Red Sox 3-2 on five hits at Fenway Park. Offensively, the White Sox got a lift from two of their lesser lights—Harry Simpson, starting in right field for the second straight game, and Esposito, filling in at shortstop for Luis Aparicio, who had twisted an ankle the day before. "Suitcase and I played sporadically out there," said Esposito, "but when he and I hit back-to-back home runs to win that one-run game in Boston, we got a real kick out of that."

The home runs came in the second inning off lefty Ted Wills and provided Pierce with a 2-0 lead. Simpson later doubled off the wall in left-center and scored the third Chicago run. That gave him two doubles and a homer in two days. Perhaps Al Lopez had finally found a hot bat. He thought he had come up with a way to do so two nights earlier, when the Sox had first arrived in Boston. To take advantage of Fenway Park's famed "Green Monster" in left field, Lopez made out a lineup that contained each of his three catchers, righthanded hitters all. "I was gonna play left field," recalled Earl Battey, "and that would've been my first and only game at another position. Lollar was gonna play first base and Romano was gonna catch. And we got rained out."

That necessitated a day-night double-header on Saturday, June 20, but Lopez scuttled his plans, sparing Battey the embarrassment of battling fly balls on national television. The afternoon contest was NBC's Game of the Week, featuring color commentator Bill Veeck, who though occupied with other pressing matters was nonetheless honoring his contract with the network, a deal that ran through the

1959 season. Veeck surely had envisioned showing off to the country this day a new-look White Sox lineup headed by Minnie Minoso and Roy Sievers, both drilling baseballs against and over the big wall in left field. Instead, his team lost Game 1 to Tom Brewer 8-2 as Early Wynn was knocked out in the second inning. Things were even worse at night, when Dick Donovan was a third-inning KO victim and rookie Jerry Casale shut out the Sox 9-0 on three hits.

With this fifth consecutive defeat, the White Sox dropped into fifth place at 33-30, just percentage points behind the surging Yankees. Cleveland's American League lead was a half-game over Detroit, one game over Baltimore and 1 1/2 games on New York and Chicago. It was the darkest day of the season for the White Sox, although their scouts did something that afternoon in Stillwater, Okla., to brighten the future: They signed Oklahoma State pitcher Joe Horlen, who would make his big-league debut just two years and three months later.

But for Al Lopez and the White Sox players, the present was all that mattered. After Pierce, Simpson and Esposito helped improve the situation the next day, the White Sox flew to Chicago for the final week of June, a brief homestand that began with the annual charity game with the Cubs Monday night, would continue with three games against Washington and climax with a four-game weekend series with the dreaded Yankees. It also began with an unlikely get-together of men who didn't always see eye to eye.

"It was right after the trading deadline," recalled Chuck Comiskey, who like Lopez had been pleased that Bill Veeck and Hank Greenberg had failed to land added offense in exchange for the likes of Jim Landis, Al Smith, Bubba Phillips, et al. "Bill and I were having sweet rolls in the Bards Room. See, Bill, when he took over, was gonna let Hank handle the player end of things while he took care of promotions. Now he looks at me and says, 'You're in charge of all players and player movements.' He says, 'Hank doesn't know one thing about these players. You've lived with these guys. You know them, their backgrounds, who signed them, what they did here, what they did there. I have to use your knowledge.'"

Fortified with this newly granted status, Comiskey went to Lopez and again volunteered his opinion that it was time to send Johnny Callison back to Indianapolis. "Callison was struggling, hitting way below .200, sitting on the bench more often than not," Comiskey said. "And I had said to Al earlier, 'We ought to send him back to Indianapolis, get him a couple hundred at-bats.' Al had said, 'No, he'll be fine.' Well, things didn't get any better, and we needed a righthanded bat more than a lefthanded bat at the time anyway (especially after the Minoso and Sievers trades fell through), so I suggested it again. So Al says, 'Why don't you go down and pick up the Indy club, and see how Ron Jackson's swinging the bat. If he's going well, we'll bring him back and send out Johnny.'"

Off went Comiskey to check on the progress of Jackson, and, in the meantime, in came the Cubs, who won the Boys Baseball Benefit Game 3-2 before 29,383. Twenty-four hours later, 23,838 fans, including some 7,500 bartenders admitted as Veeck's non-paying guests,were able to tear themselves away from the Tuesday night lineups of CBS ("Burns and Allen," "Red Skelton," "Garry Moore"), NBC ("Dragnet," "Steve Canyon," "Bob Cummings") and ABC ("Wyatt Earp," "The Rifle-man," "Naked City") to instead watch the power-hitting lineup of the Senators. Harmon Killebrew was leading the league with 24 homers and 53 RBIs, rookie Bob Allison had 18 and 46 and Jim Lemon 17 and 44. They never had a chance. Early Wynn (10-5) shut them down 4-1 with the help of the Sox's "big thumper," Sherm Lollar, who connected with Harry Simpson aboard in the eighth inning for his team-leading eighth home run.

Dick Donovan should have beaten the Washington strong boys 2-1 the next afternoon, but throwing errors by Earl Torgeson and Luis Aparicio in the ninth gave the Senators three runs and a 4-2 victory. Now Lopez was in a quandary. He couldn't afford to lose two out of three to Washington at home, particularly with the Yankees coming into town next. His plan had been to save Bob Shaw for the NewYork series, but now he might have to use him against the Senators. Then he remembered how well Barry Latman, who hadn't started a regular-season game in six weeks, had been pitching in relief (no runs, seven hits in his last 18 innings). Six weeks in the bullpen, under the tutelage of Ray Berres, had been beneficial.

"Latman," recalled Berres, "was a big kid—6-3, 210 or so. He wanted to go into like a crouch as he went into his delivery. I says, 'You're a big guy—why do you want to make yourself a little guy and not take advantage of all your size and strength?' So he made the change. He was easy to work with."

The only problem now was that Latman had started Monday night against the Cubs, two days after working 5 1/3 innings in relief at Boston. Lopez asked Latman if he could pitch again on two days' rest. Latman wasn't going to say no. "You were always scared to death that you weren't gonna pitch the next game." he said. "It was not like it is today. There were no guaranteed contracts. So you were scared to death. You'd do anything you could. You *never* said you couldn't pitch. Or they might get somebody who could."

That afternoon, June 25, Latman proved he could. Matched against Pedro Ramos, he stopped Washington 4-1 on five hits, striking out five, and even drove in the go-ahead run with a sacrifice fly. It was his first victory of 1959—after two losses—and was accomplished with his mother and his 14-year-old sister in the third-base box seats and with fellow Los Angeles native Earl Battey behind the plate. "I loved to pitch to Earl—better than I did to Lollar," said Latman. "I just seemed to get along better with Earl. And with John Romano, too. But with Lollar, I had to do everything he said. Couldn't shake him off. You had to throw what he and Lopez wanted, and that was that."

Lollar and Lopez would have wanted better than what Billy Pierce gave them the next evening in the series opener against the Yankees. In 5 1/3 innings, Pierce (8-8) allowed a two-run homer into the center-field bullpen by Hector Lopez plus four other runs and seven other hits as New York and Art Ditmar won 8-4 before a Friday night crowd of 37,909 that was more exuberant than usual. For, as Pierce was a victim in Chicago of a sixth-inning KO, Floyd Patterson was the victim in New York of a third-round TKO courtesy of Ingemar Johansson, who floored the champion seven times in the round before the bout was halted. But the fight at Yankee Stadium didn't have anything on the ones that broke out in the stands at Comiskey Park. At one point, five of them were going on simultaneously. "I remember that night," said Yankee pitcher Ralph Terry. "I was in the bullpen. And Johansson beat Patterson. It was a big upset. That night, the cops were draggin' 'em down to the bullpen and loadin' 'em on the paddy wagon. I mean, there were fights all over that place that night."

But for the presence of enough cooler heads, there might have been another on the field. Into the game, with the Yankees up by four in the seventh, came the bespectacled, hard-throwing and hard-drinking Ryne Duren, through 22 innings of a scoreless-innings stretch that would eventually reach 36. On this night, as on most others, he was throwing 100 m.p.h. smoke and not exactly certain nor concerned where his pitches were going. "He's the most exciting thing in baseball," said his manager, Casey Stengel. "When he hops over that bullpen gate, the folks stop eatin' their peanuts."

The ballplayers took notice, too. "Duren was unhittable," recalled

Sammy Esposito. "He and Herb Score in our league and Sandy Koufax in the National League—in our era, those three guys were the ones who were considered unhittable. If you hit them, it was because they hit your bat with the ball. You just couldn't see it. They were impossible to hit. One day at Yankee Stadium—in the afternoon, late innings, with the shadows—I'm in there for defense. Duren comes in, but we were ahead, so Lopez let me hit. And I swung and missed, and I took another swing and I missed. And Lopez called me back to the dugout, and I thought, 'Good, maybe somebody will hit for me.' So I get there and Al says, 'Go to right field on this guy.' And I said, 'Al, where do you think the ball will go if I *do* make contact?' And that broke him up."

Lopez was not laughing when, in the eighth inning of this game, Duren, in the process of striking out eight of the 11 White Sox batters he would face, fired two fastballs in the vicinity of Jim Landis' head, something he had done on more than one previous occasion. Landis got up and lined a single for his fourth hit of the night, but Lopez was boiling. "In the ninth," Ray Berres remembered, "when Duren came up to bat, Al brought in the little Cuban lefty, Rodolfo Arias. He told him, in Spanish, 'I want you to waste the first two pitches outside, and the next one I want you to stick in his ribs. We've got to stop this.' First time, Arias missed. Duren looked over at our dugout and Lopez yelled, 'That's right—we mean it! You can't keep throwing at Landis like that.' So the next pitch, he got him."

Duren walked very slowly toward first base, shouting oaths at Arias and at the Sox bench, who responded in kind. Umpires calmed down all hands, however, and the game proceeded without further excitement, other than Duren's striking out Luis Aparicio, Nellie Fox and Earl Torgeson in succession to wrap things up. Now the Yankees, in last place a month earlier, had the same record (36-32) and the same position in the race (third, two games out of the lead) as the Sox. Clearly, one club was on its way up. Just as clearly, that club was not the White Sox. But two things happened on Saturday, June 27, that were to help change the momentum.

Chuck Comiskey had returned from his week's stay with the Indianapolis team and convinced Al Lopez and Bill Veeck that the time had come to demote Johnny Callison, who was down to .163. "Johnny just got into a pattern where he was having trouble at the plate," said Comiskey. "The pitchers were setting him up, making him hit bad balls, stuff like that. That can happen to anyone. And it got worse and worse, to the point where he wasn't contributing anything to the offense." Comiskey's nomination for a replacement surprised Lopez, who was expecting a report on the progress of Ron Jackson. "I told Al, 'Big Ron is not the guy,'" Comiskey related. "'He's not ready, if he'll ever be ready. Now I'm gonna mention a name, and I know you're gonna shudder.' And I said, 'Jim McAnany.' And he said, 'McAnany?' I said, 'I've talked to the manager, Walker Cooper, everybody around the ballclub, and they think he's ready. Four-five games I saw him, everything he hit was a line drive. Even his outs. And he's doing a good job defensively in the outfield, which he's always done.' I said, 'You're trading outfielder for outfielder, and you won't really hurt the ballclub up here. In fact, you'll improve the ballclub.'"

Lopez wasn't completely sold. True, McAnany, 22, had hit .400—the best average in organized baseball—with 26 homers and 117 RBIs for Class A Colorado Springs the year before, but he had failed to impress Lopez either in a September call-up (0-for-13) or in an admittedly limited spring-training trial. Not only that, but the last time Comiskey had called up an outfielder in midseason from Indianapolis—in 1957—the player, Ted Beard, who had been hitting .347 in Triple A, went hitless in his first 24 at-bats with the Sox and needed a spurt at season's end to get his average up to .205. But this McAnany kid was a legitimate prospect, whereas Beard was 36 years old at the time of his summons. And, after all, McAnany was hitting .315 with seven triples, five homers and 41 runs batted in. Besides, Comiskey was persistent. He told Lopez, "I think he'll do it. Now for how long, I don't know. But right now, he's hot. He's one of the best hitters in the American Association."

At length, Lopez agreed and broke the news to Callison and put out a call for McAnany. "I was on a plane with the Indianapolis club when I got the word," McAnany remembered. "We were flying to Denver, and they got word that I was going up to Chicago. Got to Denver, got on another plane back to Chicago. Didn't even have my luggage. They said, 'Your luggage will be in Chicago the next day.' And it was."

He arrived at Comiskey Park later that afternoon, just in time for the day's second key moment. The ballgame between the White Sox and Yankees had gone to the last of the eighth inning with New York and Bob Turley, struggling this year at 6-7 but pitching this day to his 1958 Cy Young Award-winning form, leading Chicago and Bob Shaw 2-1, thanks to two Hector Lopez home runs. Norm Cash, batting for

Shaw, struck out to open the eighth, and when Luis Aparicio flied to Mickey Mantle in center for the second out, much of the crowd of 21,614 began to assume the worst: The White Sox were going to lose to the Yankees for the fifth straight time; they still couldn't beat the Yankees when it mattered. And then, remarkably, the inning, the game, the series and perhaps even the season turned.

Nellie Fox drew a walk and hustled to third on Earl Torgeson's single to right. Sherm Lollar walked to fill the bases for Harry Simpson, who had delivered before for the Sox in similar situations. Casey Stengel had lefty Bobby Shantz available in the bullpen, had he wished to play the percentages. Instead, he stayed with the right-hander, Turley, perhaps because he never seemed to have much regard for Simpson, a Yankee in '57 and '58. When the Yankees acquired "Suitcase" from Kansas City in a June 1957 deal that cost Stengel his pet, Billy Martin, New York GM George Weiss announced that Simpson would be the new Yankee leftfielder. Stengel's reaction: "I'll play who I wanna play." More often than not, it was someone other than Simpson, who disappointed Casey by hitting only .270 with 13 homers that year (after .293 with 21 the season before with a last-place club) and then by getting just one hit in 12 at-bats in the World Series loss to the Milwaukee Braves. In Stengel's mind, then, Simpson represented no serious threat.

For once, the Ol' Perfessor was wrong. Turley tried to jam Simpson on the first pitch with a fastball, but he didn't get it far enough inside. Simpson swung and drove the baseball high and deep to right field. It banged off the facing of the upper deck, next to the auxiliary score-board, for the most dramatic grand slam a White Sox batter had delivered since Tommy Byrne, another former Yankee, had beaten his ex-teammates with a two-out ninth-inning shot off Ewell Blackwell in May 1953 at Yankee Stadium. The Sox led 5-2, and Comiskey Park was bedlam. Jim McAnany, who had just arrived via taxi from Midway Airport, rushed up the ramp behind home plate to see what all the excitement was about. "Oh yeah, I remember," he said. "Harry had just hit it. When I got to the top of the ramp, first thing I saw was him rounding the bases. The place was going crazy."

The Sox then weathered long, long home runs in the ninth by Norm Siebern and Bill Skowron—both off Rodolfo Arias—to win 5-4, Gerry Staley striking out Tony Kubek to end it with runners at first and third. The sportswriters rushed to the Sox clubhouse and crowded around Simpson, who since getting into the starting lineup exactly one

77

week before had gone 8-for-26 (.308) with three doubles and two home runs. A soft-spoken sort, Simpson seemed embarrassed by all the attention. "I really don't know where the pitch was, or even what it was. I was just swinging and I got lucky," he said, almost apologetically, of his fifth career grand slam. "It felt good, really good, to hit it in a spot like that. That's the first grand slam I've hit that came in the late innings when the game was at stake."

His teammates were glad for Simpson. "He was a great guy," remembered Sam Esposito. "He was a wonderful gentleman. Real quiet. Didn't say boo, but a gentleman." Added Earl Battey: "He was pretty much a loner. You didn't see much of him. It was kind of strange, because he'd get up real early in the morning and go for these prolonged walks and then come back with a newspaper. And then he'd sit around and read the newspaper."

He likely enjoyed reading the papers the next morning, because his name was prominently splashed all over them. None of the stories mentioned that Simpson might have come to the White Sox much earlier in his career had it not been for the fact that the Cleveland Indians had brighter hopes for him than for the other black rookie outfielder they eventually chose instead to trade to Chicago. The deal went down on May 1, 1951, a three-club blockbuster that also involved the Philadelphia Athletics. All spring long, Paul Richards, then the Sox manager, had been after his general manager, Frank Lane, to trade for a flashy, speedy Cuban named Orestes "Minnie" Minoso, who had hit .339 with 40 doubles, 10 triples, 20 homers and 115 RBIs for San Diego of the Pacific Coast League the previous summer—while Richards was managing Seattle in the same league. Minoso's San Diego teammate, Simpson, had done even better: .323 with 41 doubles, 19 triples, 33 homers and a league-best 156 RBIs. Lane, while inquiring about Minoso, also made known to the Indians the Sox's interest in Simpson as well, even though Richards preferred Minoso because of his dash, versatility and better speed.

"Yes, we looked at both of them, Minnie and Suitcase," Chuck Comiskey said, decades afterwards. Comiskey, who later feuded bitterly with Lane and who even now would be in no hurry to add to the flamboyant former GM's already glistening Chicago legacy (Lane had earlier acquired Nellie Fox, Billy Pierce and Chico Carrasquel for next to nothing), was asked what caused the Sox to finally decide on Minoso over Simpson. "I think it was Cleveland," Comiskey replied, "and who they would deal. They were willing to deal Minnie before Simpson. And we had very good reports on Suitcase. My recollection of all those conversations is that we were interested in either one of them, but Cleveland seemed to be higher on Suitcase. So when it got down to the deal, they said, 'It'll only be Minoso.'"

As it turned out, of course, the Sox were overjoyed that the Indians had chosen to deal Minoso, who became an All-Star in Chicago while Simpson spent the decade drifting, suitcase in hand, around the American League. But on this weekend, the Sox were overjoyed, too, that Simpson had wound up in Chicago. Glad to be on hand, also, was Jim McAnany. "They put me up at the Piccadilly Hotel (at 5107 S. Blackstone Ave.)," he remembered, "and I went to the ballpark the next morning. And in the clubhouse, they were still talking about Simpson's homer. And then Don Gutteridge, one of the coaches, comes in and says to me, 'Hey, you're in left—get ready!' I'm thinking, 'Oh geez. And against Whitey Ford, too.'"

Ford, the brilliant Yankee lefthander, was to oppose Early Wynn in the opener of the Sunday double-header. As the crowd of 42,121 began to gather, Wynn, seeking relief from the midday June heat, was sitting with the *Daily News'* Jack Kuenster in the runway that led to the Sox dugout. At the other end of the runway were the stairs leading to the home and visitors' clubhouses, which at that time were both on the third-base side on the second level. "We were in there where it was nice and cool," recalled Kuenster. "We're just talking back and forth. So all of a sudden, I hear the clomping of spikes coming down the stairs, and here it's Hector Lopez, coming down to go out onto the field."

Lopez had been the Yankees' main offensive force in the series' first two games, with his three homers and five runs batted in. In fact, he had battered Sox pitching all year, going back to when he was still wearing a Kansas City uniform. In his last 28 at-bats against the Sox, Lopez had 13 hits, nine for extra bases. Wynn had had enough.

"As Lopez walked by us," Kuenster recounted, "Early Wynn did this deliberately—he took his spiked shoe and slashed the side of Lopez's right foot. He practically cut half the shoe off. And Lopez stops, looks down, says: 'Hey Wynn, why'd you do that for?' And Wynn just glowered at him. And then, in the first inning of that first game, Wynn faced Lopez and hit him with a pitch right in the forearm. And it was a really painful blow for Lopez. And that was it. He got one hit, a bloop single, the whole day."

With Lopez stopped, the rest of the Yankees fell in line (Mickey Mantle, for instance, was limited to one single in each game), and the Sox went on to sweep the double-header 9-2 and 4-2. There were more reasons for the sweep than the silencing of Lopez and Mantle, however.

79

First there was the successful big-league debut of McAnany, who singled to center off Ford in his first major-league at-bat, only minutes after he had gunned down Bill Skowron, trying to score on Yogi Berra's single. Remembered McAnany: "I'm out there in left field. Big crowd. I'll tell ya, I was as nervous as a whore in church. But I got the hit my first time up, and I threw the guy out at the plate. So that's probably the best thing that could've happened to me. I get to the ballpark, boom, I'm in the game. You know, I didn't have time to think."

Another factor in the sweep was the pitching of Wynn, who went the distance for his 11th victory of the year and 260th of his career and who, as was his custom, drilled not only Hector Lopez but also Norm Siebern, who had had the audacity to hit a two-run homer off Wynn in the sixth. Then there was the Game 2 performance of Dick Donovan, who threw one-hit ball into the eighth inning and evened his record at 5-5. "Dick had gotten really slider-happy," Ray Berres remembered. "And the Yankees, their righthanded hitters, would blast those sliders into right-center. So I said, 'Dick, you can't throw slider after slider. You've got to back somebody off the plate. You've got a good sinking fastball. Bust that sinker in on them.' His sinker bore in on right-handed hitters. I said, 'Gil McDougald's wearin' your butt out. For God's sake, when the situation presents itself, bust that sinker in on him a time or two, so he doesn't keep going out after your slider.'"

McDougald, incidentally, went 0-for-3 to complete an 0-for-6 afternoon. Meanwhile, the oft-maligned White Sox bats were booming. The Sox hit five home runs on the day, one each by Al Smith, Earl Battey and Bubba Phillips and two by Sherm Lollar. Lollar's two-run blast in Game 1 put Wynn ahead for good, and after one of Bill Veeck's between-games extravaganzas—this one featuring elephants, a sword swallower, a snake charmer, clowns and, of course, midgets—Lollar gave Donovan a huge lift with a three-run shot off Don Larsen with two out in the first inning of Game 2. Lollar had hit both with one of Al Smith's bats, which at 33 ounces were two ounces lighter than the ones he normally used. Lollar's decision to switch was almost as wise as the Sox's off-season decision not to switch.

"Best deal I ever made was not trading Lollar," Chuck Comiskey said. "We had the two great young catchers, Romano and Battey. We had Lollar out on the block after the '57 season. In a way, I was trying to force Lopez's hand, to catch one of our young catchers. Sherman wasn't getting any younger. So I had feelers out, throughout our league and the National League, that if somebody needed a good veteran catcher, Lollar might be available. We were always weak at third base in those days. That's why I was dangling Lollar out there, hoping to come up with a veteran third baseman. So I kept getting offered a cheese sandwich. Finally, mid-winter of '58-59, I'm still working on it. And Al says, 'Aw, Charlie, the hell with it. Why don't we just go with Sherm? I'll work the two kids in here and there. But Sherm knows the pitching staff, handles them well, and he's still hitting well.' So I said fine. So, what if I had traded Lollar?"

Chances are the White Sox would not have been in the position in which they now found themselves. They were in second place, one game behind Cleveland but now three games ahead of the real team to beat, the vanquished, fifth-place Yankees—and loaded with the confidence that came with convincingly defeating the world champions in front of a big crowd. "I said last year that the Yankees could be beaten," Al Lopez told reporters. "I said it again this season. Only thing was, my own club couldn't do it themselves. That's why I say these two games might well be the big moment of our season."

Casey Stengel seemed to agree: "We thought we had the pennant Saturday," he sighed. "Today the Chicagos got it."

But it was a bit too early to declare the pennant race over, especially when it became apparent two nights later that the White Sox's June roller-coaster ride was not quite over. Victimized by a sudden dip this time was Saturday's hero, Harry Simpson. The Sox went into Cleveland Tuesday night June 30 for a first-place showdown with the Indians and were beaten 3-1 by Cal McLish, who allowed just four hits. But the Sox had him in trouble early. In the third, they led 1-0 with runners at second and third, but Simpson tapped to the mound to end the threat. In the Cleveland third, Simpson played Dick Brown's fly ball to right into a double and then dove for and missed Vic Power's two-out liner. When the ball shot past him, Simpson jogged after it, grabbed it and, after falling down, finally let go with a weak throw toward the infield. By then, Power was rounding third and heading for an inside-the-park homer, enough to defeat Billy Pierce.

Simpson, thus 0-for-2 in the outfield, also went 0-for-4 at the plate, then took some heat from Warren Brown in the *Chicago American*: "Harry Simpson showed, both at bat and in the field, why his tour of major-league duty is not maintained in any one locality for long."

Harsh criticism, surely, for a man who three days before quite possibly had changed the course of a season. Such was the way things went for the White Sox during June of 1959. But better days—indeed, glorious days—were just ahead.

JULY

Majesty and Magic

Chicago was beside itself with excitement over the impending visit of Queen Elizabeth II, who had decided to make the city the only U.S. stop on her 45-day tour of North America. The occasion was the official opening of the St. Lawrence Seaway, which had suddenly linked Chicago with the Atlantic Ocean. The Queen, Prince Philip and their entourage were scheduled to arrive Monday, July 6, on the royal yacht *Britannia*, and Mayor Daley and his minions were working overtime to ensure every detail of the visit would go off without even the most minor of hitches. One-fifth of Chicago's police force was to be assigned solely to Queen-related duties, a fact no doubt duly noted by the city's thieves and other potential evildoers.

The entire visit, which was to last 13 hours, was carefully scripted, starting with the Queen's arrival at the foot of Congress Street. From there she would make the short walk to Buckingham Fountain, scene of the city's official welcoming ceremony. There would follow stops at the Art Institute, the International Trade Fair at Navy Pier and the Museum of Science and Industry—and, so as to make sure the royal visitors would not go hungry, Illinois Gov. William Stratton's luncheon at the Ambassador West, a pre-dinner reception for Midwest governors and mayors at the Drake and, finally, Mayor Daley's 1,000-guest dinner at the Conrad Hilton. The event was to wrap up at midnight with a spectacular fireworks display on Lake Michigan as the royal yacht departed.

Certainly no one knew then that by the time this month was over, the White Sox, too, would have taken on a regal appearance. No one could have known that, by July's end, the Sox would have grabbed the American League lead for good, gone 11-1 in one-run games during the month and won 20 of 27 overall, and actually caused Chicagoans to

dare speak of the possibility of a World Series in their city. Reasons for
the majestic ascent abounded, but chief among them was the abrupt
turnaround of Al Smith, who, with the pain in his left ankle finally
having begun to subside, batted .303 in July, led the Sox in RBIs with
18 and blasted seven home runs—all but two in the eighth, ninth or
extra innings and all but one winning or tying games. There also was
the production of newcomer Jim McAnany, who hit .322 for the month
with 16 RBIs; the offense (.299, 15 RBIs) and even more spectacular
defense of Jim Landis; the monthlong brilliance of the bullpen buddies,
Gerry Staley and Turk Lown; and the continued steadiness and leadership of Nellie Fox, who used July to present a convincing case for his
Most Valuable Player candidacy by collecting 42 hits in the 28 games
(there was one tie) and batting .359.

Not to be overlooked was the play of Luis Aparicio, who almost
singlehandedly got the month off on the right foot—pun intended—by
leading the Sox to a 6-5 victory July 1 at Cleveland. With his team
down 2-0 in the second, Aparicio, hitting in the No. 8 spot for one of
the few times all season, tripled in two runs and, when he got to third,
faked as if he were going to continue home. Second baseman Jim Baxes
fell for the move, throwing behind Aparicio in an attempt to trap him
off base. Not only was the throw unnecessary, it was wild, and as third
baseman George Strickland chased down the ball, Looie merrily trotted
home with the lead run. In the ninth, with the Sox ahead 5-3, he
walked, stole second, took third on a sacrifice bunt by Staley and scored
on Landis' sacrifice fly. The run proved huge when Woodie Held
smacked a two-run homer off Staley in the Cleveland half to make it
close. Staley, who had rescued starter Barry Latman from a two-on,
none-out jam in the sixth, gave way to Lown, who retired Vic Power,
Tito Francona and Rocky Colavito without a ball leaving the infield.

It was the beginning of a remarkable July for the two relievers and
roommates. Staley last gave up an earned run on July 4 and then closed
the month with a string of eight appearances, covering 15 1/3 innings,
without surrendering another. For the month, he had an earned-run
average of 1.88 over 24 innings. As for Lown, he allowed five runs,
four earned, across 20 2/3 innings for a 1.74 ERA. He also won four
games, while Staley saved three. Each made 11 appearances (not a great
amount by today's standards, but Sox pitchers threw 10 complete games
during the month, more than many staffs now collect in an entire
season). The two were similarly close off the field as well.

"He was the best roomie I ever had," said Lown. "It worked out so nice. We were like brothers. It was like we were one. What I wanted to do, he wanted to do. What he wanted to do, I wanted to do. When one of us wanted to take a walk, the other was there, too. If one of us wanted to go eat, the other went."

"We liked the same restaurants," Staley remembered. "We didn't carouse around bars and all that stuff. We took in movies—went out to see stuff. Who wanted to sit around the lobby or the room all the time? In some of those big cities, it was nice just to get out and watch the public."

Mainly, they'd walk. "And maybe do some shopping, and that's about it," said Lown. "But you know, we never talked that much about baseball. About pitching, either. Everything else under the sun, but not that."

"What the heck," Staley reasoned, "we saw enough of it on the field."

One explanation for the pair's success in July and throughout 1959 was that pitching coach Ray Berres had seen enough of them on the field and in the bullpen to get both straightened out when they ventured away from what had worked best for them in the past.

"The off-season before, I remember Al and Chuck were talking about using Staley in a deal," Berres said, referring to Al Lopez and Chuck Comiskey. "And I was lying in bed one night, and I started thinking about Staley. And I remembered distinctly that every time he'd be ready to get called in, and he was loose, he fooled with that knuckleball of his. And I remembered that every time he left the bullpen, after having thrown so many knuckleballs just to keep loose, it affected his sinker.

"So I called Chuck and I told him, 'Don't move Staley until we see him in spring training, 'cause I've got an idea what's happened to him and I'd like to prove it to myself and to you and Al both that the knuckler is taking away from his sinker, the control of it and the velocity.'"

In Tampa, Berres convinced Staley to concentrate on his sinkerball and put the knuckler on the back burner. "I didn't use it very much," Staley confirmed. "If I'd get ahead of a good hitter, maybe I would try a knuckler. But otherwise, I'd use the sinker at least 90 percent of the time."

"And gee," said Berres, "he went on to have an outstanding year. He'd throw that sinker, and that ball would be at the knee or below, and it would sink with some velocity. Before, he wasn't throwing that good hard sinker. It was more of a drifting sinker. And I'd noticed that it was always after he'd been throwing that knuckleball."

"Before" had been 1958, when Staley's ERA had climbed to 3.16 after being at 2.06 in '57, his second with the White Sox, who had acquired him on waivers from the Yankees at the behest of then-manager Marty Marion, his former St. Louis Cardinal teammate and manager. In '58, Staley had struck out only 27 batters. A season later, emphasizing his hard sinker, he would strike out 54.

As for Lown, the '58 season had been his first with the Sox but hardly his first in Chicago. He had pitched 3 1/2 years for the Cubs, beginning in 1951, before being sent down to Los Angeles of the Pacific Coast League, where he had two big years before returning to the Cubs for the '56 and '57 seasons. He was successful both years, leading the National League with 67 appearances in '57, but he wasn't happy.

"At Wrigley Field," he said, "you had Ernie Banks' wind blowing out, boy oh boy. Driving to the ballpark, as I approached it, I'd look at the flags to see which way the wind was blowing and say a 'Hail Mary' if the wind was blowing out. And most of the time it was. But I found out later that the Cubs had wanted to get rid of me. I'd had a fabulous year in L.A. in '55 (12-5, 2.13 ERA in 61 games, 96 strikeouts in 114 innings), and when it was over, the general manager out there, John Holland, called me in and said, 'We're selling you back to the Cubs.' And I told him, 'I had a good enough year. Someone else will buy me. I don't want to go back to the Cubs.' Because they had done me dirty as far as money goes. A couple years later, Holland was named general manager of the Cubs. And I think he remembered that conversation."

If this Lown fellow didn't want to be a Cub, Holland figured, he should be granted his wish. In spring training of '58, after he hadn't been used much, save for a few appearances in "B" games, Lown knew what was coming. "I told my wife and kids, 'We're leaving. I don't know where, but I have this feeling that I'm leaving this club.' It was just a matter of where and when."

Where was Cincinnati. When was May 8. "The Cubs traded me for a pitcher with a bad arm—Hershell Freeman," Lown said, laughing. It wasn't the last Cub trade to elicit laughter, of course, but the Cubs were not actually sending Lown to Cincinnati. Al Lopez, who believed the White Sox had lost the pennant in 1957 because they lacked a reliever who could come into a game late and overpower hitters, had been greatly impressed when Lown worked the final five innings of the '57 Cubs-Sox boys benefit game that August and struck out six while allowing only two hits and no walks. "I did a hell of a job against them," Lown remembered, "and I had my good fastball that night." Lopez couldn't get Lown from the Cubs, who simply didn't trade with their crosstown rivals at that time. It was only after Lown had gone to the Reds, who had expressed interest in veteran Sox first baseman Walt Dropo—then 34 but capable of regularly reaching Crosley Field's left-field fence, 328 feet away—that the Sox were able to land the pitcher they thought could help them. The deal was announced as separate waiver purchases of $15,000 each, one day apart, but it was, essentially, a trade.

"So everyone was satisfied," said Lown. "Lopez got me and the Reds got Dropo. And the Cubs got rid of me. And it was the best thing Holland could have done for me."

Ray Berres still had to do something for Lown. Again, the coach had been doing some observing and thinking, the latter of which he had plenty of time for on his daily, 142-mile round trip between his home in Silver Lake, Wis., and the ballpark. "I had heard Turk on the radio once, and he had said, 'I pleased the crowd in Wrigley Field every time I threw that blooper pitch. They'd get a big kick out of it.' So I remembered that, and I also remembered him throwing it in the bull-pen, and I also remembered that every time he threw it, it took him three, four, sometimes five pitches to get back with that good fastball. See, he kind of choked the ball when he threw the blooper pitch, and then it would take him a while to readjust his delivery. So we took that pitch away from him. I told Sherman (Lollar), 'We won't even signal for it.'

"One time he complained to a friend of his who was also an acquaintance of mine. This guy told me, 'Turk doesn't like the way he's being handled.' And I says, 'Hey, don't let Al Lopez hear that. We picked him up for 15,000 bucks. We're his last stand. He can probably have another couple years with us if he's satisfied to do what we got him to do—throw the fastball. As long as he realizes that.'"

To his credit, Lown did. His blooper pitch—he called it the "butterfly"—was sent to the scrap heap, as were, to a lesser degree, his slider and curveball. And his career, like Staley's, was back on track. After the two roomies' teamwork in the July 1 game at Cleveland, they were busy again the next two nights in Detroit, but now it was Al Smith's turn to step, no longer gingerly, into the limelight. Almost since the opening week of the 1958 season, Smith had been, as Warren Brown put it, "the target for some of the most shameful vocal abuse ever put upon a White Sox player." His sin? He had taken over in left field for South Side hero Minnie Minoso. Had Smith's Sox debut been as memorable as Minoso's in '51, when he homered off the Yankees' Vic Raschi his first time up, the fans might have adopted him as their new darling. But he didn't, and they didn't. Instead, he had an off year, hitting .252 with only 12 homers, 58 runs batted in and just three stolen bases. Of course, it didn't help any that Minoso, in Cleveland, had hit .302 with 24 homers, 80 RBIs and 14 steals. So far, 1959 was even worse. Smith entered July with a .223 average to go with three home runs and 15 RBIs. What few people were aware of was the pain in Smith's left ankle, which he had jammed while sliding into home plate at Detroit in the Cleveland Indians' final game of 1957.

"A bone chip developed, but they told me the ankle wasn't broken, so I went home to Chicago figuring the ankle would get better," recalled Smith, who still lives in Chicago. "In December, I was traded to the White Sox. The trade didn't bother me. I was glad to come here, 'cause my home was here. But what did bother me was I went to spring training and I wasn't able to maneuver my foot. I didn't really have any spring training at all. I could hardly run. But they never told the sportswriters that. I played more than 130 games that year on that bad ankle, but I paid for it. I got it from the fans. I wasn't much of a replacement for Minnie."

The way he was going now, he wouldn't have been much of a replacement for Ted Beard. But then, suddenly, the pain in the ankle began lessening. "Somewhere around the last of June or first of July," Smith said, "I didn't have to wrap it so tight. It had bothered me when I'd take off, to start running. If it had been the right ankle, I wouldn't have been able to play at all. Because, as a righthanded hitter, you're putting your weight down on it."

The Al Smith who had played so well for Al Lopez in Cleveland finally was going to show up in a White Sox uniform. On July 2, he hit a grand slam during a five-run ninth-inning rally that wasn't quite enough in a 9-7 loss to the Tigers in Detroit. The next night he struck again. Not long after Gary Player had shot a final-round 68 to win the British Open and Alex Olmedo of the U.S. defeated Rod Laver to win the men's singles title at Wimbledon, Smith added his name to the headlines, when, with two out in the 10th, he drove a 3-2 pitch from Detroit's Tom Morgan into the Briggs Stadium left-field upper deck for a 6-5 Sox victory. The Sox were now 8-2 in extra-inning games, and Smith had driven in the winning run in four of them. But they were still a game behind, because Cleveland had beaten Kansas City as Herb Score, striking out 14, improved his record to 9-5. Score, beginning to resemble the pre-injury superstar of '55 and '56, now had 110 strikeouts in 114 innings. A revived Herb Score, the White Sox knew, would make the Indians difficult to overtake in the second half. (As it happened, Score pitched only 46 more innings and won no more games in '59.)

Besides Score, also worrisome to the Sox—perhaps because of the presence of so many former Yankees—were the Kansas City A's, to whom they paid a visit July 4-5. They hadn't won a series all year from the Athletics and were 3-7 against them overall. Something had to be done about that, the Sox players realized. "You could feel things getting tighter," recalled Jim McAnany, "because the games against Kansas City became very important. We sensed it. The guys, they didn't talk much about it, but you knew it was in everybody's mind."

So, while some 500,000 Chicagoans and suburbanites celebrated the 4th of July by watching a mock invasion assault by Marines at Montrose Beach, followed later by a giant lakefront fireworks show, the Sox assaulted lefty Bud Daley and his successors for 17 hits in Game 1, five of the hits by Jim Landis and four by McAnany. These fireworks were provided by home runs from John Romano, Bubba Phillips and Sherm Lollar, the latter's a two-run tie-breaking shot in the seventh that gave Bob Shaw (5 1/3 innings of one-hit pitching in relief of Dick Donovan) a 7-4 victory. And though the Sox lost the second game 8-3 as ex-Yankee Jerry Lumpe drilled a two-run homer off Billy Pierce and ex-Yankee Johnny Kucks baffled them over 4 2/3 innings to rescue ex-Yankee Rip Coleman, they rebounded Sunday afternoon to win a game they needed badly, because Cleveland was busy completing a three-game sweep of Detroit and a loss would have meant a three-game deficit heading into the All-Star break. Instead, the Sox beat a pitcher, Ned Garver, they hadn't beaten in two years and did so in the kind of stirring fashion that was to mark the bulk of their victories the rest of the month.

Down 3-1 in the eighth, the Sox cut the lead to a run on a homer by Luis Aparicio, his fifth of the year. With one out in the ninth, Al Smith tied it with his sixth homer and third in four days. In the 10th, Aparicio singled, stole his 25th base and scored on Nellie Fox's single. Turk Lown, finishing four innings of one-hit relief, got the win and the Sox headed home to Chicago, where, though it mattered little to them at the time, their eventual World Series opponents, the Los Angeles

Dodgers, had swept the Cubs in a double-header before 32,728 at Wrigley Field to move within a half-game of National League co-leaders Milwaukee and San Francisco.

Not all the Sox flew to Chicago. Aparicio and Fox, top American League vote-getters in the All-Star balloting—then done by the players, coaches and managers—departed for Pittsburgh along with Early Wynn, Billy Pierce and Sherm Lollar to represent the Sox in Tuesday's game against the National League. Aboard the flight, too, were coaches Tony Cuccinello and Ray Berres, invited by their former manager, Casey Stengel, to be part of his All-Star staff. Another of Stengel's former players, Al Lopez—who had played for Casey both with the Brooklyn Dodgers and Boston Braves—had respectfully declined an All-Star invitation, preferring the tranquility of his bayside home in Tampa. Before he left, Lopez, noting the Sox were 9-2 in extra-inning games and 16-4 in contests decided by one run, joked: "If we get nothing but extra-inning and one-run games the rest of the way, we're a cinch." Inwardly, he was worried about the inconsistency of two of his supposed big winners, Pierce (8-10) and Dick Donovan (5-5), both of whom had been shelled by the A's in Saturday's double-header. Pierce's ERA had zoomed to 4.20, Donovan's to 3.87. "Give us 20 wins total from Pierce and Donovan in the second half," Lopez said, hopefully, "and we'll win the pennant." Had he known then that he would only get 10 more wins total from the pair, Lopez might have remained in Tampa the rest of the summer.

The hot rumor at the All-Star festivities was that Lopez might not be remaining in Chicago beyond that summer. The word was that Bill Veeck was considering bringing in the bombastic and belligerent Leo Durocher, now working, like Veeck, part time as an NBC baseball analyst, to manage the White Sox in 1960. Of course, the source of the rumor was Leo himself, who casually mentioned to a couple of columnists that though he had received no formal offer, he had discussed the possibility of managing the Sox with one of Veeck's stockholders, New Yorker David Marx. The last thing Veeck wanted to do was alienate Lopez, especially in the middle of a pennant race. Reached in Chicago, Veeck laughed off the story and suggested Durocher was hoping for employment in the proposed Continental League, whose backers were shooting for a 1961 opening in locales like New York, Houston, Dallas-Ft. Worth, Minneapolis-St.Paul and Toronto. Said Veeck: "I haven't discussed Durocher as a prospective manager. In fact, the first I knew that he was letting the world know he was available was when this story from Pittsburgh was called to my attention. Maybe Leo's getting ready for the third major league. I do know he isn't getting ready for the White Sox."

Chicago, meanwhile, had been ready for Queen Elizabeth, whose one-day visit had shunted into the shadows such visiting luminaries as Groucho Marx, Mel Torme, Mort Sahl and Les Brown and his Band of Renown—all in town performing at various venues. A million and a half people had lined the route of Her Majesty's procession from Buckingham Fountain, down Lake Shore Drive, through the Loop and then on to Navy Pier. TV, radio and newspapers provided full coverage, the *Chicago American* even coming out with a "Royal Souvenir Edition," whose main page one story was written by Hal Bruno, much, much later one of ABC television's top political commentators, and was headlined by the gigantic words, "SHE'S HERE."

With the Queen having departed, though, attention turned to Pittsburgh's Forbes Field, where the National Leaguers defeated the American League All-Stars 5-4 despite starter Early Wynn's solid three-inning stint (one run allowed) and Nellie Fox's two hits. The sight of Fox and Luis Aparicio together in the middle of the AL infield was, in a way, a tangible reminder to everyone as to why the White Sox were where they were in the standings: 43-35, in second place, two games behind Cleveland, 2 1/2 ahead of third-place Baltimore and three ahead of New York. Both mighty mites were fielding well, Fox was hitting .330 with 41 RBIs and Aparicio was at .291 with a major-league-leading 25 stolen bases, just six fewer thanWillie Mays' majors-best total of 31 for the entire 1958 season. Sox fans were aware that Little Looie was on pace to steal 50 bases—no big-leaguer had stolen that many since George Stirnweiss in 1944—and when 36,743 of them turned out Thursday night, July 9, to watch the Sox resume the schedule against Cleveland, a few brought along something not heard at Comiskey Park in several years—the old "Go-Go" chant.

Originated during the 1951 season, when speedy Sox rookies Jim Busby and Minnie Minoso combined to steal 57 bases and helped transform Comiskey Park from a ghost town into a place of pandemonium day after day, night after night, the chant, like Busby and Minoso, eventually had faded away. Yes, Aparicio and Jim Rivera and Jim Landis and others still had been stealing bases, but the "Go-Go" cry steadily had dissipated as Paul Richards' running, daring Sox of the early '50s evolved into a more conservative club in mid-decade under Marty Marion. But now, in the second half of the '59 season, the shouts of "Go! Go!" were to slowly but surely return—especially whenever Aparicio reached base—and the White Sox again would be known across the nation as the Go-Go Sox.

The second-half fun began in the first inning, when Herb Score made the mistake of letting Aparicio, the leadoff man, get on base, this time with a single. The crowd knew Aparicio was going. Score knew Aparicio was going. Aparicio knew he was going. He had studied Score's moves, his reactions, and something else.

"I almost fell over when he told me this," Jim Landis remembered, "but he said that he watched the pitcher's eyes. And I got out there after he tells me this and tried watching the pitcher's eyes, and I'm saying there's no way I can see the guy's eyes. But that's what he said, and I know he was serious."

"Some pitchers, yes," confirmed Aparicio. "They would have a certain look in their eyes when they gonna throw to first base. And after three-four years of stealing bases, I found out I can steal easier off lefthanded pitchers—some from their eyes, some from their moves, because every pitcher got a different move. So I just tried to find out what they do different when they gonna throw to first base and when they gonna throw to home plate. They gotta do something different."

Aparicio, having first seen Score the second day of the 1956 season, knew when the Cleveland lefty was going to throw home. With "Go! Go!" shouts ringing in his ears, he took off for second base and made it easily for his 26th theft. Nellie Fox grounded out to second baseman Jim Baxes, enabling Aparicio to take third, from whence he then scored on Landis' sacrifice fly. It was the quintessential 1959 White Sox rally: one run on one hit, thanks to Aparicio's speed, Fox's unselfishness and Landis' fly ball—and, too, the crowd.

"Remember how they all used to holler 'Go! Go! Go! Go!'?" asked Bob Shaw. "The involvement of the people, the enthusiasm. That was something. Oh yeah, I still hear it. I talk about that a lot, when people ask me about the old days and about the '59 White Sox, how you could hear 'em yelling 'Go! Go! Go!' A lot of enthusiasm. It really got us going."

It got the opposing pitcher going, too. "The idea isn't the crowd yelling 'Go! Go!'—although that's certainly part of it," said Billy Pierce. "But you know that that runner is gonna go. The same thing with Maury Wills with the Dodgers. I always said I was lucky in 1962 (when Pierce was with the Giants and Wills was stealing 104 bases). He never stole a base on me. But there was only one reason: He never got a hit off me. Except one time, when he got a single and it rolled through the outfielder's legs and he wound up at third. But a good speedy baserunner, leading off, is gonna upset a pitcher."

Aparicio wasn't leading off in the fifth, with the Sox down 2-1, but Score was nonetheless concerned about him. This time, he put him on with a walk. So Aparicio was at first and Bubba Phillips at second with two out for Fox, who reached on an infield hit to fill the bases. Landis followed with a single to left for two runs, and the Sox and Pierce were on their way to a 4-3 victory and to within a game of the lead. Their biggest fan—Mayor Daley, plus his wife, "Sis," and daughters Mary (20) and Eleanor (18) and sons Richie (17), Mike (16), John (12) and Billy (10)—were on their way by train to Los Angeles for the national mayors' conference and a Disneyland vacation. They would be gone for at least 14 days but most assuredly would be back for the Yankee series July 28-30 and probably for the Sunday, July 25 double-header against Baltimore. The Daleys seldom missed a Sunday double-header.

"The mayor," Chuck Comiskey remembered, "would leave religiously at 5:30 at Sunday double-headers, because Sis would have dinner on at 6. The boys would've been eating all day—popcorn, hot dogs—but he'd kinda cut 'em off about an hour before they were gonna go home. And I'd kid the mayor: 'How are they gonna eat dinner?' 'They'd *better* eat dinner. Or else their mother is gonna get me.'"

The Indians at last got Early Wynn, who had beaten them seven straight times, on Friday night, July 10, shelling him out in the fifth inning of an 8-4 Cleveland victory before 41,588 people, the majority of whom sat through a pair of rain delays totaling 1 hour 17 minutes hoping the Sox could come back and make a game of it. They did. In fact, the Indians did not clinch this one, thus regaining their two-game lead, until the ninth, when they scored three runs against Bob Shaw. The inning's big hit was a bases-loaded, two-run, two-out single by Tito Francona, who ended up 4-for-5 on the night and was now hitting .407 over 135 at-bats.

"Francona, he absolutely owned me," Shaw remembered. "I could throw a ball today, and if he was standing within 10 feet of it he could whack a base hit somewhere, I'm certain of it. He just wore me out. The only time I could ever get him out was toward the end of my career, when I was throwing a spitball. I could get him out with a spitball, but I couldn't get him out with anything else."

The next afternoon, as Clark Gable and his wife, Kay Williams, celebrated their fourth anniversary in St. Gilgen, Austria (Ms. Williams must have figured the marriage was living on borrowed time—she was Gable's fifth wife), the steel industry's chief negotiator, R. Conrad Cooper, emerged from his latest bargaining session with the steelworkers' union and said he saw "no possibility of an agreement before Tuesday's strike deadline." That was not good news for the many steel plants on the Far South Side and in Northwest Indiana and for the 90,000 people who worked in them. There was, however, a cheering note from 35th and Shields, where the White Sox defeated the Athletics 8-3 as Barry Latman held Kansas City hitless over the final six innings. "For the A's," wrote Warren Brown, "Roger Maris was the only annoyance Latman had." Maris, now hitting .308, drove in all the Kansas City runs and, added Brown, in a remarkable bit of prescience, "looked so fine that any day now the Yankees may be expected to make a deal for him."

While the Yankees were getting hammered a fourth straight game in Boston and the Indians were splitting a pair with Detroit, the White Sox swept Sunday's double-header from Kansas City 5-3 and 9-7 to draw within a game of first place. The keys were Al Smith (5-for-8 with a homer on the day) and Jim McAnany, who, after making two outstanding catches in right field the day before, contributed a bases-loaded triple to left-center off lefty Bud Daley in the first inning of Game 1 and another, this a liner down the right-field line off right-hander John Tsitouris, in the fifth inning of Game 2. McAnany, in 37 at-bats since his June 27 callup, was batting .378 with 11 RBIs and had made a believer of the once-doubting Al Lopez: "He's a fine-looking player. He's in the lineup to stay."

Chuck Comiskey felt vindicated ("He made me look awfully good for about two months—I thanked him for not making me look bad"), and Jim McAnany felt elated.

"Those were two big ballgames," he said. "That was kind of a turning point. It seemed to mean a lot to the club, because Kansas City had really been rough on us earlier. And that's when I realized I was really contributing. Before, all I wanted to do was make the bus. Not that I was numb, but I felt I was a lucky guy. I just was in the right place at the right time, and when I came up I did well in my first game. No doubt if I hadn't started off well I would've been out of there just as fast as I'd gotten there. No question in my mind. But I like to think I got there because I had worked hard. I was small, I didn't have the talent a lot of guys had. But it had been a dream of mine, and I worked hard to get there."

Now he wanted to stay, so he was willing to do whatever it took to make sure he did, even if it meant being No. 8 in the batting order. "My job," he said, "was to get on base, somehow, however I did it. The reason was Lopez did not want the pitcher to lead off the next inning. He didn't care what I did, as long as I didn't make the last out. That was my role."

A .378 batting average, which was to climb to .432 by midweek, was proof McAnany was not making many outs, let alone the last one. "What had helped," he said, "was getting new glasses. I used to wear those regular, everyday frames. And I was in a closed batting stance, and the left frame, the corner of it, would block out my vision. I would lose that inside pitch. So they fitted me with wrap-around glasses, and I opened up my stance just a tiny bit. And I didn't have that problem anymore. It made a world of difference. I owe a lot to that optometrist."

As the White Sox flew to Boston the next day, Monday, July 13, they owed a debt of gratitude to the Red Sox, who were completing a five-game sweep of the Yankees at Fenway Park. New York was now 6 1/2 games back of Chicago, which was one behind Cleveland, a team the White Sox had beaten nine times out of 14. Confidence was growing on a club that was already a pretty unified bunch.

"I never saw any jealousy," McAnany said. "No animosity. Everyone wanted each other to do well. You talk about a team effort, this was it."

Remembered Jim Landis: "It was a good blend of young and old. It really was. The best part of it—and I've always said this was a big part of our winning—was we got along so well. Maybe seven to 10 guys go out and have a bite to eat together on the road. Just relax and enjoy each other. And even when we were at home, four or five couples would go out for dinner together. There was great unity. I can remember sitting in an outdoor restaurant in Washington, almost 20 guys sitting there, having a belt, getting ready to have dinner. We'd just sit around and bullcrap for a couple hours. You know, nothing wild, just having a nice time.

"I remember six or seven of us going to an Italian place—Esposito, some other guys—and every meal there I'd have spaghetti. And I can remember Bob Shaw, who was a real health nut, always trying to convince me: 'God dang it, I keep telling you, you gotta put just butter on it. No sauce!' And every time, I'd still have my sauce. He'd just shake his head. But it was nothing wild, crazy. It was just a very mellow, fun time. But a bunch doing it together."

Often a bowling alley was the meeting place of choice. "The guys would be bowling—Fox, Sherm Lollar, two-three other guys, every time we'd get into a town, they'd always go bowling," said Turk Lown. "You could go down to the bowling alley, and you could join them, no problem. Nothing would be said. Or you'd go in the bar at the airport to have a beer or something, and you'd meet a couple of the guys, and you'd sit down and it'd be like brothers."

There were, too, the constant card games. "I would say the most fun we had was getting out to the ballpark early and playing cards," said Earl Battey. "We were a great card-playing team. We played a game called 'Oh Hell,' a kind of variation of bridge. And we played a lot of Hearts."

"And," added Al Smith, "we played poker. Nellie, Sherm, four or five of us, if we had a rainout, we'd go play poker. We'd play a dollar limit. That kept our mind occupied."

Race, insisted Battey, was no barrier. "The black guys and the white guys got along well. We used to socialize. I was always a big jazz fan. And when I saw Landis down in Sarasota, at the Sox's fantasy camp, that's what he was tellin' all the guys: 'Man, when we were traveling, Earl and I used to hang out at all these jazz places.' It was always us, Esposito, Rivera ... we'd go to all the jazz joints in whatever city we were in."

One reason for the team's togetherness was the mind-set of veterans like Pierce, Fox, Lollar and Rivera, who had been with the White Sox for years—Pierce since 1949, Fox since '50 and Lollar and Rivera since '52. "You gotta give credit to those four to have those things happen—couples going out together, guys hanging around together on the road," Landis said. "They set the tone good that way. They weren't afraid of losing their jobs. They felt that, 'Hey, if we're gonna win, we have to help you—meaning the younger players. They weren't afraid to help the young guys. They didn't see them as a threat."

"The veterans treated me so well," McAnany recalled. "I had my locker right in between Nellie Fox and Sherm Lollar. And those two were great gentlemen. They treated me like I had been there all along."

This feeling was nothing new, said Luis Aparicio, who had come up to the Sox in 1956. "We had a lot of veterans, like Early Wynn and Sherman. Especially Sherman, he really helped me, in showing me the attitude I should have for the game. When I broke in, he and Fox were there. I got a lot of help from those guys. I don't think I woulda made it if it wasn't for them. I'd just gone from two years in the minor leagues and I come to the big leagues, with a lot of stars there. But their attitude to me was great."

Billy Pierce explained the veterans' theory: "Just because a bunch of us had been in a number of All-Star Games, that didn't make us better than anybody else. Everybody was out there working together to make us a winner. That was the idea. You needed everybody."

Another reason for the closeness of this White Sox team was that, unlike earlier Chicago clubs that had been built entirely through Frank Lane's trades and purchases, this one contained nine players—more than a third of the team—who had been signed by the Sox and had come up through the farm system. (The '56 team, for example, had contained only two—rookies Aparicio and Sammy Esposito.) Landis and Battey had been together in 1953 at Colorado Springs; Aparicio, Battey and Rodolfo Arias had spent 1954 in Waterloo, Iowa; Aparicio and Esposito were teammates all of '55 at Memphis; and McAnany, John Romano, Norm Cash and Barry Latman had spent that season together in Waterloo. Romano, Latman and Landis were at Memphis in '56, and for a time that same year Landis joined McAnany and Arias in Colorado Springs. And so it went. Cash and McAnany were at Waterloo again in '56; Latman and Romano were teammates at Indianapolis in '57; and Romano, Cash, Latman and, briefly, McAnany were at Indy in '58.

"We were kinda all the same age," said McAnany, "and we all came through the system. I think that's what we felt good about. All the hard work was paying off. We were all happy for each other, and we were close. And a lot of that comes from the camaraderie you develop in those bus leagues."

Now they were on the bus again, riding from Logan Airport to their hotel in Boston. "We used to stay in the Copley Plaza," recalled Chuck Comiskey. "Old hotel, ritzy hotel. You could walk over to Fenway Park. At the hotel, there was a lady at the desk, looked about 85 years old, and she knew every ballplayer that ever came in there. She was like a mother hen to them. And she would lay out their mail, with their keys, right out there on the front desk. Now, in the meantime, our players had decided that since they were from Chicago, they ought to all have guns. So about 10 or 12 of them are carrying these .45s— water pistols. They all come in and she says, 'Oh, how are my boys?' And somebody says, 'I was expecting a special package. Could you look to see if it's back there?' And she turns around to look for it, and they pull out the squirt guns and they let her have it. And she's looking up to the ceiling to see where the water's coming from. Next day they squire her down to a nice shop and buy her three or four new dresses."

That night, Tuesday, July 14, only hours before the nation's sixth steel strike since World War II began, the White Sox struck early and often against lefty Ted Wills and his relief to cool off the Red Sox 7-3, Billy Pierce evening his record at 10-10. John Romano—catching more and more when opponents used lefthanded pitching, with Sherm Lollar moving to first base—had a single and a home run, and the amazing Jim McAnany collected two more hits to raise his average to .390. His biggest hit came in the fourth. With runners at second and third and one out, Boston's recently hired manager, Billy Jurges, ordered an intentional walk to Bubba Phillips and brought in righthander Murray Wall to face McAnany. Jurges, under whom the Red Sox had gone 6-1, apparently had been celebrating his team's conquest of the Yankees too much to have heard of the Chicago rookie's penchant for delivering with the bases loaded. McAnany lined Wall's first pitch into center field for two runs, and the White Sox were ahead to stay.

They were almost ahead in the standings as well. Whitey Ford and Ryne Duren had teamed up that same night to edge Herb Score and the Indians 1-0 at Yankee Stadium, and the Sox were just .002 out of first place. In Washington the next day, Senate Rackets Committee Chairman John McClellan (D-Ark.) told Teamsters boss Jimmy Hoffa he was a "fountainhead of corruption." Also in Washington, another senator, Hubert Humphrey of Minnesota, announced he was a candidate for the 1960 Democratic presidential nomination. In Chicago, where the College All-Stars were preparing to meet the world champion Baltimore Colts in the annual College All-Star Game, coach Otto Graham was impressed by the potential of a 235-pound tackle from Syracuse named Ron Luciano. In Boston and New York, it rained, forcing doubleheaders in both locales the following afternoon, July16.

While the Indians were losing both of their games to the Yankees, the White Sox were splitting at Fenway, winning the opener 4-3 on Lollar's tiebreaking double in the seventh before losing 5-4 in Game 2 despite cleanup hitter Romano's three hits and two RBIs. Even with the loss, the Sox were in first place by a game and heading to New York, where they were about to play two of the most dramatic games in their history.

The first was on Friday night, July 17, when Ralph Terry and Early Wynn battled in a pitchers' duel for the ages. As 42,020 people sat enthralled, Terry took a no-hitter into the ninth, Wynn a one-hitter. The score was 0-0. Wynn had been aided greatly by several marvelous defensive plays, most notably one by Jim Landis, who robbed Mickey Mantle of an inside-the-park home run with a sensational catch out by the monuments of past Yankee greats, at that time some 460 feet from home plate.

"You look back," said Landis, doing just that, "and you say, 'My God, you hit the ball that far and you don't get anything for it?' If I'd hit a ball that far and somebody had caught it, I think I'd shoot him."

Now, leading off the ninth, Jim McAnany shot one past Terry into center field, thus taking care of the no-hitter. Wynn bunted in front of the plate, but Yogi Berra's throw to second was too late to get McAnany. Now came another bunt, this one by Luis Aparicio, moving the runners to second and third. Nellie Fox, his hitting streak at 13 games and his batting average at .332, was given an intentional walk, loading the bases for Landis, who lined a 1-2 fastball into right field for a two-run single. Wynn, after allowing the second and final New York hit of the night, closed out his 2-0 victory with the help of a sparkling 3-6-3 double play begun and ended by Earl Torgeson, who took the relay from Aparicio just in time to get Mantle at first. Umpire Ed Rommel not only called Mantle out, he threw him out for bumping him during the raucous rhubarb that ensued. When order was restored, Berra popped to Fox, Wynn had his 12th win, the Sox were still in first by a game and veteran New York writers were calling what they had just witnessed the most exciting, most captivating game at Yankee Stadium since Don Larsen's "perfecto" in the 1956 World Series.

A Chicago writer, Warren Brown, managed to get his reaction to the game printed on Page 1 of the next day's *Chicago American*: "Man and boy, I've been playing, watching or writing about baseball for most of the present century. Yet I can't recall any other game as supercharged for thrills, especially of a spectacular defensive nature, as Early Wynn's 261st victory."

All Brown needed to do was wait a few hours. Bob Shaw, who had grown up on Long Island, opposed the aforementioned Larsen in another game that left both the participants and the spectators emotionally drained. "I'm pretty sure the whole family was there," Shaw said. "I know my dad was there for sure. He was a Giants fan, my sister was a Yankee fan and I'd been a Dodger fan. That one I remember well. The thing is, I go to bed the night before, thinking, 'My God, how the hell are we gonna top this?' And then to have a hell of a ball- game to follow that one up. And that's really what it took to beat 'em. That worked out great."

Shaw was great, both pitching and hitting. The Sox were down 1-0 in the fourth—it would have been 2-0 but for Al Smith's gunning down Hector Lopez at the plate on Bobby Richardson's second-inning single—before Jim McAnany doubled to score Smith (3-for-4) and Shaw singled to score McAnany.

Larsen and Shaw thereafter matched zeros. Then came another thrilling ninth inning. With one out, Yogi Berra singled to right, and when Norm Siebern did the same, Berra's pinch-runner, Bobby Shantz, raced to third. Now Hector Lopez, the noted Sox-killer, approached the plate, intent on repeating that age-old Yankee ninth-inning magic. Sensing the same thing, Al Lopez approached the mound, took the baseball from Shaw and waved in Gerry Staley. The Yankee Stadium crowd—the paid attendance was 27,959, but well in excess of 30,000 were on hand—created a clamor worthy of such a terrific ballgame. Staley threw one pitch. Hector Lopez ripped a one-hopper at Nellie Fox, who threw to Luis Aparicio, who relayed to Earl Torgeson for a game-ending double play. On a day on which Lawrence Welk had fired Alice Lon, his "champagne lady," for showing too much knee on Welk's TV show, the White Sox, still one ahead of Cleveland and now 19-5 in one-run games, had again shown the kind of championship class that had them thinking about champagne showers.

"When we left that Stadium that night," said Jim McAnany, "we felt it. A lot of it had to do with that series in New York."

To Casey Stengel, a lot of it had to do with McAnany, or whoever that rookie outfielder was.

"Last spring," said Stengel, talking to Chicago writers after the game, "I didn't know Lopez was gonna come up with that McSweeney in right field. They've been a real ballclub since that McSweeney come up. First time I see him, he throws one of my men out at the plate in Chicago. He makes catches, he runs, he hits good. You ain't had a bit of trouble in right field since he got there. Before that, you had nothing else but trouble."

There was to be precious little trouble the rest of the month for the White Sox, a double-header setback that Sunday in Yankee Stadium notwithstanding. Losses to Whitey Ford and rookie Eli Grba—a graduate of Bowen High School on Chicago's Southeast Side—coupled with Cleveland's split at Boston left the Sox in second place but just .001 in arrears. That was nothing compared to the record peacetime deficit announced the next day by the Treasury Department: $12.5 billion for fiscal 1959. There was other news on this July 20, as the Sox returned to Chicago for what would be a memorable homestand. Blues singer Billie Holiday was buried in New York City, dead at age 44 from a heroin overdose. President Eisenhower said he saw no hope for a quick settlement to the steel strike. Listening closely was Bill Veeck, who announced that all striking steelworkers, as well as steel management personnel, would be his guests at that Saturday's Sox-Baltimore contest. "They might as well come to the ballgame," Veeck reasoned. "They're not working."

The Sox were about to begin work on a new string of victories, five altogether, the first four of them by one run. There would then come one of those July rarities—a Sox loss—followed by six more wins. "It was right after the All-Star break," recalled Earl Battey, "that we started believing we were going to do it—when we started putting together little spurts. Winning five or six in a row, and then we would lose one and then win four or five more. We never had any prolonged losing streaks."

Said Bob Shaw: "As we progressed and we were doing well, you became cognizant of the fact that, hey, we've got a pretty good ballclub and it looks like we can do it." Added Jim Landis: "We started winning a pretty fair share of games, and at the same time, the Yankees weren't really controlling anything. And I think a lot of guys just started picking up that tempo and saying, 'Hey, we can.' Plus, the skipper saying all along about the Yankees, 'They're ripe—they are ripe.'"

The same attitude had reached the front office, Chuck Comiskey remembered. "We started winning some games that maybe we didn't have a right to win. Then, I think you start to say, 'The good Lord is shining on us,' you know what I mean? The other guy pitched a good game against us, a five- or six-hitter, and we eke out a 2-1 victory. And we had a lot of those games. And those same games, in the previous years, we did not win."

One such game was on Tuesday night, July 21, a night forever to be revered among Boston trivia buffs as the night the Red Sox, at long last, became the final major-league team to break the color line, sending out Elijah "Pumpsie" Green as a pinch-runner in the eighth inning. A half-inning earlier, as 32,116 people (including 3,582 bartenders admitted as guests of that patron saint of all bartenders, Bill Veeck) screamed for a run to break a 1-1 tie, Luis Aparicio drew a walk from Red Sox starter

Tom Brewer, took second on Nellie Fox's sacrifice bunt and scored when Landis, trying to check his swing, blooped an RBI single over first base. The scoreboard had just flashed the final from Cleveland, where 46,912 had seen the Indians' Cal McLish beat the Yankees 5-1. The Sox had to win to keep pace. Dick Donovan (7-5), with more help from Landis, who raced back to haul down Frank Malzone's ninth-inning drive at the center-field bullpen fence, made the 2-1 lead hold up, getting Jackie Jensen on a checked-swing roller to first with two on to end it. "That," Veeck informed Boston writers, "was one of our easier games."

And it was one of Donovan's best. "Donovan, he was hilarious," Landis remembered, laughing. "On the nights he pitched, on the dugout floor, one foot over on either side of him, could be all the crap you wanted. But right in front of him had to be spic and span. That and his towel. He always had a towel, and he always had it folded just so. And Rivera would sit and throw stuff onto the floor and unfold the towel while Dick was out there on the mound. And Dick would come back in after each inning and clear it all up again. And the towel would be unfolded, and he'd just fold it right back up. I don't think it ever dawned on him. He was in such a zone, his mind was so focused. And never, 'What the hell's goin' on here?' None of that. He was into it that much. But when he didn't pitch, he'd be the guy pulling some kind of trick."

Donovan didn't pitch the next day, when Jim Rivera turned 37, "Porgy and Bess" (starring Sidney Poitier and Dorothy Dandridge) made its Midwest premiere at the McVickers and another "Tricky Dick," Vice President Nixon, left with wife Pat for Moscow and an 11-day tour of the Soviet Union. At Comiskey Park, the Sox trailed Boston and rookie Jerry Casale 4-2 with two out in the seventh when Nellie Fox doubled, Jim Landis walked, Sherm Lollar singled for one run and Billy Goodman doubled to make it 4-4. In the ninth, after a second straight shutout inning by Turk Lown, Fox singled, moved up on Landis' bunt and scored on Lollar's single for a 5-4 victory.

Next came yet another thriller. On Friday night, July 24, the Orioles' Hoyt Wilhelm was sailing along with a three-hitter, leading the Sox and Billy Pierce 1-0 in the eighth inning. Jim McAnany was on first with two outs and Fox was up. The Indians, who had split the final two games of their series with New York, had just beaten Washington 5-2. A Baltimore victory would move Cleveland into first place by a half-game. The only good news for the Sox so far was that a 22-year-old farmhand, Gary Peters, had thrown a no-hitter for Indianapolis to beat Minneapolis in the American Association. Now, Fox would make sure there was more good news.

Fox, who already had two of the Sox's three hits, drove one of Wilhelm's knucklers into the gap in right-center for a game-tying triple. He was left stranded as Wilhelm got Landis to end the inning, but the 29,274 fans on hand figured victory was at hand. So did the White Sox. Recalled Al Smith: "It got so that by the end of July and the first of August, we figured we couldn't be beaten. We had a feeling on the bench that we were gonna win." He remembered the dugout seating configuration: Coach Johnny Cooney, sign-stealer supreme, sat in the corner, closest to home plate. Next came Al Lopez. On the bench next to Lopez was a towel. "No one," said Smith, "sat on that towel. We all said, 'That's where Jesus Christ sits.'"

It was Smith who provided the divine finish this time. With one out and the bases empty in the last of the ninth and the score still 1-1, Smith swung at a Wilhelm flutterball and met it perfectly. The ball sailed on a line toward the left-field stands, near the foul pole. When the ball disappeared into the seats, Comiskey Park erupted. Pennant fever was building. And why not? Teams that win games this way win pennants. "As soon as I hit the ball," Smith said that night, "Wilhelm started walking off the mound. When I saw him do that, I knew the ball was gone." Said Smith years afterward: "Wilhelm was tough, but I hit him pretty good. Not for a high average, but you'd get a pitch from him every now and then that you could handle. Sometimes he'd throw that knuckler too hard and it wouldn't do anything. If he had the wind facing him, the ball would do more. I think it was blowing out that night. But I hit a line drive, and I remember it just made the first or second row."

More drama followed the next afternoon, although it was different from the drama created earlier in the day in Moscow, where Richard Nixon and Nikita Khrushchev engaged in what became known as "the kitchen debate." In the kitchen of a model home on display at the American Exhibition, the two men aired their differences on everything from Berlin to the status of women, with Nixon telling the Soviet leader, "You must not be afraid of new ideas. After all, you don't know everything." There was nothing new at Comiskey Park: Baltimore and the White Sox were at it again, another low-scoring, pitcher-dominated ballgame. Already the two clubs had played a 17-inning game and one of 10 innings, plus two others decided in the ninth. Still to come were an 18-inning 1-1 tie in August at Baltimore and a 16-inning 1-0 Orioles victory in September at Baltimore. In this one, before a crowd swelled to 25,782 by some 13,000 Veeck guests—7,445 steelworkers, 2,977 honor students and 2,778 Pony Leaguers—Billy O'Dell was leading Bob Shaw 2-1 as Sherm Lollar stepped up to open the home ninth. Lollar hit O'Dell's first pitch into the lower deck in left for his 13th home run, and the game was tied. And it would stay tied for a while. Shaw, winning pitcher in the 17-inning victory over the Orioles on June 4, lasted 11 innings this time before giving way to Turk Lown.

"Those Baltimore games," Shaw said, shaking his head in recollection. "Well, you kinda got yourself prepared: 'Hey, I gotta bear down here, do a good job, because this is the way it's been.' You do the best you can no matter what, but you just *knew* you'd better do well against them, because there weren't gonna be too many runs scored either way. So you just hope it comes out in your favor."

Thanks to Lown and Harry "Suitcase" Simpson, it did. Lown (7-2) held the Orioles scoreless for six innings before the Sox broke through in the 17th again. Jim Landis singled, took off for second on a steal attempt and kept going to third as Lollar singled to center. Baltimore manager Paul Richards, with nobody out, ordered Al Smith walked intentionally to set up a force at any base. Jim Rivera obliged, grounding into a first-to-home forceout. Time was called. Sammy Esposito went in to run for Lollar at third, and Simpson came up to hit for Bubba Phillips. Simpson had batted only three times since June 30, each as a pinch-hitter. Only Larry Doby, who hadn't appeared in a game since June 20, was a more forgotten man on the club. But the Baltimore pitcher was Billy Loes, off whom Simpson had hit a game-winning homer (for Kansas City) in April and a bases-loaded single in May. This time, with the infield and outfield playing shallow, Simpson sent a drive that bounced to the wall in right-center, sending Esposito across with the winning run at 5:47 p.m., 4 hours 17 minutes after the game's first pitch. Observed Simpson: "I guess I hit Loes pretty good."

Simpson's game-winner was not the only thing that enabled Al Lopez to breathe a bit easier that evening. News had arrived from Detroit that Yankee slugger Bill Skowron, in the lineup again after missing two weeks with a bad back, had broken his left wrist in two places on a play at first base. Reaching over into the runner's path for a typically inaccurate throw from the scatter-armed third baseman, Hector Lopez, who already had made two errors in the game, Skowron had collided with Detroit's Coot Veal. "The Moose," having hit 15 homers with 59 RBIs in just half a season, was out for the year. So were the Yankees, in fourth place and eight games out of first. Now, perhaps, Al Lopez could finally relax a little.

"I roomed with Al at Brooklyn in 1934," said Ray Berres. "He was an entirely different player than he was a manager. As a player, he just had to pretty much worry about himself. He was very affable, kidded around, carried on. He was very, very serious as a manager. And all the years he managed, he had stomach problems. He'd be taking all those damned pills."

"Lopez couldn't keep food down," said Jerome Holtzman, then covering the club for the *Chicago Sun-Times*. "He'd eat soup all the time. He'd go out for dinner and have a couple bowls of soup."

The steady diet of one-run thrillers wasn't helping Lopez's stomach troubles, surely. So the next day, Early Wynn and Al Smith, two of his favorites, provided the perfect remedy. Smith hit his ninth home run, an inside-the-parker, with two on and two out in the fourth, and Wynn threw a two-hitter as the White Sox "routed" the Orioles 4-1 in Game 1 of the Sunday double-header before 35,207 on Bill Veeck's latest promotion, S & H Green Stamp Day. Green Stamps were the rage at the time with housewives, few of whom were coming to Veeck's ballpark.

"I came up with the idea," Veeck said, "because I've been worried about the almost complete nonexistence of women at Comiskey Park." Thus, he gave each woman attending the double-header an S & H stamp book with 100 Green Stamps, plus a coupon redeemable for 50 more stamps. Also, there were countless between-games giveaways, including food items, a rotisserie grill and even a new convertible.

Milt Pappas, 20-year-old Baltimore righthander, put an end to the festive mood, not to mention the Sox's five-game winning streak, with a five-hit shutout in Game 2, but matters improved immediately the next day when Boston's Jerry Casale three-hit the Indians 4-0 in Cleveland. Now the Indians and White Sox were both 56-40 and tied for the lead. Baltimore was in third place, 7 1/2 games behind, New York fourth at 8 1/2 back and Kansas City fifth, nine games out. On top of the popular music standings was "Lonely Boy," by Paul Anka. And feeling a bit lonely as he arrived in Chicago for a three-game series was Yankee manager Casey Stengel. Not only was he without Bill Skowron, but four more of his players—Gil McDougald, Tony Kubek, Bob Turley and Bobby Richardson—were at Henrotin Hospital with assorted ailments, and only Richardson was expected to be available for Tuesday night's series opener. Even so, Stengel hadn't lost his sense of humor. When a visitor to his Del Prado Hotel suite at 53rd Street and Hyde Park Boulevard brought up that day's official announcement of the birth of the Continental League, Stengel said: "That's great. Now a manager can get fired in three leagues instead of just two."

Not that Stengel himself had to fret about job security, although when this series ended, some people back in the front office in New York certainly had to be wondering what in the world had happened to their Yankees. A loss Tuesday night, July 28, a rain-shortened tie on Wednesday night and a defeat Thursday left them in fifth place at 48-51, 10 1/2 games out. Their in-league farm team, Kansas City, had won 11 straight, was 50-49 and in third place, two games ahead of them. Thus, the White Sox, for so long bullied by the Yankees, now had helped sink them to new depths of embarrassment.

It hadn't been easy, of course. Tuesday night's game, played before 43,829 people, including Mayor Daley and his sons, went down to the final out. The catalyst, as he had been all season, was Nellie Fox, who singled home his roommate, Billy Pierce, in the fifth inning for a 2-1 lead, then singled again in the eighth ahead of a two-run homer into the centerfield bullpen by Mr. July, Al Smith, his seventh home run of the month. In Cleveland, the Indians had split a double-header with Boston. In Chicago, the Sox were ahead 4-1. A victory would put them back in first place by themselves. But a three-run lead was too much. Pierce opened the ninth by giving up a single to Hector Lopez, then watched Luis Aparicio bobble Elston Howard's grounder for an error. Rookie Fritz Brickell singled to score Lopez, and Marv Throneberry's fly ball to right sent Howard to third. Don Larsen, in a pinch-hitting role, sent Howard home with a sacrifice fly. Ah, now it was 4-3. Comfortable again, Pierce fired a called third strike past Bobby Richardson to end it. Comiskey Park was bedlam. Among the more joyous celebrants was Mayor Daley. "This is the greatest sports year in Chicago's history," he shouted above the din, publicizing the upcoming Pan-American Games without actually mentioning them. "But it won't be complete until the Sox are playing in the World Series."

The World Series was on Bob Shaw's mind the next night, when, despite predictions of stormy weather, another 43,599 packed Comiskey Park. After giving up a two-run, game-tying homer to Yogi Berra in the sixth inning, just minutes before a monsoon hit the South Side and washed out the contest, Shaw turned on himself. Aware the Dodgers had gone into first place in the National League by a half-game over the Giants and by a game over the Braves, and aware the Sox could have extended their lead over Cleveland to 1 1/2 games had he not thrown the gopher ball to Berra, Shaw remarked, "We're not gonna make it to the Los Angeles Coliseum by throwing pitches like that."

Better pitches were thrown by Early Wynn the next afternoon, a day that happened to be a special one for future Hall-of-Famers. In Cincinnati, Cardinals rookie Bob Gibson, age 23, shut out the Reds 1-0 for his first major-league victory. In San Francisco, Willie McCovey, age 21, made his major-league debut and collected two singles and two triples in four at-bats in the Giants' 7-2 romp over the Phillies. In Chicago, Wynn, age 39, spoiled Casey Stengel's 69th birthday and Yankee rookie Eli Grba's homecoming with a six-hit, 3-1 victory before 30,858. Al Smith drove in two more runs to help Wynn (14-6), who struck out nine, equal his victory total of 1958, when he lost 16. In '58, too, he had gone 0-6 against the Yankees. So far in '59, he was 3-0 against them, having allowed three runs in 27 innings.

"I think maybe we rested him too much last year," Al Lopez said after the game. "We were thinking about his age, and we were giving him four and five days' rest. Today he pitched with three days' rest. His control is much better this year than it was last year, when he had more rest. I guess age doesn't mean anything to him."

"Early was really amazing," agreed Sam Esposito, many years later. "He was one of the few guys who could pitch up high and get away with it. He'd throw the ball up at the letters and very seldom would he get hurt up there. That's what was amazing. When he's 38 or 39, he can't throw as hard as he did before. When they throw hard and they're young, that's different. But he was getting away with it at 39. He'd make you go up and reach for it. And the umpires knew he was throwing it up there, and they gave him the high strike."

Wynn had given the White Sox an extremely big victory on this afternoon, because the man he had been traded for, Minnie Minoso, drove in all of his team's runs in Cleveland's 4-3 decision over Boston that night. Thus the Sox, almost an afterthought when this month began and the Queen's visit dominated the newspapers, remained front page material—and one game ahead of the Indians. Their battle royal at the top of the American League was to rage four more weeks, until a climactic weekend series in Cleveland. But before that, several key ballgames, plus a key acquisition, were still in store for Chicago.

AUGUST

Hello Klu, Goodbye Cleveland

As July became August, Vice President Richard Nixon mingled with Nikita Khrushchev and other Soviet dignitaries in Moscow and extended the premier an invitation to visit the U.S., an offer Khrushchev heartily accepted. In Chicago, Mayor Daley blamed the Republicans in control in Springfield for the lagging pace of work on the Congress Street expressway. In the northwest Chicago suburb of Elk Grove Village, new three-bedroom homes with attached garages were being sold for as little as $17,500, four-bedroom homes with two full baths for $21,750. In the southwest suburb of Orland Park, for $190 down and monthly principal and interest of $99.80, a family could move into a new $17,300, three-bedroom home. At the neighborhood National food store, a 1 1/4-pound loaf of bread was going for 19 cents, a pound of bacon for 49 cents, a tube of tomatoes for 19 cents and six 12-ounce bottles of Coke for 45 cents—plus deposit. Downtown, Jimmy Stewart and Lee Remick were starring in "Anatomy of a Murder" at the Woods Theater, "A Hole in the Head"—starring Frank Sinatra and Edward G. Robinson—was playing at the Oriental and Rod Steiger was "Al Capone" at the Cinestage. And, over at the Empire Room of the Palmer House, Nelson Eddy was beginning a one-week stay.

Though the months had changed, the White Sox's opponents had not. The Washington Senators had opened a weekend series at Comiskey Park on Friday evening, July 31, and had been beaten 7-1, held to one run—for the second time in five weeks—by Barry Latman. Again he had been aided by an Earl Torgeson home run, as had been the case in Latman's previous victory over Sievers, Killebrew & Co. on June 25.

Now, with August upon them, the Sox had won 23 of their last 31

107

games and were leading second-place Cleveland by a game. Yet even against the sad-sack Senators, who were in the midst of a 16-game losing streak, runs for Chicago were exceedingly difficult to come by. On Saturday afternoon, the White Sox managed only one hit off young Camilo Pascual in seven innings and trailed 1-0 when they came to bat in the ninth. Pitching now was Dick Hyde, a bespectacled righthander from Downstate Illinois who threw almost underhanded, a kind of forerunner of Dan Quisenberry.

With one out, Norm Cash batted for Sammy Esposito and drew a walk. The crowd of 30,435, almost half of them Little Leaguers, began making the sort of ruckus usually produced only by the night-game customers. Then, when Torgeson lashed a single to right, sending Cash racing to third, the place really began rocking. The fans knew, as the players and management had begun to suspect, that this was their year, and that this game was just another one-run victory waiting to be snatched from the loss column. Wrote Bill Veeck: "When the fans became convinced ... that after 40 years their time had finally come, they got behind the team and almost pushed us to the pennant. We'd come into the ninth inning, three runs behind, and they'd fill the park with a sort of electric excitement that told us they *knew* that one way or another we were going to pull it out. So there'd be a base on balls and an error and a squibbling hit and a wild pitch and a sacrifice fly, and we'd win."

Sure enough, Jim Landis came through with a hit, not a squibbling one but a line drive to center field. Rookie Bob Allison came over to try to cut it off, but the ball skipped away from him, and first Cash and then Torgeson came across, Torgeson sliding home just ahead of the throw to catcher Steve Korcheck. The Sox, despite collecting just three hits all afternoon, had won 2-1. They were now 25-5 in games decided by a run and were two games ahead of the Indians.

The next afternoon, an even stranger and more exciting ending was in store for the 26,866 believers on hand. Russ Kemmerer, a right-handed pitcher of middling ability who one year hence would be pitching for the White Sox, was pitching against them—and, as Pascual had, quite effectively. He carried a two-hitter and a 2-1 lead into the ninth. Then it started. Luis Aparicio opened with a single, and the "Go! Go!" chant began in earnest. Kemmerer threw to first to keep Looie close. With that came the inevitable boos from the crowd. Another throw over. More boos. Another throw. More boos, louder this time. Finally, Kemmerer threw home, and Nellie Fox put down a splendid bunt. Korcheck, the catcher again this day, hustled out from behind the plate, picked up the ball and then fired it wildly past first baseman Roy Sievers and down the right-field line.

Aparicio, never hesitating, sped home with the tying run and Fox wound up at third with the potential game-winner. Now came the obligatory intentional walks to Al Smith and Sherm Lollar to fill the bases and set up a force at any base. Manager Cookie Lavagetto's decision made sense, not only from the standpoint of percentage baseball but also because the next hitter, Billy Goodman, was fighting a losing battle to maintain a batting average of .190. But here, with the infield and outfield pulled in close, and the crowd in an uproar, Goodman lined a drive to left field that would have been an out in any other situation but in this case sailed over the head of the drawn-in Lenny Green. The Sox had won another improbable one, 3-2. Their record in one-run games was now 26-5.

"But you know," said Jim Landis, reminiscing one brutally cold January afternoon in the warmth of the Hyatt Regency Chicago, "to be honest, I never felt any pressure in those one-run games, because we got so adapted to that style of play. We expected the games to be close. After a while, that's how your mind gets to working: 'Hey, here's another one—let's go get it.'"

The constant straining for runs was causing concern in the front office, however, if not in the clubhouse. And when, after a day off for an experimental second All-Star Game in Los Angeles, the Sox left on a 13-game road trip and scored a grand total of nine runs in the journey's first five games—one of them an 18-inning, 1-1 tie with the Orioles halted by Baltimore's city curfew—Bill Veeck, Chuck Comiskey and Hank Greenberg hurriedly went into conference at Comiskey Park and huddled over the waiver list. Their target was a veteran lefthanded hitter who could deliver the long ball. They already had Sherm Lollar and Al Smith capable of doing so, on occasion, from the right side. Their top home run hitter from the left side was Earl Torgeson, with all of eight. The Opening Day optimism surrounding the power potential of Norm Cash and fellow lefthanded-hitting rookie Johnny Callison had long ago faded. Harry Simpson, a defensive liability, was confined to pinch-hitting duty. And Larry Doby, who had had one at-bat since June 20 and had been bothered again by back pains, had finally been sent to San Diego of the Pacific Coast League to make room for a much-needed 10th pitcher, rookie Ken McBride, soon to turn 24.

Eventually, the front-office trio narrowed its choices to two men whose acquisition would not cost any key personnel. Both were reserve first basemen in the National League—George Crowe of the St. Louis Cardinals and Ted Kluszewski, alias "Big Klu," of the Pittsburgh Pirates and of southwest suburban Argo. Both earlier had had big years with the Cincinnati Reds, especially Kluszewski, the NL home run and RBI champ in 1954, when he collected 49 and 141. He had also led the league in hits in '55, a season in which he had belted 47 more homers. He had taken to cutting off his uniform sleeves at the shoulder tops so as to expose his bulging biceps to enemy pitchers, a development that eventually had led management to design a sleeveless uniform for all Reds players. Klu, one could argue, had become the symbol of an entire ballclub. However, late in the 1956 season, the 6-foot-2-inch, 245-pounder had begun experiencing back pain. During the off-season, the problem was diagnosed as a slipped disc, and Klu sat out most of the '57 season, providing teammate Crowe, at long last, an opportunity to show what he could do as a regular.

Crowe, a large man himself at 6-2, 210, had been a backup with the Reds and, before that, with the Braves. Because of his race, his debut in organized baseball had not come until 1949, when he was already 26—at least—and after he had spent two years with the New York Black Yankees of the old Negro leagues. That's where Veeck and Greenberg, then at Cleveland and heavily scouting black talent, first became aware of him. In his three minor-league seasons, he had hit .354, .353 and .339 with RBI totals of 106, 122 and 119. But it was not until 1957 that he finally got a chance to play every day, and he responded with 31 home runs, 92 RBIs and a .271 batting average. Now, with the Cardinals, a club with three other first basemen in Bill White, Joe Cunningham and the aging Stan Musial, he was mostly a pinch-hitter but a dangerous one. And, if need be, he could step in and play first base occasionally.

In short, his role in St. Louis almost mirrored that of Kluszewski's in Pittsburgh. The White Sox saw them both as potentially the type of experienced veterans who could provide a lift, physically as well as emotionally. But, as usual, there was a difference of opinion between Greenberg and Comiskey as to which of the two would be the best man for the job. Greenberg wanted Crowe, who was hitting in the neighborhood of .285, and Comiskey wanted Kluszewski, who was down around .250. Comiskey did not want Crowe, who, fairly or unfairly, had developed a reputation among baseball's establishment as a bad influence on young black players, who knew Crowe as "Big Daddy" and admired him for his unabashed independence.

"We used to see George Crowe in Tampa every spring with the Reds," said Comiskey. "So I knew about him. But in the meantime, I put it right to Tony Cuccinello, God love him. He was like Al Lopez's right-hand man. He did a lot of checking around the National League. He comes to me one day and says, 'I don't get much of a good report on Crowe. What do you know about him?' 'The only thing I know about him, Tony, is he's kind of a clubhouse lawyer and a little bit of a troublemaker.' Tony looked at me and says, 'Those are the kinds of reports I'm getting. Most of the coaches over in that league are saying, 'Geez, be careful. He's a very moody guy.'"

Comiskey had gone to Veeck, who, despite his long friendship with Greenberg and earlier knowledge of Crowe, was keeping out of the fray. Recalled Comiskey: "I'd said to Bill, 'I think Klu would be great—if he's *alive*. Local guy, from Argo High, shows those big muscles.' And I never mentioned my conversation with Cuccinello, but I said, 'I hear stories. I've heard reports. I don't know whether Crowe's the kind of guy who'll do it for us, where he'll take the pressure. That's gonna be a pressure situation. Plus he's got kind of a bad attitude in the clubhouse. Now, if Klu is alive, or even warm, he could be the guy who could do something for us. But there again, he hasn't been playing regularly, either.'"

To help make the decision, Veeck dispatched two scouts, one to follow Crowe for a week, one to follow Kluszewski for a week. After the week was over, the scouts were to switch assignments, all the time gathering information on the two players from people in the National League. In truth, Crowe provided the more impressive performance, hitting a ninth-inning pinch grand slam against the Dodgers on August 13 in St. Louis, and another ninth-inning pinch homer, this one with the bases empty, on August 22 in Cincinnati. The Sox operatives even had a chance to compare notes when the Cardinals and Pirates met August 19-20 in Pittsburgh. There they bade each other farewell until Tuesday, August 25, when they were to report their findings to Veeck et al. in Chicago.

Meanwhile, in the American League, the White Sox had struggled through a 7-5-1 road trip, one of the losses a 2-1 setback August 15 at Kansas City when Jim Rivera messed up what was supposed to have been a suicide-squeeze bunt by Jim McAnany. McAnany got the bunt down, all right, but Rivera broke too late from third base and was trapped in a rally-killing rundown. "But I didn't miss the sign," said

Jungle Jim, responding to critics who assumed he had. "I got the sign. I just forgot to run." The miscue upset Al Lopez, already upset by other developments that week. That same night, for one, he had lost Billy Pierce, who came out of the game in the second inning with a hip injury. "I went down in my delivery," recalled Pierce, who didn't pitch again until Labor Day, September 7, "and I couldn't get back up. Something in the hip. It was really nasty. That wasn't the most painful injury I ever had in baseball, but for just that one day, ooh. And it didn't go away right away, either. I'd try to bend over, and I couldn't do it for a while."

Earlier that week in Detroit, when the Tigers—especially Harvey Kuenn and Al Kaline—were busy pounding Pierce 8-1, the lefty had pained Lopez by throwing too many sliders—or so Warren Brown, in his *Chicago American* column, had strongly hinted. "I had changed my style of pitching," Billy said, several decades later. "I was throwing more hard sliders than fastballs by then, because I could throw it for a strike as well as I could a fastball. I'd keep it down and in on the right-handers so they'd hit it on the fists." This particular evening, the Tigers repeatedly were hitting Pierce's sliders on the sweet part of the bat, angering Lopez. "You could throw too much of anything," Pierce said, "but there got to be a point where some of the old-timers, of which Al was one, would call the slider 'a nickel curve.' But I didn't throw that type of slider. I threw a hard slider."

Remembered Jim McAnany: "Lopez was angry at Billy for throwing a home run ball, and then he yelled at me 'cause I wasn't playing over far enough for Harvey Kuenn. He'd motioned me over, but I guess I didn't move over far enough. And he's yelling at me. And I said, 'What's he hot at me for?' And Jim Landis said, 'He's just ticked at Billy. But he's not gonna say anything to Billy.'"

Now Pierce was going to miss three weeks, as had Dick Donovan, who had returned from elbow problems just in time to absorb a 7-2 beating from the A's in Kansas City the day after Pierce went down. Thus, when the troublesome Orioles came calling at the start of a two-week homestand and won two out of three, the White Sox had lost four of their last five games. What had been a four-game lead a week earlier was down to 2 1/2. But now came Friday night, August 21, designated as Nellie Fox Night, and the always-accommodating Senators, 5-13 against Chicago thus far in 1959. Just hours after Congress had voted officially to admit Hawaii as the 50th state, almost 38,000 came out to see Little Nell, who entered the evening with a team-leading .322

112

average and a league-leading 158 base hits, showered with gifts—including two cars and a motor scooter—from fans, teammates and club management. Years later, Bill Veeck, grinning mischievously, remembered the most expensive item presented to the Pennsylvania native: "We gave him a boat that night, a 26-foot sailboat. There was no water, of course—except for a little creek—within 100 miles of his house. Ultimately, he sold the boat and bought some land he had wanted. We would've given him the land, of course, but you can't tow a piece of land into a ballpark."

When Fox's haul was finally cleared off the field, it was the Senators' turn to perform the role of gift-givers. Luis Aparicio opened the home first with a base hit off lefty Chuck Stobbs, and the old ballpark began reverberating with the familiar "Go! Go!" cries. Looie set sail for second, but Stobbs threw behind him, trapping him off first. Aparicio, however, like all great base stealers, kept right on going, at full speed, toward second, and Roy Sievers, the first baseman, threw the ball into left field. Looie was safe at second with his 39th steal of the year. Now came the night's honored guest, Fox, and Stobbs nailed him in the back with a pitch. Then Aparicio and Fox worked a double steal as Jim Landis struck out, but catcher Clint Courtney, like Sievers before him, heaved the ball into left field in his attempt to apprehend Aparicio, and the wee Venezuelan got up and came home. After Sherm Lollar failed, Bubba Phillips grounded a single to center to score Fox, and another typical '59 Sox rally was in the books and Chicago was en route to another one-run victory. This one was a 5-4 win made possible mostly by John Romano and Jim Rivera. With the Senators ahead 3-2 and the bases filled with two out in the sixth, Romano, batting for reliever Gerry Staley, smashed one past third baseman Harmon Killebrew for the tying and go-ahead runs. Romano was now 6-for-9 (he finished a league-best 8-for-13) as a pinch-hitter, a role generally reserved for a veteran, not a rookie.

"It didn't make any difference to me," Romano remembered. "I just wanted to grab a bat and get the hell up there. 'Cause after sitting down in that bullpen all the time and not getting much chance to play, I wanted to get up there."

Romano did not require the preparation that countless veteran pinch-hitters have claimed they needed. "That's a lot of baloney," he said. "First of all, I'd never faced any of the pitchers we were gonna play against, so how was I gonna prepare myself? It was my first year in the big leagues. But how do I explain 8-for-13? I dunno. I just hit, that's all. I could always swing the bat. And I loved the fastball. You couldn't throw one by me with a cannon. The pitch that really screwed me up was the slow, off-speed stuff. But they never found that out."

With Romano having taken care of the offense, Rivera took care of the defense. In the eighth, with the lefty-swinging Courtney facing Turk Lown with a man on base, Al Lopez called time and sent Rivera racing out of the dugout to replace Jim McAnany in right. Courtney promptly belted a blast that seemed headed for the lower deck, but Rivera went back to the wall, leaped and made an incredible catch. "Took that one right out of the fans' hands," Jungle Jim said proudly, many years afterward.

The next afternoon, Messrs. Veeck, Greenberg and Comiskey were given a stark reminder as to why their scouts had been on the road for almost two weeks now. They watched as the White Sox mounted an assault of three singles and a walk against Washington's Russ Kemmerer, but because Barry Latman once again baffled his Senator cousins and because one of the three hits the Sox collected was delivered by Phillips with Lollar on third base, Chicago was a 1-0 winner and still 2 1/2 games on top.

More confirmation of the Sox's biggest problem, if indeed any more was needed, came during Sunday's double-header, when 44,520 turned out to see the Yankees' Art Ditmar defeat Early Wynn 7-1 with a three-hitter in the opener and Ralph Terry blank the home team through six innings of Game 2. That made it two White Sox runs in 23 innings. Oh, well, maybe it was just too hot to hit: For the sixth straight day, temperatures were in the 90s, the humidity stifling, with no relief in sight. Finally, leading off the last of the seventh, Lollar drove his 19th homer of the year into the seats in left to break a scoreless tie. Some shoddy Yankee defense helped provide four more runs in the inning, more than enough for Bob Shaw, who improved to 13-4 with a six-hit, 5-0 shutout.

When the Sox somehow scrounged around for four runs the next afternoon against the Yankees and Don Larsen to win 4-2, with Ray Moore and Turk Lown combining to strike out Mickey Mantle four times, Chicago's lead over the Indians was at two games. But the front office and, at long last, even Al Lopez were completely convinced a move had to be made, particularly with a four-game series coming up that weekend in Cleveland. So on the morning of Tuesday, August 25, the Sox brain trust gathered at the ballpark to hear the scouts' reports and make a decision on Ted Kluszewski and George Crowe.

"We're sitting in Greenberg's office," Chuck Comiskey remembered. "Hank's there, Bill's there, Lopez is there, I'm there. We're waiting for the scouts. Greenberg, in the meantime, is pushing Crowe. 'We've got the deal. Let's make the deal, get him right up here.' That's when Veeck stepped in and said, 'Let's wait 'til the scouts get up here.' OK, so the scouts come in, and the first one says, 'I wouldn't have that goddamn Crowe on this ballclub if he came over here for free. I can't get a good report on him from anybody.' Greenberg jumps out of his chair and points at me: 'You talked to him before he got here!' I said to the scout, Bill Norman, 'Bill, when was the last time I saw you?' He said, I dunno, Mr. C, must've been three weeks ago—we had lunch up in the Bards Room.' 'Have I talked to you this morning?' 'No, I haven't talked to you.' Greenberg says, 'You've been pushing Klu all the time, Comiskey! What the hell, he's hitting .250, Crowe's hitting .285.'"

Lopez, silent until now, finally spoke up, calmly asking the scouts, "Give us a rundown on these two guys." The reports on Kluszewski, as Comiskey and Lopez recalled them, began something like this: He hadn't been playing much, was doing some pinch-hitting and was probably out of condition. "All of it was not positive," Comiskey admitted. "Just telling where he was at the moment. However, they also said, 'But guys in the National League said if you're looking for a guy to give you some pop, take Klu. He can still swing the bat, even though he might be 20 pounds overweight. Get him in here, put him on a little regimentation as far as his weight goes, and he can probably do the job.'" And as for Crowe? Recalled Comiskey: "They said, 'The other guy, he'll have a hot day for you, then he'll go four-five days where he's not productive. Plus you may have an attitude situation on a ballclub.'"

At length, everyone looked at Lopez, who, as Comiskey well knew, did not want anybody on his team who might rock the boat. Remembered Comiskey: "Lopez says, 'As far as I'm concerned, it's Kluszewski.'"

And that was that. The deal was finalized: Harry "Suitcase" Simpson, grand-slam hero of June 27, and Triple-A Indianapolis infielder Bobby Sagers went to Pittsburgh, and Kluszewski came to Chicago. But Hank Greenberg was still pleading his case to Bill Veeck at lunchtime. "He has Bill cornered: 'How can you take a guy like that?'" Comiskey related. "Bill said to him, 'Look, that was the consensus. Two scouts followed them, they crisscrossed. Why send the scouts out, pay the hotel bills and have them talk to the people in the other league if you're not going to listen to them?' Later on, Bill says to me, 'Boy, you really got under Greenberg's skin.' I said, 'Bill, I couldn't care less. I don't have to sleep with the guy.' The only thing I wanted was somebody who could give us some pop. I wanted a guy who could do the job for us. I told Bill, 'I don't care if he's black, white, green or orange, or what ballclub he's with. I don't care. Get the guy who can help us.'"

Kluszewski did indeed help. First of all, he didn't exactly take his time reporting to his new club, as some players were wont to do. Many years later, before a game at Wrigley Field, when he was serving as the Reds' hitting instructor, he looked back on that eventful day. "I was very excited, very much so, because what most people didn't realize was that I had never played in a World Series until then. In fact, I made it to Chicago that same day. Got the news in the afternoon and made it here that evening. My family—some of my brothers—they felt that I had finally made it to the major leagues, coming to the White Sox. I was a little of both—a Sox fan and a Cub fan. But Sox Park was a lot closer to Argo than Wrigley Field, so the ballgames I saw were at Sox Park. Most of the family were Sox fans. Of course, in '59 they were *all* Sox fans. But none of them were there that first night, because they didn't expect me to get to Chicago that fast."

The 27,002 paid customers at Comiskey Park for that night's game with Boston had heard the news of Big Klu's acquisition and imminent arrival—the news had made headlines in both Chicago afternoon newspapers, the *American* and *Daily News*. Quite naturally, then, the fans were brimming with anticipation. And in the home seventh, with a runner on, one out and the White Sox down 3-2 to Boston's Frank Sullivan, out of the home dugout strode a very large man with a No. 4 on his back. Everyone knew who it was, and the crowd rose for a standing ovation. Then, even though Kluszewski rapped into a 4-6-3 inning-ending double play, he received another standing "O" on his way back to the bench. The fans saved their loudest cheers for later, however. The Sox were behind 4-2 with one out in the ninth, their lead about to be reduced to one game because the Indians' Cal McLish, with Rocky Colavito homering twice in Cleveland, had beaten the Yankees for the fifth time that season. Al Smith slapped what looked for all the world like a routine grounder toward short, but the ball hit a pebble and jumped over the head of Don Buddin for a base hit. That was the start. Next came singles by Norm Cash and Jim Rivera for one run and

Johnny Callison at the Sox's Tampa training base on the day he turned 20 years old—
March 12, 1959

Photo Courtesy of
UPI/Cobis-Bettmann

'59 Summer of the Sox

Nellie Fox turns a double play after forcing out Cleveland's Rocky Colavito in a game at Comiskey Park on May 27.

Two Sox rookies on the road–

Johnny Callison (left) and **Norm Cash** make a photo stop on the Freedom Trail in Boston on the club's East Coast road trip in June.

Batboy John Roscich **and coach** Don Gutteridge **are the first to greet** Earl Torgeson **after his 17th-inning home run, defeated Baltimore 6-5 on June 4.**
Photo Courtesy of Chicago Tribune

Nellie Fox **(left) and winning pitcher** Bob Shaw **admire the sweet spot of** Harry "Suitcase" Simpson's **bat, which produced an eighth-inning grand slam to beat the Yankees 5-4 on June 27.**

Photo Courtesy of Chicago Tribune

'59 Summer of the Sox

Luis Aparicio slides past Cleveland shortstop Woodie Held for a stolen base during the White Sox's July 9 victory over the first-place Indians.

Photo Courtesy of AP/ Wide World Photos

Jim Landis steals second base during the July 16 double-header at Boston's Fenway Park. Red Sox shortstop Don Buddin reaches for the late and wide throw.

Photo Courtesy of AP/Wide World Photos

Photo Courtesy of Chicago Tribune

1959 White Sox team photo taken in the late morning of Saturday, August 1, 1959, hours before Larry Doby was sent to San Diego (Pacific Coast League) and replaced on the roster by rookie pitcher Ken McBride.

Top Row: (from left) Earl Torgeson, Billy Pierce, Luis Aparicio, Barry Latman, Norm Cash, Dick Donovan, batting practice catcher Joe Heinsen, Earl Battey, Jim McAnany.

Row 3: Trainer Ed Froehlich, traveling secretary Bernie Snyderworth, Early Wynn, Rodolfo Arias, Ray Moore, Turk Lown, John Romano, Bob Shaw, Sammy Esposito, Jim Rivera, Bubba Phillips.

Row 2: Clubhouse man Arthur Colledge, Billy Goodman, coach Tony Cuccinello, coach Johnny Cooney, coach Don Gutteridge, manager Al Lopez, coach Ray Berres, Gerry Staley, Sherm Lollar, Nellie Fox, clubhouse man Sharkey Colledge.

Row 1: Larry Doby, Jim Landis, batboy John Sala, batboy John Roscich, Al Smith, Harry Simpson.

'59 Summer of the Sox

Al Smith poses before the game with his best fans– all named Smith, Smit, Schmidt, Smythe, etc. – on Smith Night, August 26. Even with all this backing, Al didn't have his biggest

Photo Courtesy of Chicago Tribune

night, to say the least. The buttons held and worn by the fans read, "I'm a Smith and I'm for Al."

Sox rightfielder Jim McAnany leaps to take an extra-base hit away from the Yankees' Norm Siebern during the July 19 double-header at Yankee Stadium.

Photo Courtesy of AP/Wide World Photos

Rookie catcher **John Romano** signs autographs for his many admirers outside the Sox clubhouse before the September 1 game against Detroit.
Photo Courtesy of Chicago Tribune

Jim Rivera, with his trademark head-first slide, beats **Bob Cerv's** throw to the plate to give the Sox a 3-2, 10-inning victory over Kansas City on September 8, in front of 46,598 at Comiskey Park. **Rivera scored on a single by Luis Aparicio.**

Photo Courtesy of Chicago Tribune

'59 Summer of the Sox

Luis Aparicio, Jim Rivera and Al Smith celebrate in the visitors' clubhouse after the White Sox's 4-2 pennant-clinching victory in Cleveland, September 22. Smith and Rivera hit back-to-back home runs and Aparicio turned Vic Power's grounder into a game-ending double play.

'59 Summer of the Sox

Bill Veeck (center), and his wife, Mary Frances, get a police escort through the crowd at Midway Airport as they await the arrival of the Sox's plane from Cleveland in the early hours of September 23.

Photo Courtesy of Chicago Tribune

Sherm Lollar and Jim Landis enjoy being part of the victory parade through the Loop on Thursday, September 24, two days after the pennant-clincher.

Photo Courtesy of Chicago Tribune

'59 Summer of the Sox

Ted Kluszewski swings and drives his first home run of the World Series opener into the right-field seats. He added another homer his next time up.

Photo Courtesy of Chicago Tribune

Photo Courtesy of UPI/Corbis-Bettmann

Nellie Fox heads home from third as **Sherm Lollar** grounds into a double play in the fourth inning of Game 5 of the World Series in the Los Angeles Coliseum. The run was the only one of the game, which was played before a record postseason and regular-season crowd of 92,706.

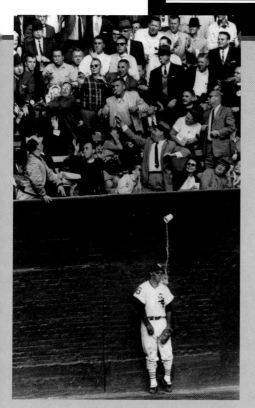

Reaching for Charlie Neal's first home run of Game 2, a fan in the front row loses his beer, which showers down on Sox left-fielder Al Smith. Smith later met the fan on a ticket-sales call.

Photo Courtesy of Chicago Tribune

A pair of "Double D's," Don Drysdale (left) and Dick Donovan, meet before battling each other in Game 3 of the World Series, the first series game played west of St. Louis.

Photo Courtesy of AP/ Wide World Photos

Jim Landis makes a diving catch on **Junior Gilliam's** line drive in the first inning of Game 3 of the World Series in the Los Angeles Coliseum.

Jim Rivera runs down **Charlie Neal's** long drive to right-center to save the White Sox's 1-0 Game 5 victory in the World Series.

'59 Summer of the Sox

another single by John Romano—putting him at .700 as a pinch-hitter on the year—to tie the game. Finally, in the 10th, with Sherm Lollar on first with two gone, reliever Mike Fornieles, once with the White Sox, delivered a 1-2 curveball and Billy Goodman drilled it up the alley between rightfielder Jackie Jensen and centerfielder Gary Geiger. Lollar, lead-footed though he was, scored without a play. That made the Sox 30-8 in one-run contests and 1-0 with Kluszewski.

"Looking back," said Jim Landis, "I think too much was expected of him. You know, 'Here's the big home run hitter to help us down the stretch.' But I knew his power numbers had fallen off. And when he came over, I figured it was gonna be tough on him for a while because the papers were goin', 'Wow, we got our power guy.' But as far as temperament and attitude, he fit in so great with the club, he really did. He was one of those quick, one-liner guys. Took the kidding real well. He was good for the club. I'm not saying he didn't do us any good with the bat, either, but there were a lot of other good things that he brought to the ballclub."

"I know Kluszewski helped us a lot," said Al Lopez, "I think more morale-wise than anything else, because it gave the other fellas confidence."

And it provided the missing link. "What really picked us up," said Al Smith, "was when we got Big Klu, 'cause there wasn't nobody hittin' the long ball in our lineup other than Lollar and myself. He added some punch to that lineup. And we had a lot of fun with him too."

"Early Wynn took him on as his private project," Chuck Comiskey revealed. "Now I don't know whether Lopez had told him, 'Hey, Gus, get this guy in shape.' But they would put on the rubber suits and they would go out and run—and run. And do calisthenics. When they took off the rubber suits in that clubhouse, everybody left the place. I mean, we thought the stockyards had a smell. Oh, man.

"And Klu took a lot of batting practice when he first got here. And ballplayers admire other ballplayers. He started ripping a couple into those right-field upper-deck seats, breaking the backs of seats in the lower deck, driving the ball into right-center—and the whole ballclub, the attitude's there, they're all pulling for him. In the clubhouse, they're needling him: 'When are you and Wynn coming back in to dress? We want to be the hell out of here!' So there was a real good attitude. And he always had 60 to 80 tickets he'd leave for his family and friends. Everyone from Argo would come in."

On Klu's second night with the White Sox, there were Kluszewskis from Argo and Smiths from everywhere at the ballpark. It was "Smith Night," Bill Veeck's grand idea to get the fans, once and for all, off the back of Al Smith, still being booed at times despite his remarkable July. What better way to do that, reasoned Veeck, than to create Smith's own rooting section behind him in the left-field seats? Thus, anyone showing a piece of identification indicating his name was Smith—or Smythe, Smit or some other such derivative—was granted free admission and given a blue-and-white badge that read: "I'm a Smith and I'm for Al." All told, 5,253 Smiths showed up, joining 22,497 paying customers (plus various guests of management, among them Fidel Castro's 9-year-old son, in town for the opening of the third annual Pan American Games). The concept was brilliant, the results less so: Smith struck out twice, hit into a double play and dropped a fly ball in the midst of the Red Sox's decisive four-run seventh-inning rally as Boston won 7-6.

Recalled Smith, decades later: "I remember I had my milkman out there that night. He was a Polish fellow. I went out there to autograph some of the fans' tickets before the game started. And I saw him out there and said, 'How the hell did you get out here?' He'd gotten somebody's tax bill, had the name 'Smith' on it. That's how he got in. I told him, 'Well, you be my bodyguard out here tonight.' But they booed just like they always did."

Now, because Rocky Colavito had just solved Yankee closer Ryne Duren for his 38th homer to give the Indians a 5-4 victory, Cleveland's eighth straight triumph, the Sox's lead was down to one game. Smith Night had been a disaster, and Nellie Fox had gone 3-for-33 since *his* "night." Veeck quite likely was beginning to have second thoughts about his promotional genius. The following afternoon, though, as the Pan American Games began with colorful opening ceremonies just a few blocks away at Soldier Field, Fox collected three hits, John Romano three RBIs and Ted Kluszewski—in his first Sox start—two hits in four tries and Barry Latman went 8 1/3 innings to beat Boston 5-1. The lead was at 1 1/2 games, and the club departed for Cleveland in good spirits and confident it would perform well in the four critical games there.

"I felt, and I think most of the guys felt, that we were on a good roll, and we weren't worried going in there," remembered Jim Landis. "The way everything was going—we were playing good baseball—I don't think anybody panicked. We just felt we had the better ballclub and surely the better pitching. I don't think anybody expects to win four out of four on the road, but we expected at least a split or to come out better than that."

Cleveland fans were anticipating the same from their club, with its collection of characters (Billy Martin, Jimmy Piersall and Mudcat Grant) and clouters (Colavito, Minnie Minoso, Tito Francona and Woodie Held). The Tribe had won eight in a row, and the townspeople were near hysteria. Tickets were going fast; huge crowds were expected. It was the biggest baseball weekend in Cleveland since the unfortunate 1954 World Series. And the sportswriters had all sorts of angles awaiting them. The Indians were being run by Frank Lane, who had traded for so many of the current White Sox. The Sox were being run by Bill Veeck, who had brought Cleveland a world championship in 1948, and by Hank Greenberg, who'd been in charge of the 111-game winners of '54. The '54 club had been managed by Al Lopez and had included 23-game winner Early Wynn and regular leftfielder Al Smith. The '59 Indians were led not only by ex-Chicago hero Minoso but also by the .370-hitting Francona, dealt by the Sox to Detroit in June 1958 in a deal that also involved Bob Shaw. And Friday night's starter for Chicago was to be none other than Shaw. Opposing him was Jack Harshman, once a big winner for the Sox—before the arrival of Lopez, who quickly soured on him and had him banished to Baltimore after the '57 season.

Lane, some 20 years later, recalled his feelings as the big series commenced: "Of course I had mixed emotions. I didn't want to be beaten out of a pennant, but if I was gonna be beaten, I'd rather be beaten by the team I'd left in Chicago: Billy Pierce, Nellie Fox, Sherm Lollar, Jim Rivera ..."

A throng of 70,398 packed the mammoth lakefront stadium for the series opener on Friday night, August 28. The few sports fans who didn't show perhaps were more interested in the middleweight title bout between Carmen Basilio and champ Gene Fullmer that evening in San Francisco. Shaw and Harshman dueled like heavyweights for five innings, each taking some punches—the score was tied 3-3—but remaining on their feet. Then, in the seventh, Mudcat Grant, who had replaced Harshman in the sixth, was touched for singles by Nellie Fox and Jim Landis, the latter's third hit of the game. Up stepped Sherm Lollar, who sent one deep to left. Back toward the 6-foot-high wire fence drifted Minnie Minoso. He jumped up and, for a split second, had the ball in his glove. But he collided with the fence on his leap, enough to jar the ball loose. Minnie watched in disbelief as fans behind the fence battled for the ball, which had dropped over the barrier for a three-run, game-deciding homer, Lollar's 20th home run of 1959.

Minoso took some ribbing later from his old roommate, Earl Battey. "I kidded him: 'Hey, you're playing for Cleveland now, but it's like you're still playing for us!' 'Course, he didn't like that."

Remembered Frank Lane, his eyes brightening: "Minnie couldn't wait for the ball to come down. He jumped up to catch the ball, and he knocked it over the fence. And I can still see Minnie, on his hands and knees, trying to reach through the wire fence, trying to get at the baseball. And as badly as I felt about it, I couldn't keep from laughing."

Al Lopez was in no mood for laughter the next afternoon. As a Ladies Day crowd of 50,290 began to gather for Game 2 of the series, the White Sox manager learned that his scheduled starter, Ken McBride, had come down with tonsilitis and was running a 102-degree temperature. Already short of pitchers—Billy Pierce was still on the sidelines because of his sore hip—Lopez now had to decide between Ray Moore, an emergency starter the previous Monday against New York, or the far more reliable Dick Donovan, who had worked eight innings Tuesday night. Donovan preferred four days of rest between assignments and thus was penciled in to start one of the games of Sunday's double-header. "Tricky Dick," therefore, was laying low.

"I'll never forget that afternoon in Cleveland," said Donovan, even though 35 years had passed since. "I'd pulled a tendon in my elbow in July, missed about three weeks. But by now, my arm was OK again. I'm standing out in the outfield during batting practice, and (pitching coach) Ray Berres comes out and says to me, 'Hear about McBride?' 'No.' 'He's sick. He can't pitch.' 'Oh really?' I'd learned long ago, you never volunteer. But he says to me, 'Can you pitch?' 'Yeah, I can pitch.' He walks away. Ten minutes later, Lopez comes walking out toward me. 'McBride's sick. He can't pitch.' 'Yeah, I heard.' 'Can you pitch?' He looks at me with that look. 'I can pitch.'

"I volunteered for absolutely nothing. I still don't volunteer for anything. But I was honest. And Lopez was absolutely delighted that I was able to pitch. In fact, he sat down and we chatted. And that's what he told me. This is self-praising, and I don't mean it that way. But he was absolutely delighted."

That was before the game. Imagine how Lopez must have felt when it was over and Donovan had shut out the Indians 2-0 on five hits, two of them bloops, to move the Sox 3 1/2 games in front. He was in trouble in only one inning, the second, when the Tribe loaded the bases with one out. But Donovan squirmed out of that predicament and then waited for his teammates to get to 22-year-old rookie Jim Perry, winner of 10 games to date. The match was scoreless with two out in the seventh with Jim Landis at first base with his third hit of the day and sixth of the series, enabling his batting average to climb to .275. Earl Torgeson next lined a single over short, and Landis was off to the races, third base his intended finish line, even though most baserunners gladly would have settled for a one-base advance on a ball hit to left field. "I remember that very well," Landis said. "Some things happen that I'll always remember. I just had my mind made up that, no matter what, third base was where I was gonna go." Minnie Minoso, in left, must have figured that, too, because he hurried in to grab the ball so he could nail Landis at third. But Minnie fumbled the ball, and that caused Landis—and third-base coach Tony Cuccinello—to instantaneously change their plans. Landis, seeing Cuccinello waving him home, never stopped at third, instead sprinting all the way to the plate. Minoso finally fired to third baseman George Strickland, who whirled and threw home, but Landis was sliding in safely with the only run Donovan would need.

"That game, not because I pitched it, but that game was a big, big, big ballgame," Donovan said. "Because if we win it and then we lose two on Sunday, at least we broke even. We came there with a game-and-a-half lead and we leave with a game-and-a-half lead. But if we lose that game and Cleveland beats us a double-header Sunday, well, then ..."

Even with 66,586 fans cheering them on, however, the Indians were unable to halt the momentum the Sox had gained from winning the series' first two games. Cleveland's chances had looked good, what with Cal McLish (16-6, and 3-0 vs. Chicago) and Gary Bell (14-10) going against Early Wynn, making his fourth try for victory No.17, and Barry Latman, 7-5 but working again on only two days' rest—as he did four times in '59. "Barry was just a kid," said Jim Landis, "but if we had a rotation problem, he'd say to Ray Berres, 'Here, give *me* the ball.' And most of the time he got the ball, he went out and did a good job."

This was to be one of those times. And as for Wynn, he wasn't going to fail a fourth time in a row, especially when the opposition was Cleveland. The Indians' hopes began sagging in the sixth inning of Game 1, when the Sox batted around to score five times and wipe out a 2-0 deficit. Wynn, whose record against his former club improved to 8-1, started things with a home run. Luis Aparicio's 44th steal, Landis'

121

RBI double, a run-scoring single by Billy Goodman, a walk with the bases loaded and a hit batsman under the same circumstances were the inning's other highlights. After the 6-3 victory, the Sox scored five runs in the first three innings of the nightcap, the crusher coming in the second when Latman, with the bases filled, sent Rocky Colavito against the fence in right-center for his fly ball. John Romano, playing so Sherm Lollar could get some rest, scored easily from third, and Al Smith, catching the Indians completely by surprise, tagged up at second base and, never thinking to pause at third, raced all the way home. George Strickland, again at third base, took the relay throw, but when he turned around, expecting to see Smith on the bag, Smith instead was beginning his scoring slide. Afterward, Smith, grinning, said: "The only one at third base in a Sox uniform Strickland could possibly have tagged was Cuccinello."

Nearly 40 years later, Smith recalled something else about that play in Cleveland. "Colavito had a strong arm, but he was wild. And Cuccinello had a sign where'd he'd like bug out his eyes when I'd come to third base. I'd always tell him, 'Don't wave me in—I'll just look at your eyes.' If his eyes were bugged out real big, that was my sign to go." He had seen in Cuccinello's eyes that Colavito had overthrown the cutoff man, so he'd sped home for a 3-0 lead. Goodman's two-run single in the third and Smith's two-run homer in the fifth made it smoother sailing for Latman, who gave up a three-run blast by Colavito (his 39th homer) in the fourth and a solo home run by Woodie Held (his 25th) in the fifth and then turned things over to Turk Lown. Lown responded with four shutout innings, and the Sox, 9-4 winners, were 5 1/2 games ahead and ready for a joyous plane ride back to Chicago. Awaiting them at Midway Airport was a crowd, equally joyous, estimated by police to be in the vicinity of 10,000. When the Sox's plane rolled to a stop, it was surrounded immediately by the celebrants, some of them carrying signs reading, "Welcome Home, Champs!" Most of the players, with help from Chicago's finest, were, at length, able to reach their cars and make their way home. However, Jim Rivera, as though he had just coached a Rose Bowl winner, was hoisted onto the shoulders of a few of his admirers and given a victory ride all the way to his waiting Cadillac.

"Gosh yes, it was a heck of a crowd," Jim Landis remembered. "The feeling was tremendous. And after we got off the plane, we didn't exactly hurry home to our apartments, let's put it that way. There was Bob Shaw, myself, Norm Cash, a bunch of us guys. We took a little extra time getting home. We were *very* happy."

SEPTEMBER

Power Out, Sirens On

Nikita Khrushchev was making final preparations for his trip to the United States, and Dwight D. Eisenhower was wrapping up his visit to Western Europe. Two new trouble spots had developed in the world: The government of Laos was appealing to the United Nations for help in its fight against North Vietnamese-backed communist rebels, and the exiled Dalai Lama was likewise pleading for aid as Chinese troops carried out "reforms" back in his Tibetan homeland.

The Pan American Games were wrapping up in Chicago, where news of that city's admission as the ninth and newest member of the National Basketball Association, starting with the 1960-61 season, caused such a tremor that the *Tribune*, in trumpeting the event, ran a three-inch wire-service account on Page 3 of the sports section. In Chicago there was far more interest in the budding romance of Aristotle Onassis and Maria Callas.

It was the first week of September in 1959. Kids everywhere were preparing to go back to school. Teenagers tuned in to their favorite disc jockeys in hopes of hearing hits like "The Three Bells" by the Browns, "Sleep Walk" by Santo and Johnny, "Poison Ivy" by the Coasters, "Just Ask Your Heart" by Frankie Avalon, "Mack The Knife" by Bobby Darin, "Mr. Blue" by the Fleetwoods and "Put Your Head On My Shoulder" by Paul Anka, who, though still a teenager himself, was already obscenely wealthy.

It was the first week of September in 1959, and it was a marvelous time to be a White Sox fan. The four-game sweep of Cleveland had brought on World Series fever, and, all over Chicagoland, people were discussing such normally foreign concepts as "the magic number" and World Series tickets. Even longtime Sox stars like Billy Pierce and Nellie Fox, roommates for the ninth straight year, were getting caught up in the excitement.

"As the year went along," Pierce said, "and the breaks seemed to be going our way a little more than they had—especially in those one-run games—we'd say, in the room at night, 'Hey, we got a good chance this year.' And of course, now, when September came around, we thought, 'We've got a great chance.' Especially when you knew that New York wasn't the team right behind you. You know, that was the team that had beaten us so many times, and they weren't there. If they had been in second place instead of Cleveland, you'd be worrying a little more."

But the Yankees, in fourth place, were 16 1/2 games back as the new month began, so even when third-place Detroit arrived at Comiskey Park Tuesday night, September 1, and beat the Sox 4-0 before what to Bill Veeck had to be a disappointing crowd of 27,218, spirits were still high. After all, the Sox had never had much success with Jim Bunning, the AL strikeout leader who was 10-2 lifetime against them after his three-hit shutout this night. At least Bunning, who struck out eight, had failed once again to fan Fox, which, as Jim Landis remembered, certainly was worth something—to Fox, anyway.

"Nellie and Bunning were good friends," Landis said, "and they had a bet, every time Bunning faced us: Fifty bucks—in those days, you know, that was a little bit of money—that he would strike Nellie out. And you would've had to watch, but Bunning would get two strikes on him but never the third. And sometimes, Nellie would even get a base hit with two strikes on him, and you'd watch Bunning on the mound—his reaction—and it was worse than if he'd lost the ballgame.

"They had that standard bet, every game. And Jim never did collect."

Not until, that is, the 1965 season, when Bunning was pitching for the Philadelphia Phillies and Fox was a player-coach with the Houston Astros.

Remembered Bunning, now a U.S. senator: "They called Nellie over from the first-base coach's box and had him pinch-hit. And he took a very close third strike. And he shattered that bat over home plate, he was so mad."

Such was not the case the night of September 2, 1959, when Fox collected three hits, scored three runs and drove in four during a 7-2, 11-4 sweep of a twilight-night double-header before 43,237. His bases-loaded triple in the fifth inning of Game 2 off Detroit's Tom Morgan capped the Sox's second 11-run inning of the season. The triple came long after Fox had singled in Luis Aparicio, who had stolen his 46th base, with the second run of the inning. The third run, which tied the score, came in on a single by Ted Kluszewski, who by now was wearing No. 8, the uniform number seemingly reserved by the Sox during the '50s for veteran first basemen—e.g., Ferris Fain, Walt Dropo, Ray Boone—who had seen better days elsewhere. In Klu's eight trips to the plate this night, he had delivered four hits. It was a big night for another newcomer to the club, Joe Stanka, a 28-year-old rookie purchased from Sacramento to coincide with the September 1 expansion of rosters. The tall righthander relieved starter Barry Latman in Game 2 and threw 3 1/3 innings, allowing one run and one hit, and picked up his first major-league victory.

Stanka was to have been accompanied to Chicago from the Pacific Coast League by Larry Doby, who had been sent to San Diego by Bill Veeck on August 1 to make room for pitcher Ken McBride, with the promise he'd be brought back September 1 for the stretch run. "I was there for about a week or two, working out, trying to get in shape, because I hadn't been playing," Doby recalled. "And then I got into the lineup, and I hit a triple, and I broke my ankle sliding into third. And that was the end of my career."

Doby's teammates hadn't forgotten him, however. They would vote him a half share ($3,637.59) of their World Series loot. But surely Doby would have preferred being there, in Chicago those first few days of September, as his new team, the White Sox, prepared for another weekend series with his old team, the Cleveland Indians. Sportswriters from all over arrived in town on Thursday, September 3, the day before the three-game series was to begin. Among them were New York heavyweights Red Smith, Frank Graham and Leonard Koppett. The Indians, still 5 1/2 games behind, landed at Midway Airport at about 10:30 that night and headed directly to their Chicago home, the Knickerbocker Hotel, well aware they needed a sweep—or, at the very worst, two out of three—in order to stay alive.

The Sox's Earl Battey, meanwhile, had taken advantage of the open date in the schedule to offer congratulations to a former schoolmate who happened to be in town. "There was a girl on our Pan-American Games team from my high school, Jordan High in Los Angeles, named Earlene Brown. And most of the track athletes were staying at the dorms over at the University of Chicago." So Battey, who lived close by in Hyde Park, went over for a chat. "I hadn't seen her since high school," he said. Since high school, Brown had accomplished quite a bit, including gold medals in both the discus and shot put at Soldier

Field earlier that week. But Brown knew that Battey had done fairly well for himself since high school, too, and that a good reason for the lack of excitement for the Pan Am Games was the excitement Battey's baseball team had been creating.

That excitement, and the White Sox's lead, was to crest on Friday night, September 4, when 45,510 folks from the city, the suburbs and downstate and from Indiana, Iowa, Wisconsin and Michigan jammed into Comiskey Park for a typical 1959 White Sox thriller. RBI singles in the second by Jim McAnany and Luis Aparicio off Jim Perry put the Sox up 2-0, but Early Wynn ran into some trouble in the fifth. After Jim Baxes drove his 15th home run into the upper deck in left to make it 2-1, the Indians put two on with two out for Minnie Minoso. Minnie sent what appeared to be a certain two-run triple toward right-center, but then, out of nowhere, came Jim Landis, who'd been shaded to left-center. The gap, once huge, between baseball and outfielder was closing fast. Finally, Landis, at full speed, reached up, made the catch, bounced off the canvas bullpen fence, just to the right of the 415-foot marker, and headed back toward the dugout as though this was no big deal. The old park, however, erupted with a roar of eardrum-shattering proportions. Up in the press box, Jerome Holtzman, covering the game for the *Chicago Sun-Times*, marveled anew at this latest in a series of Landis miracle catches.

"Landis," he said, "made everything look easier than it really was. And that hurt him. Willie Mays made everything look tough. And Kluszewski told me, after he'd come over to the White Sox and had been over here for about two weeks, he said: 'Landis is a better center fielder than Willie Mays.' Now, he'd played in the National League for all those years. Kluszewski said that. And I really felt good that he had, because it supported my belief."

Another unbelievable play lay ahead, this one by leftfielder Al Smith. Again Minoso, whom Smith had replaced, was involved. With two out in the eighth and Wynn still ahead 2-1, Minoso doubled to right-center. Tito Francona followed with a line single to left. Smith, charging, grabbed the ball on the first bounce. Minoso was rounding third, heading home with the tying run. Smith let go with a bullet throw, low and powerful, that reached catcher Sherm Lollar on one hop. Minoso leaped into his slide, and Lollar dove at him with ball in glove. Plate umpire Frank Umont made the call, and broadcaster Bob Elson, a bit more exuberant than usual, passed it on along the White Sox radio network: "He's out! He's out at Chicago!" Again Comiskey

Park rocked from the deafening noise. It is doubtful that Umont could hear, let alone understand, the stream of epithets Minoso was hurling his way.

"I was safe...safe...safe," Minnie moaned after the game. "Maybe Umont don't see it. I dunno. Everybody see play but him."

Whether he saw it or not, it was the play of the week, maybe the year. The Sox, having regained their collective breath, added a run in their half and then, with Gerry Staley relieving Wynn (18-9), held off the Indians in the ninth to win 3-2, Staley striking out Baxes and getting pinch-hitter Elmer Valo on a pop-up to end it with the tying run on base. The lead was 6 1/2, and though Cleveland rebounded to beat Bob Shaw 6-5 Saturday afternoon—despite ninth-inning homers by Smith and John Romano—and Dick Donovan 2-1 Sunday afternoon on Vic Power's two-run double in the ninth, the Sox were still in command. Even so, of those three weekend games, Al Lopez remembered most vividly the Sunday defeat that would have restored the Sox's 6 1/2-game advantage.

"See, you never feel safe until you clinch it," he said. "We had a chance to really hurt Cleveland that day, and Donovan was pitching a real good game. And he made a mistake, hung a high slider to Vic Power, and he hit a double into right-center to beat us the ballgame. I really felt bad about that game, because we had them put away."

The White Sox recovered to put away the Kansas City A's twice the next day in a Labor Day double-header before the third straight surprisingly low turnout, this time 26,368—following Saturday's crowd of 26,920 and Sunday's 34,269. Blame for that could go to the heat (Monday's temperature was 96, the fourth straight day of 90-plus), or to rumors that proved false (news outlets kept claiming there was a paucity of tickets available) or, if one really wanted to stretch, to Monday's Pan American Games Closing Ceremonies at Soldier Field or Monday's opening by Jimmy Durante at the Chez Paree.

Blame, however, could not be assigned to the White Sox. They defeated Kansas City 2-1 in Game 1 Monday behind Billy Pierce, who before giving way to Turk Lown went seven innings in his first appearance since his hip injury August 15. Then they routed the A's 13-7 in Game 2 behind Ted Kluszewski, who, having entered the second game with a .350 average on the strength of 14 hits (all singles) in 40 at-bats as a member of the White Sox, crashed two long home runs, evoking memories of the Big Klu who had terrorized National League pitchers for so many seasons.

127

I　Said Kluszewski, several years later: "You know, you don't play for a while, and hitting is such a fine art that you just kind of lose that little edge of getting that bat out there. Home run hitting is the type of thing where you have to commit yourself a little sooner. I was probably defensive for the first couple of weeks with the White Sox, just trying to make contact."

That's all he had done in the first game of the Labor Day double-header, when his single scored Nellie Fox from second and Jim Landis all the way from first, Landis duping rightfielder Roger Maris into thinking he was stopping at third. As Maris held the ball, Landis kept running and scored standing up. Pierce, happy to be back on the firing line, made the two runs hold up.

"The hip started feeling better," he said, "and I won a couple ball-games the last month. But it was frustrating being out. It was one of those things that took you out of the swing of things for a while. And you want to be there. You know, 'Here we are, we're in first place.' You want to help out. But I couldn't help anybody that way. If you're not at your best, those hitters are too good."

There was plenty of good hitting by the White Sox in the third inning of Game 2. With the Sox down 4-1 to A's starter John Tsitouris, Luis Aparicio, who earlier had stolen his 50th base of the season, opened with a triple and scored on Fox's infield out. Landis, in the midst of a brilliant day, doubled and Kluszewski followed with his first homer, a shot off the upper-deck facade in right. John Romano walked and Al Smith blasted his 15th home run for a 6-4 Chicago lead. Jim Rivera, next up, hit his second, and the rout was on. Three innings later, Fox singled, Landis tripled and Kluszewski homered, this a less prodigious blow into the right-field lower deck. That gave him five RBIs for the game and six for the afternoon.

"Yet Landis was the star of that double-header," Jerome Holtzman argued, noting that Landis had two singles, two doubles and two triples in eight official at-bats, scored four runs and drove in two. "You know, Earl Torgeson made the remark one day, comparing Aparicio and Landis. He said, 'Landis plays every day like he's gonna be sent down. Aparicio plays like he's got it knocked.'"

No doubt many observers figured Landis now had it knocked, what with the red-hot, menacing Kluszewski batting behind him in the No. 4 spot. Landis challenged that theory. "Things didn't change a heck of a lot after we got Klu," he said. "The pitchers had always tried to make sure Looie, Nellie and myself hit the ball. They didn't want us to walk.

That was their first priority. And I'm sure they got chewed out if they walked one of us, because they knew it was gonna be a run, somehow. So it was, 'Keep those guys off the bases.' So I don't think it mattered who was hitting fourth, Klu or whomever. We knew that's the way the pitchers were gonna approach things. So we got our pitches to hit, because they didn't want to walk us."

Kansas City's Bud Daley walked only one Sox batter during the next evening's game, played in front of 46,598 people—including 18,350 women admitted free on Ladies Night—and he carried a 2-1 lead over Early Wynn into the Chicago ninth. But this was 1959, and one-run ninth-inning deficits were hardly worrisome to the White Sox. Sherm Lollar, enjoying the night off as John Romano did the catching, came off the bench to open the inning with a pinch single. Romano sacrificed Sammy Esposito, Lollar's pinch-runner, to second, and Al Smith lined a single to left to score him.

Then, after Wynn set down the A's in the 10th, Jim Rivera opened the Sox half with a bloop over second baseman Wayne Terwilliger's head. Jungle Jim, thinking two-base hit, got himself trapped between first and second, and faked a retreat to first. Terwilliger bought it, throwing to first baseman Kent Hadley. Rivera took off for second and made it safely with a head-first dive as 46,000 hearts skipped beats. Wynn followed by bunting foul for strike three, one of the few mistakes he made on this night (six hits and zero walks allowed in 10 innings), but Luis Aparicio drilled a hit to left and Rivera, stirring up a veritable dust storm at home plate, slid in head first to beat Bob Cerv's throw for the victory, Wynn's 19th, the Sox's 12th in 14 extra-inning games and 33rd in 44 one-run contests. Said Rivera to reporters, through clouds of cigar smoke: "How'd ya like that for an evening of thrills, fellas?"

The Sox, with magic number now down to a lucky 13, took their thrill show on the road the next night to Washington, where fans in "our nation's capital," as Bob Elson would say, saw the league leaders' typical offense on display at the outset. Aparicio drew a walk from Tex Clevenger, stole his 51st base, took third on Nellie Fox's infield out and scored on Jim Landis' sacrifice fly. Later, in the seventh, the Sox broke a 1-1 tie when errors by Senators shortstop Billy Consolo and third base-man Harmon Killebrew and hits by Smith and Rivera and a sacrifice fly by Aparicio provided four runs and a 5-1 triumph for Bob Shaw, his 15th win of the year.

The next day, Thursday, September 10, Jerome Holtzman decided to go over to a luncheon/reception for the White Sox set up by

Illinois Rep. John C. Kluczynski and to which the Illinois congressional delegation—and Vice President Richard Nixon, the noted baseball fan—had been invited. Sure enough, Nixon showed, but only seven Sox players did—John Romano, Billy Pierce, Turk Lown, Gerry Staley, Bob Shaw, Barry Latman and the recently arrived Joe Stanka.

"Nixon," Holtzman said, "knew who Stanka was. Here's a guy who had just been brought up from Sacramento, and Nixon—maybe he had been briefed, I don't know—but he knew who he was. And I was there, and it amazed me that he knew. I was standing there, writing down the quotes as the players walked by. Nixon knew all about Staley and Lown, and he also mentioned Pierce's near-perfect game (against Washington in June 1958), when Ed Fitzgerald broke it up with two out in the ninth."

Nixon also noted that the Senators had won six of the seven games he had attended that year, so he promised the Sox players he would stay away from Griffith Stadium that night. It didn't matter: Dick Donovan gave up home runs, both two-run shots, to Killebrew (No. 40) and Jim Lemon (No. 29), and Camilo Pascual stopped the Sox on four hits to win 8-2, despite the presence of reinforcements from Indianapolis: catcher Camilo Carreon (American Association Rookie of the Year), pitcher Gary Peters, third baseman J.C. Martin, first baseman Ron Jackson and outfielders Joe Hicks and Johnny Callison, who had hit .299 with 10 homers and 46 RBIs in 79 Triple-A games.

"I'd gone back and had a pretty good time," Callison remembered. "In fact, I thought they'd call me up. Hell, I was hitting .400 for a while. But they didn't bring me back. Until September."

And even then, he would not see action till the final weekend of the season. But that was all right; there was a pennant to be won. The White Sox made scant headway toward that goal the following evening in Baltimore's Memorial Stadium, going scoreless in 25 innings of a twi-night twin bill to lose 3-0 in nine to 20-year-old Jack Fisher in Game 1 and 1-0 in 16 to 20-year-old Jerry Walker in Game 2, on Brooks Robinson's two-out RBI single (Billy Pierce and Barry Latman were the hard-luck Sox pitchers). Game 2 was the makeup of the August 6 18-inning 1-1 tie, in which the Sox had failed to score over the final 15 innings. So, in effect, Lopez's Lumbermen had gone scoreless in 40 consecutive innings at Baltimore.

"Well, it was a big ballpark," Lopez recalled, "and they had damn good pitching. We both had good pitching, good defense. So all the games turned out real close. We had an awful time trying to win games there."

Added Pierce: "We could not hit in that ballpark. We beat them a lot of games, but it was never 10-2. It was 3-1, 2-1, 4-3. The dimensions, the way it was laid out, it just threw the hitters off balance. I'll bet if you check the records, we hit for a lower average in that ballpark than anywhere else. And no home runs hardly at all."

Cleveland had lost in Washington, so the Sox, even after the twin setbacks, were still four games ahead and the magic number was down to 10, but there were some concerns. Jim Landis, probably the team's most valuable player the last five to six weeks, was suffering from a badly bruised thigh, injured during the Cleveland series in Chicago when he slid back into first on a pickoff attempt. The injury had contributed to an 0-for-18 slump that had dipped his average to .271.

Remembered Jack Kuenster of the *Chicago Daily News*: "His leg was practically rubbed raw. A bluish color—all bruised from the hip all the way down his leg." Said Landis: "It was weird. I landed on my right thigh real hard, and all of a sudden I got all these bruises and boils and everything."

Before each game, Landis had the thigh treated and wrapped by trainer Eddie Froelich. He continued to play, in pain, an inspiration to his team. But now, this Saturday in Baltimore, his team needed more than inspiration. After three straight defeats, their longest skid since June, the Sox needed a win. Who better to provide it than Early Wynn, the club's big winner all season long? Ol' Gus, scowling and battling, turned in his usual strong performance, scattering seven hits, striking out five and registering the obligatory hit batsman. His victim this time was Brooks Robinson, whom Wynn nailed with a fastball his first time up, payback for the young third baseman's game-ending hit the night before.

While his teammates finally broke their Baltimore drought at 41 innings, Wynn blanked the Orioles until the eighth before settling for a 6-1 victory, giving him 20 wins for the fifth time in his career. He might have had a more difficult time had it not been for a move by Al Lopez that previewed a maneuver to come in the World Series. Lopez, hearing the bespectacled rookie Jim McAnany's complaints about the tough sun in right field, moved him over to left and switched Al Smith to right. "The kid told me he couldn't see the ball in the sun," Lopez told reporters. Remembered McAnany: "I used to have the damnedest time with those flip-down glasses. He probably saved my bacon, getting me out of the sun field."

Meanwhile, Landis, who had singled in the first Sox run, was saving nothing. Bad thigh and all, he stole home in the eighth (for the last of his 20 steals on the year and his first in a week and a half) after having sparked a three-run rally by beating out a bunt. But the slide into the plate was the final straw. The next day in Boston, after Bob Shaw (16-6) had beaten the Red Sox 3-1 on a rare home run by ping hitter Billy Goodman ("I hit a fastball—what the hell else could I hit over the fence?"), Landis was admitted to Boston's Sancta Maria Hospital with what doctors said was cellulitis inflammation of tissue next to the skin, the result of a ruptured blood vessel. Landis, from his new quarters, explained why he had not gone the hospital route earlier: "I wanted to play every day. I didn't want to let the team down at this stage of the race."

Fortunately, thanks to the once-hated Yankees, who had swept that day's double-header from the Indians before 40,870 in New York, there wasn't much of a race left. The White Sox were now 5 1/2 games ahead with 10 games to go, and the magic number was down to six. Any combination of Sox victories and Cleveland defeats adding up to six meant a pennant for Chicago. No wonder Bill Veeck announced that same day, Sunday, September 13, that the club would begin accepting mail orders for World Series tickets. He also revealed his plan for how the tickets—at least those not already earmarked for season-ticket holders and for major-league baseball personnel—would be distributed. In a special drawing, 60 percent of the available tickets would go to Chicago, 20 percent to the suburbs and 20 percent to out-of-towners. Of Chicago's share, 35 percent would go to the North Side and 65 percent to the club's main fan base on the South Side. Imagine, then, Veeck's surprise when, a few days later, the first application drawn was from a North Sider—and a Cub fan to boot. But for the most part, the ticket allocation went off pretty much as Veeck had hoped.

"We had the tickets selected by lot," he recalled. "We had a group of outstanding citizens do the selecting, so there wouldn't be any accusations of favoritism. Which pleased a lot of people and got a lot of other people annoyed. Because customers of customers of customers didn't get tickets, and the real fans did."

The identity of the Sox's October opponent was still anyone's guess. That same Sunday, the Giants' Jack Sanford beat Philadelphia 1-0 on Dusty Rhodes' sacrifice fly, Cincinnati beat Braves ace Warren Spahn 3-2 and Pittsburgh beat the Dodgers 4-3. So, with two weeks to go, the Giants had a two-game lead on both Milwaukee and Los Angeles. And, promised San Francisco city fathers, the brand new Candlestick Park, originally scheduled to debut on Opening Day 1960, would be ready in time for the World Series.

Just then, the White Sox, with Landis laid up, went into a bit of a tailspin, and new, gnawing fears enveloped some of the faithful, who wondered if maybe all this World Series talk wasn't just a bit too premature, wasn't perhaps putting a jinx on their heroes. The Sox lost Monday, September 14, in Boston by a 9-3 count as Dick Donovan was KO'd in his own backyard during a six-run sixth. In that same inning, Turk Lown, on his first pitch, gave up a three-run homer to rookie call-up and future White Sox coach Jim Mahoney, who at the time was hitting .056 for Boston after hitting .212 with zero home runs in 103 games at Triple-A Minneapolis.

The White Sox moved on to New York, where they split two games Tuesday and Wednesday, Billy Pierce winning 4-3 and Early Wynn losing to rookie Jim Coates 3-1, before returning home to lose two of three that weekend to Detroit. They were still without Landis, who had been flown from Boston to Chicago that Wednesday and was being treated at Mercy Hospital. "When Landis went out of the lineup," Jerome Holtzman remembered, "they put Bubba Phillips in center field and Billy Goodman at third. And they just weren't the same club. And they didn't clinch until Landis came back."

No, but they had gotten closer to the prize, mostly because the Indians were losing as well. In fact, after Bob Shaw finally defeated his former teammates, the Tigers, and Jim Bunning 1-0 on Friday night, September 18, before 37,352 at Comiskey Park, the magic number was down to two. Who cared that Khrushchev was in the United States on a never-thought-possible visit? The White Sox were one victory and one Cleveland loss from their first pennant since 1919.

Taking nothing away from Sherm Lollar—whose fifth-inning home run, his career-best 21st, gave him 14 game-winning hits, eight of them homers—the hero of this night was Shaw, who threw a five-hitter for his 17th win and received a scare only in the ninth. That was when the Tigers' Gail Harris led off with a deep drive to right. Shaw, Lollar and Jim Rivera, the rightfielder, all thought the same thing: home run. But this was 1959. A slight breeze held up the ball just enough, and Rivera caught it up against the bricks. "I backed up against that wall so hard," Rivera told the writers, "the seat of my pants is covered with green paint."

Harvey Kuenn, next up, drew the only walk allowed by Shaw, and Al Kaline lined one toward left, but Al Smith was there for the second out. Charlie Maxwell singled to right, Kuenn racing to third, and up stepped Frank Bolling, whose ninth-inning, three-run homer off the left-field foul pole in 1958's second game had helped start Dick

Donovan and the White Sox toward a forgettable season. But again, this was 1959. Bolling swung at yet another of Shaw's sinking fastballs—Lollar said Shaw threw only 12 curveballs all night—and drove it on the ground to third baseman Sammy Esposito, who speared the ball and threw to Nellie Fox at second for a game-ending force. The night air rang with the crowd's roar and, a few minutes later, with the last of Bill Veeck's 1959 fireworks spectaculars.

"I remember that one," said Shaw, who had been 0-3 against the Tigers until that evening. "You get traded away by Detroit, and then you beat them in a game like that. That was very exciting. That was a big thrill for me."

And it was a big thrill for pitching coach Ray Berres. "I think Ray Berres deserves a lot of credit for developing Bob Shaw," said Al Lopez, "because he's the one who really worked with him in the bullpen, developing his delivery."

And Berres was the one who had recommended the Sox get him from Detroit. He had watched Shaw throw in the Tigers' bullpen down the left-field line at Briggs Stadium early in the '58 season and had been both distressed and impressed. "Everything he was throwing," Berres remembered, "was a promiscuous pitch. But finally I happened to see him throw a pitch—his last, disgusted throw as the game was ending—where the ball went 'zip.' It really moved down. And he didn't even notice it."

Berres filed the moment away in his memory until he learned the Sox were talking deal with the Tigers a month or so later. "I said, 'Geez, if you ever get a chance to get him, let's take a chance on the guy.' Nobody seemed to be interested. I said, 'He's young, he has a good arm. I happened to see him do something that, if we can get him to do it repeatedly, I think he'll be of some help to us.'"

So the Sox got the Tigers to throw him into the deal that brought Ray Boone to Chicago that June 15. A grateful Berres went to work immediately. "When he came to us," he said of Shaw, "I told him what I had seen. I told him, 'If you do it our way, you can help us and help yourself. Are you willing to go through this transition?'"

At length, Shaw agreed. "So as time went on," Berres related, "we'd sit and talk. And every time a pitch would get away from him, I'd explain why. It was timing. He'd go to the plate with his arm dragging alongside his right leg. He'd drop the ball down by his right leg. By the time he got his arm up to the focal point of his delivery, his body was already gone. His leverage, everything, was spent. Consequently, he had a late delivery with his arm, so the ball was flying all over the place."

Eventually, Berres' preaching got through. "He went to extremes with it," said Berres. "It was funny. He was really conscientious about it, because he saw how it helped his control, he saw the movement, he saw how it helped his breaking ball. One day Lopez and I were in a cab, driving down Michigan Avenue, and Al says, 'Hey, Ray, look at your protege.' Bob's walking along Michigan, looking in the windows and practicing that delivery. Whenever there was a mirror or a reflection, he'd practice it. And all of a sudden he got it."

"What Ray basically taught," Shaw said, "was really quite simple. You've got to break your hands, get the hand out of the glove, keep your weight back, get your arm up. It wasn't all that elaborate. Just basic fundamentals, and he knew 'em, and there are really very few people in the country who know what they are."

After Shaw's performance that night against Detroit, very few people thought it was going to take another four days before the White Sox would clinch the American League championship. But it did. There was no clinching on Saturday, when Cleveland won at Kansas City and the Sox lost to Detroit 5-4 despite a long, ninth-inning pinch homer by rookie Norm Cash. Nor was there a clinching on Sunday, when the Indians again beat the A's and a somewhat disappointing crowd of 27,284 on a cool, sunny afternoon saw Harvey Kuenn and Al Kaline hit home runs off Detroit native Billy Pierce (now 12-20 lifetime against his hometown club) in another 5-4 Tiger victory. A sensational diving catch in left-center by Johnny Groth—a former Sox outfielder and a Chicago native, yet—helped prevent the magic number from being trimmed to 1. The lead was down to 3 1/2 games. On top of that, Jim Bunning, called upon by Tiger manager Jimmy Dykes, the longtime Sox manager, to relieve in the ninth inning, avenged Sherm Lollar's game-winning Friday night homer off of him by hitting Lollar with a pitch on the right hand, causing a substantial bruise. The frustration was beginning to even get to Lopez, the normally pleasant, patient Senor who now was in the practice of ordering photographers out of his office.

"You only take pictures when we get beat," he had complained loudly after Saturday's defeat. "Why don't you come when we win? Where were you last night? Go over and take pictures in Detroit's clubhouse. They're feeling pretty good."

The outburst had to have been a bit startling to those who followed the White Sox regularly, like Jack Kuenster and Jerome Holtzman. "He was the finest manager I ever met or had to deal with in my life," said Kuenster. "Not only as a tactician, but as a man who got along with the press. He was very good. He knew we had a job to do, and you could go into his office, even after a tough loss—he might stall for a while, go in and take a shower, and you might have to wait on him—but he'd come out and in a very solemn way he'd tell you what the club should've done and what mistakes were made and why he made certain moves."

Added Holtzman: "Lopez was a very courteous man. He treated the writers with respect. He was terrific with me. And not just me. He was terrific with everybody."

Holtzman was also moved by the respect Lopez commanded. "Lopez captained every team he played on. Did you know that? Brooklyn, Boston, Pittsburgh. All the Sox players called him 'Mr. Lopez.' He was held in such respect that even Dick Donovan, who was kind of a flip guy, called him 'Mr. Lopez.' Maybe the only one who didn't was Early Wynn, but he was an older guy who'd been with him for years. But Aparicio, to this day, whenever he sees Lopez—and I've seen it many times, at the Hall of Fame and elsewhere—he still calls him 'Mr. Lopez.'

"You know, Lopez inherited Ray Berres and Don Gutteridge from the Marty Marion (managerial) regime. And he kept them. And they became his greatest boosters. Which is very unusual."

It was even more unusual than Lopez's hollering at photographers. But that was going to be a mere aberration in this gloriously successful season. Any lingering doubts that all would end well should have been dispelled earlier in the month, when Edmund Gwenn, who had played the part of Kris Kringle in "The Miracle on 34th Street," passed away, 20 days shy of his 82nd birthday. "The Miracle on 34th Street" was being swept away by "The Miracle on 35th Street," which reached its culmination on Tuesday night, September 22, in Cleveland.

On September 22, 1959, Nikita Khrushchev and his entourage flew from San Francisco to Des Moines and spent the afternoon touring the John Deere factory and a meat-packing plant, where he sampled his first American hot dog. In New York that day, the UN voted once again, this time 44-29, against the admission of Red China. In Chicago, where it was partly sunny with temperatures in the 80s, jury selection was under way in the murder trial of Duncan Hansen. In Cleveland, the White Sox arrived at the huge lakefront stadium confident that this would be the night. True, Jim Perry, the scheduled Cleveland starter, was a tough pitcher, but the Sox had Early Wynn going for them, and Bob Shaw, having had three days of rest, was available in case Wynn were to falter. Plus, the Sox had beaten the Indians eight out of 10 in this place in '59. And Jim Landis, just out of the hospital, was back in uniform, although he was not yet robust enough to play a full nine innings.

Back in Chicago, televisions switched to Channel 9 at 7 p.m. for WGN's telecast from Cleveland. Jack Brickhouse and his new color analyst, Cleveland immortal Lou Boudreau, that evening blew away the competition, which included "Wyatt Earp" and "To Tell the Truth" in the first hour, "The Rifleman" and "The Naked City" in the 8-9 p.m. hour and "The Andy Williams Show," with Shari Lewis and Johnny Mercer among the guest stars, in the 9-10 p.m. slot. But Brickhouse and Boudreau had the clear advantage of a brilliant ballgame.

The crowd of 54,293 at what was then called Municipal Stadium held hope, however unreasonable, that if the Indians could win this night, cutting the Chicago lead to 2 1/2 games, a pennant was still possible. After this game, the White Sox would have three games left with the Tigers in Detroit, while the Tribe would finish at home with four against plummeting Kansas City. But the Sox felt a sense of urgency.

"We pretty much thought we had it," said Bob Shaw, "but in sports you don't take anything for granted. You know, it's, 'Let's win the damn thing and get it over with.'"

It was not going to be easy. Not only was Landis missing from the starting lineup, but so was Sherm Lollar, his right hand still hurting. Thus, the catching duties fell to the rookie, John Romano, who was startled to see his name on Al Lopez's lineup card.

"It was a big shock to me," Romano remembered. "I couldn't believe it. I was telling myself, 'The most important game of the year, and he's putting me in there?' I couldn't believe it."

Regardless, there he was, catching Early Wynn in a game that could mean the pennant. For Romano, this was the pinnacle of what had been a memorable rookie season. "To catch these guys ...I'm a kid, 24 years old, and I'm catching Early Wynn and Billy Pierce and all these guys—and Staley too? Holy cripes, it was unbelievable. I mean, it was such a fantastic year for me, just being there."

And this would be a fantastic night. The first big play came in the second, when Minnie Minoso tagged at third and tried to score on

137

Rocky Colavito's fly to Al Smith toward the line in medium left. Minnie hadn't yet learned his lesson. Recalled Smith, proudly: "Minnie and I used to have a bet—who could throw out the other guy. That year, he didn't throw me out once. I threw him out three times." This was the third.

So the game was scoreless in the Chicago third, when Bubba Phillips opened with a single—the first hit off Jim Perry—and scored on Luis Aparicio's double to right. After Nellie Fox walked, Billy Goodman doubled to right-center for a 2-0 lead. It stayed that way until the fifth, when Jimmy Piersall's RBI single made it 2-1 and put Cleveland runners at first and third with one out. But Vic Power, in a hint of what was to come, hit a sharp grounder to Aparicio. He fired to Fox to force Piersall, and Fox relayed to first baseman Ted Kluszewski for the double play.

Now came the key inning, the sixth. Mudcat Grant relieved Perry, who had been lifted for a successful pinch-hitter, rookie Gordy Coleman, the previous half inning. Romano tagged a Grant fastball high and deep to straightaway center, but Piersall caught the ball up against the fence, at the 410-foot marker. Next came Smith, who sent one deep to left. This one went over the fence. "I'd played in Cleveland so long I knew the ball was gone when I hit it," Smith said. Now it was 3-1. Next up was Jim Rivera. "I got a fastball, shoulder-high, boy," he recalled, grinning. "I hit it to right-center, into the old bullpen there."

So suddenly it was 4-1, and Al Lopez went into action. With a three-run lead, he waved in Earl Battey to take over the catching, and, after Colavito's deep sacrifice fly to center scored Tito Francona to make it 4-2, he waved in Bob Shaw to take over the pitching. Shaw got Woodie Held to bounce into a Goodman-to-Fox force to end that inning, then managed to steer out of trouble in the seventh and eighth, getting his nemesis, Francona—on a smash, of course, to Fox—to end the former and getting Russ Nixon on a 4-6-3 double play to end the latter.

Now came the ninth. Lopez sent Jim Landis, in his first game appearance in nine days, out to center and brought Phillips in to play third in place of Goodman. Lopez also summoned Sherm Lollar, bruised hand and all, to do the catching. This, after all, was it. Lopez was going to win it with his "A" team on the field. Shaw went to work. Held popped to Fox for the first out, but Jim Baxes singled off Shaw's glove, and Ray Webster went in as a pinch-runner. Jack Harshman, the pitcher who had hit six homers as a member of the White Sox three seasons before, batted for Grant and lined a single to right. The big crowd came to life, and so did the the Sox bullpen. Turk Lown and Gerry Staley began throwing, and Billy Pierce prepared to do so. Carroll Hardy ran for Harshman. Up to bat stepped Piersall. Out by second base, Aparicio said something to Fox. "It was funny," Aparicio remembered, "but I kid to Nellie, 'Hey, we need to make a double play.'"

They didn't get it right away. Piersall ripped a low liner toward Fox. The ball short-hopped him and squirted away for what went as a base hit, loading the bases. Now Lopez walked to the mound, looking toward the bullpen, where Lown, Staley and now Pierce, too, was throwing. The batter for Cleveland was Vic Power, a righthanded hitter. Next up was Francona, a lefty. "I was very close to being in that ballgame, as it turned out," Pierce recalled. "I was warming up to come in and face Francona." But Lopez here wanted a righthander. Lown hoped for the call. "It was a choice between Gerry or me," he said, "and he took Gerry. I would've liked to have gone in. I loved those spots. But it was Power who had hit that liner to third that time before off me, and maybe Lopez remembered that and decided to bring Gerry in."

Staley had figured he would be the man. "The decision is, did you want a strikeout (i.e., Lown) or did you want to take a chance and make them hit the ball (i.e., Staley)? A situation like that, a ground ball gives you a chance to get a double play and get out of the inning." Sure enough, Lopez wanted Staley, who was more than ready.

"Actually," he said, "I could've walked in cold from that bullpen to the mound and taken six or seven pitches and been ready. I didn't throw hard enough to where I needed that much warm up. Half a dozen pitches and I'd be ready to go."

All he needed against Power, when play resumed, was one pitch. Above the din of more than 54,000 voices, Jack Brickhouse had the call: "Webster on third, Hardy on second, Piersall on first, and dangerous Vic Power is up. One out. Here we go. Power is 1-for-4, an infield single—there's a ground ball...Aparicio has it! Steps on second, throws to first...The ballgame's over! The White Sox are the champions of 1959! The 40-year wait has now ended!"

Remembered Staley: "When he hit it, I knew it was on the ground, and that it was headed in the right direction—to Aparicio. As long as he fielded the ball clean, we were at least gonna get one out and we'd still be one run ahead."

Aparicio had gotten two outs, by himself. Some believe he did so, instead of tossing the ball to Fox, because of the previous play. Aparicio insists otherwise. "The ground ball Vic Power hit was right toward second base, and I was running toward the base. I just catch the ball and keep running, tag the base and throw. I don't think there was a reason to flip to Nellie."

With or without Fox, the double play was completed at 9:43 p.m. Chicago time, setting off a celebration on the field and countless more back home. An estimated 20,000 people gathered in the Loop to salute the victory, 3,000 alone jamming the intersection of State and Madison streets. Thousands more began heading for Midway Airport, where the Sox's plane was scheduled to land around 2 a.m. Meanwhile, Fire Commissioner Robert Quinn, a close friend of Mayor Daley and just as passionate a Sox fan, ordered the city's air-raid sirens turned on as part of the festivities. It may have been the wrong move: Hundreds and hundreds of Chicagoans, apparently unaware that Chairman Khrushchev was in Des Moines and thus more than likely would not order a strike on Chicago, rushed from their homes and from bars and searched the skies for approaching Soviet bombers. Others scrambled into bomb shelters.

"The sirens' wail," wrote Bill Veeck, "made the night memorable, since there was no way for the people of Chicago to know whether the sirens were announcing the White Sox victory or the impending arrival of the Russians. I mean, if you were a White Sox fan, you had to figure that it was just your luck for The Bomb to be dropped right after the White Sox won the pennant. What else could follow 1919?"

Newspapers and TV and radio stations were flooded with outraged calls, and people for the next several days were demanding Quinn's scalp. But Daley, asked to comment that very night while he waited, with 25,000 other fans at Midway Airport, for the Sox's return, shrugged it all off: "It was no one's fault. It was all done in the hilarity of the occasion. It was done in accordance with the City Council proclamation."

That proclamation, passed six days earlier, had stated in part: "Be it further resolved that bells ring, whistles blow, bands play and general joy be unconfined when the coveted pennant has been won by the heroes of 35th Street, the Chicago White Sox." Apparently to Quinn, and maybe to Daley as well, an air-raid siren was simply just another whistle. In any event, Quinn, to no one's surprise, kept his job.

Meanwhile, back in Cleveland, the on-field celebration had long since moved into the clubhouse, where Al Lopez and Chuck Comiskey embraced while their players smoked huge cigars, danced victory jigs and gave each other showers of beer and champagne. "In the clubhouse," recalled Bob Shaw, "it was fabulous. You win it, and it's a great feeling. It makes you feel good, too, to know you had a key role in it, and you figure you're gonna get a nice raise for next year. But I don't know. I don't think money was as big a deal as it is today."

"I was a spectator in that game," remembered Jim McAnany, "but in that clubhouse afterwards, I know a lot of those guys really appreciated it. Not that I didn't, but here I am in my first year in the big leagues. I didn't know at the time the magnitude of it. A little later on, I started realizing what it meant. But for Billy, Nellie, Sherm Lollar, Jim Rivera, those guys—I really felt happy for them, because I know it really meant so much to those guys. And they were really great people."

Rivera had repaired to a different section of the clubhouse with one of his closest friends on the team. "I went into one of the stalls, in the bathroom there," said Sammy Esposito, "and I was drinking a beer, and Rivera was sitting in the next one, drinking a little champagne. We were just talking very calmly in there."

Jim Landis, who had barely worked up a sweat, was sitting quietly in front of his locker, not certain how to react. "It's funny," he said. "You can play all year, and play real hard, but if you're not (starting) in that particular game, the one that wins it all, you feel funny, like, 'What am I doing here? I didn't help.' It was a funny, lost feeling, it really was. But Earl Torgeson, he knew. He came over, made me feel a lot better. It was real nice of him."

Also feeling like he didn't belong there, for far better reasons, was Johnny Callison. "I remember everyone dancing around in that little clubhouse," he said. "But I really couldn't get that excited. You know, I wasn't part of it. I didn't think I was part of it."

They were all part of the ride home, still memorable after all these years. "We were drinking champagne," said Jerome Holtzman. "Lopez and I drank from the same glass. And I kept that glass for years. I had it marked. But somehow the marker fell off or something, and now I don't know which one is the right glass."

Said Al Smith, laughing: "Early Wynn, Klu and I stood up all the way on that flight back from Cleveland. I shouldn't say this, 'cause we could get in trouble with the FAA. But we landed standing up. We never sat down. First you're high from winning the game for the pennant. And then you're high from the champagne."

Jack Brickhouse remembered the flight for other reasons. "We did a telecast from the plane. We did interviews with the players. And I remember Early Wynn going up to the pilots, saying, 'If you fellas want to take a coffee break, I'll be glad to take over for a while.' Rivera doing his dance in the aisle. All those thousands of people at Midway when we got back. They did almost $20,000 worth of damage to the fences, you know. They found out where the plane was coming in, of course. Now that I think about it, I guess we told them." And the fans had been listening. The welcoming party now included Bill Veeck and his wife. Veeck had arrived shortly after midnight, having driven all night from Downstate Bloomington, where he had delivered speeches to five different audiences. The Veecks, helped by police, joined the mayor and his wife and, when the Sox plane rolled to a stop at exactly 2:08 a.m. next to the Air National Guard hangar, together they made their way up the ramp to be the first to greet the players.

"I remember the crowd at the airport," said Bob Shaw. "I mean, we were exhilarated, we were happy. But when you got off that plane and saw all those people waiting for you, that really gave you goose bumps. You can't lose sight of that. That's probably one of the things that bothers me most today, with the money part of it. In other words, these guys are making tremendous money, and I don't begrudge their making it. But what bothers me very deeply is that I remember when we were playing, the average blue-collar working man could take his kids to the ballpark. And that was part of what we called America's sport, baseball. Today, if you have two, three kids, you just can't run to the ballpark. It gets pretty expensive, so I think it reduces the chance of young kids going as much as they could years ago. And that kinda bothers me. Because let's face it, it's the kids and the people who come to watch you play that really make this all exciting."

It's what made it so exciting that night 40 years ago. The crowd was so large that Esposito, who lived with his parents in Roseland on the Far South Side, didn't even try to fight it. "We couldn't get a cab, we couldn't get anything," he recalled. "So we went across the street, grabbed a beer and waited it out. But the crowd was unbelievable at the airport. You couldn't move. I don't think I got home till 4 in the morning."

Some players were able to escape. "Earl Torgeson and I got into a cab together," said Billy Pierce, "and I'll never forget, coming down 55th, Garfield Boulevard, people had flares on the lawn, they were sitting outside. And this was way past 2 in the morning."

At least the players could sleep in the next day because there was no game until Friday in Detroit. There were, however, other matters to be concerned with, such as Wednesday evening's 500-guest gala thrown by Bill Veeck at the Williford Room of the Conrad Hilton, plus Thursday's ticker-tape parade through the Loop, which attracted 700,000 people— doubtless some of them curious office workers—and which ended with a rally and speeches at City Hall.

There was also the yet-unresolved National League pennant race. On Wednesday afternoon, Veeck and Al Lopez, both early risers anyway, went over to Wrigley Field to get a firsthand look at the San Francisco Giants, who were attempting, without success, to shake off the effects of the previous weekend's three-game sweep by the Dodgers. The Sox bosses saw Cal Neeman blast a knuckleball from future White Sox reliever Eddie Fisher out of the park in the 10th inning for a 9-8 Cub victory. That night, Roger Craig and the Dodgers shut out the Cardinals in St. Louis while the Braves were losing 5-4 in Pittsburgh. So, with four days left, Milwaukee was tied with the Dodgers—who would be at Wrigley Field over the weekend—and two ahead of the Giants. It was still too close to call.

Still to be decided, too, was the voting of World Series shares, a topic the Sox took up during that final week. Earl Battey went into the meeting with an agenda. "I was back and forth between the minors and Chicago for several years—'55, '56, '57," he said, "and the White Sox always finished second or third. And I was always thankful to the guys who'd been on the team all year, 'cause they always voted me some money. And I always said, 'If I'm ever in that position, I'm gonna take care of the guys who were there for only half the year or a quarter of the year or even the guys who got called up after September 1.' So when it came time to vote, I argued and fought for those guys who weren't there the whole time."

One such person was Harry Simpson, traded to the Pirates on August 25 and thus cut out of the record Series pot, which would pay out a full share of $11,231 for each member of the winning team and $7,275 for each losing club member. Battey and several others had argued on Simpson's behalf, noting his many contributions, not the least of which was his grand slam against the Yankees.

"I recalled that home run," Battey said, "and I know a lot of the players recalled it, too, because Suitcase wound up going over to Pittsburgh, and Pittsburgh came in fourth place. And I recall that there was a ruling from the commissioner's office that if he went to a team that finished in the first division, he wasn't entitled to any money from the team he had left. So instead of a first-place share, he got a fourth-place share. We all felt badly."

Simpson's winnings? The Pirates' full share, which was $588.99, or $6,686 less than what he would have received had he not been traded. Said Battey: "That's when Bill Veeck tried to rectify the situation." What Veeck did was to make sure Simpson ended up with a World Series ring. He also got him back from the Pirates that winter and invited him to spring training. And though Simpson was cut the day before the season opener, Veeck ensured that he would remain in the Sox system for the next few years, through the 1962 season.

As for the 1959 season, the White Sox closed it out over the weekend of September 25-27 at Briggs Stadium in Detroit under the direction of Coach Tony Cuccinello, while Al Lopez stayed in Chicago to scout the Dodgers. Friday's pitcher was Billy Pierce. "After he'd hurt his hip," Ray Berres remembered, "he didn't get his velocity back. Billy was struggling that month. Tony took over the club that last weekend, with the instructions to get Billy ready for the second game of the World Series. And Al said, 'His outing will determine my decision, whether or not to start him.' And anyway, geez, Billy got racked. And you can get racked with good stuff once in awhile, but his velocity wasn't there, his control wasn't there. And I think that was the deciding factor."

Pierce lasted only two innings, giving up three runs and five hits, one a homer by Al Kaline, before Dick Donovan entered to work five scoreless innings, but the Sox lost anyway 6-5. Back in Chicago, Lopez watched the Dodgers beat the Cubs 5-4 in 11 on Gil Hodges' homer. He also saw a rookie reliever, Larry Sherry, get out of a two-on, one-out jam in the 10th by striking out National League MVP Ernie Banks on three pitches and getting Walt Moryn on a tap to the mound. That evening, Lopez motored up to Milwaukee and saw the Braves lose 6-3 to the last-place Phillies, who got a three-run homer from their third baseman, Gene Freese.

The next afternoon, Early Wynn tuned up for the Series opener, going five innings for his 22nd victory as the Sox, with a solo homer from Earl Battey and a grand slam from Johnny Callison, won 10-5. Lopez, meanwhile, at Wrigley Field, witnessed the Cubs' 12-2 pounding of Johnny Podres and L.A., which, coupled with Warren Spahn's 3-2 decision over the Phillies—despite another Freese home run—meant the Dodgers and Braves were tied going into the season finale.

On Sunday, September 27, Lopez, satisfied he had seen enough of his possible Series opponents, returned to his club in Detroit. The *Sun-Times'* Jerome Holtzman, noting that Luis Aparicio had sat out Saturday's game, was not in this day's lineup either and was still at 54 stolen bases, two shy of the Sox's club record set by Wally Moses in 1943, sought out Lopez. "I still remember it now," he said. "Before the game I went up to him and said, 'Hey Senor, Looie needs two stolen bases to tie the club record.' And Lopez told Cuccinello, and Cuccinello talked to Aparicio, and Aparicio went into the lineup."

In the first inning, Aparicio singled and then, running on a rookie catcher named Jim Shoop, easily stole second. Shoop's throw sailed into center field, and Aparicio could have walked to third base. Instead, he stayed put, then set out for third on the next pitch and slid in with steal No. 56. He then scored the first of five first-inning runs that helped Bob Shaw notch his 18th win. "And then," said Holtzman, "Looie took himself out of the game. And that's how he tied Wally Moses' record. But that's how it was in those days. Records weren't that important."

Won-lost records were, and the Sox's final mark, 94-60, was five games better than Cleveland's and 15 better than New York's. It was also better than the 88-66 records with which Milwaukee and Los Angeles finished, the Dodgers having beaten the Cubs 7-1 on Roger Craig's six-hitter and homers by Charlie Neal and Johnny Roseboro, and the Braves having downed the Phils 5-2 behind pitcher Bob Buhl and before 48,642 at County Stadium. So now, the White Sox, raring to go, would have to wait until at least Thursday rather than the usual Wednesday Series opener as the Braves and Dodgers battled it out in a best-of-three playoff for the title.

By Wednesday or so, recalled Jim Landis, "a lot of the real excite-ment was wearing off because we had to wait three days for the other league's playoff. I'm not saying that's what beat us, but I know in my own heart a little edge went away. You know, 'Let's go!' So I don't care what anybody says. For me, anyway, a little bit of my edge was lost."

Whatever edge the Braves might have had was lost in Monday's playoff opener at Milwaukee, when Roseboro's homer off Carlton Willey broke a 2-2 tie in the sixth and Larry Sherry, the first-year man signed by one-time Sox coach and manager Red Corriden out of Los Angeles' Fairfax High School, shut out the Braves over the final 7 2/3 innings in a 3-2 Dodger victory. After the game came word that Corriden had passed away at age 72 while watching his protege perform on TV. Now, with the Braves near their demise, the teams flew to Los

Angeles for the next day's game at the Coliseum, the football and track stadium serving as the Dodgers' home until their new digs at Chavez Ravine were ready. Neither Lew Burdette nor Warren Spahn could hold a 5-2 ninth-inning Milwaukee lead, and then, in the 12th, with two on and two out, shortstop Felix Mantilla charged in and grabbed Carl Furillo's slow tap and threw low, past first baseman Frank Torre and into the Dodger dugout, Gil Hodges scoring from second with the game- and pennant-winning run.

More than a month before, Nellie Fox had said, "You know who we want to play in the Series, don't you? Look at that Coliseum out there in Los Angeles. Ninety thousand seats. Now you know who we're rooting for."

Fox and the White Sox had been granted their wish.

OCTOBER

No More Champagne,
but Plenty of Sherry

The shocking realization that the White Sox actually were going to be in a World Series was finally beginning to sink in, and among the happiest with Chicago's role as host were its restaurant and hotel owners, who conservatively estimated between $10 million and $12 million would be spent at their establishments during the Series' first two days. The city's hotels expected an influx of at least 10,000 out-of-town guests. Among them were the Dodgers, who had arrived at the Conrad Hilton at 8 a.m. Wednesday, September 30, after their red-eye flight from Los Angeles, plus a horde of sportswriters who had descended upon the LaSalle Hotel, which was serving as World Series headquarters. And the proprietor of a barber shop in the Palmer House reported having had two interesting customers, both in town for the Series: an Alaskan Indian and a male Hawaiian hula dancer.

Attempting to capitalize on the festive mood, merchandisers around the area announced one "World Series sale" after another. Lytton's tied theirs in with an anniversary sale, with imported worsted suits going for $53.50, Mansfield's men's shoes for $13.85 and fur-trimmed women's coats for $98. Maurice L. Rothschild put two-trouser suits by Don Richards on sale for $69.50, and at Wieboldt's, Maytag washers and Philco dryers were going for $169 and Westinghouse and Frigidaire 11-cubic-foot refrigerators for $199.

There were no such sales on tickets for Game 1, set for Thursday, October 1. Seven-dollar reserved grandstand seats were being scalped for $50, and $10 boxes were commanding up to $150. About 500 people, who just wanted a seat, camped out overnight outside the Comiskey Park bleacher gate to be first in line for the 1,300 $2 bleacher tickets that were to begin being sold at 8 a.m. Thursday. Another 3,000 to 4,000 standing-room tickets were also available at $4.10 each. Loop office workers knew they'd be able to sneak away to the nearest watering hole for a few innings, but, for those who perhaps wanted to make an afternoon of it, the Sheraton Towers at 505 N. Michigan Ave. was offering, free to the public, theater-sized closed-circuit TV in its seventh-floor ballroom, which held 1,500.

Meanwhile, on the eve of the Series, Bill Veeck had rehired Al Lopez for 1960 at a salary said to be in the vicinity of $60,000, while Cubs owner P. K. Wrigley, trying to steal some of the newspaper space from the White Sox, fired his manager, Bob Scheffing, and replaced him with Charlie Grimm, who had served as Wrigley's manager in two earlier stints. The only reason for the move had to be publicity: Scheffing had taken the Cubs from 62-92 and last place in his first year, 1957, to 74-80 and fifth place in '59. Said the Phillies' Eddie Sawyer: "The way I see it, Bob Scheffing was manager of the year in our league, and now he isn't managing anymore. Sometimes this game is hard to figure."

What was harder to figure was baseball's choice of radio broadcasters for the World Series. Sharing the duties on the games, carried in Chicago over WMAQ and WCFL, were to be Byrum Saam, "voice" of the Phillies, and the Yankees' Mel Allen, who got to do Series games practically every year as it was. Veeck had argued for Bob Elson, who had been broadcasting Sox games, without any postseason reward, since 1930.

Like most of Veeck's petitions to baseball's rulers, this one fell on deaf ears—although he had championed, with success, the cause of his local radio men in the 1948 Series. At least the Sox would be represented on the Series telecasts, available in Chicago on Channel 5 and Channel 9, by Jack Brickhouse, who was teaming with the Dodgers' Vin Scully.

Brickhouse and Scully, in their pre-Series preparations, no doubt studied both clubs' strengths and weaknesses. The Dodgers, like everyone else, had the edge in offense and power: World Series veterans Gil Hodges (25 homers, 80 RBIs, .276 average) and Duke Snider (23, 87, .308) had support from fellow long-ball hitters Wally Moon (19, 74, .302), Charlie Neal (19, 83, .287) and Don Demeter (18 homers). The Dodgers also had good hitters in Junior Gilliam (.282) and Norm Larker (.290), and rookie shortstop Maury Wills, called up from Triple-A Spokane in June, had gone on a 24-for-37 binge in September that enabled him to finish at a respectable .260.

The Dodgers' pitching seemed to compare favorably with that of the White Sox. Los Angeles had no 22-game winner like Early Wynn or 18-game winner such as Bob Shaw, but Roger Craig had gone 11-5 with a 2.06 earned-run average since his return from the minors in late May, and rookie reliever Larry Sherry, a minor-leaguer until June, finished 7-2 and 2.30 with 72 strikeouts in 94 innings. Don Drysdale had been 15-6 at the start of August before fading to finish 17-13, but the side-arming smokeballer with a penchant for knocking down batters had led the National League in strikeouts with 245 in 271 innings. There were also Johnny Podres (14-9), hero of the Dodgers' 1955 Series triumph; fellow lefty Danny McDevitt (10-8); longtime relief specialist Clem Labine and the still-developing 23-year-old Sandy Koufax, erratic but capable: He had struck out 18 Giants on August 31. Altogether, he had fanned 173 in just 153 innings.

Where the Sox clearly had an edge was on defense, particularly at shortstop (Luis Aparicio over the rookie Wills) and second base (Nellie Fox over Neal) and in the outfield (the Dodgers had no one to match Jim Landis or Al Smith). But there was no great edge in overall speed: They had no 50-base stealer like Aparicio, but the Dodgers had shown they, too, could run: Gilliam had swiped 23 bases, Neal 17, Moon 15 and Wills, warming up for much bigger years to come, 8. And their manager, Walter Alston, was confident that the Sox's speed would be held in check by his catcher, Johnny Roseboro, who had thrown out an astounding 59 percent (24-of-41) of would-be base-stealers that season.

Still, oddsmakers, taking into account the home-field advantage, had established the Sox as 6-5 favorites to win the Series. And when the fans began arriving in the late morning that Thursday, the home team was pumped, from the front office on down.

"There's a number of things you want to do," recalled Chuck Comiskey. "First of all, you want to bring the big flag to Chicago. And then, you want to defend the American League honor. The league factor was very big. Don't think it wasn't."

Gerry Staley, who had pitched in both leagues, was thrilled just to finally be in the Series after 13 years in the majors. "That's everybody's goal, to get to the World Series. I'd missed the Cardinals' pennant in '46—I first came up in '47. And I'd joined the Yankees too late in '55 to be eligible for the Series. I threw batting practice for them in the Series, but I couldn't even sit in the dugout during the game. So I'd just go back to the hotel and watch the game on TV."

In his hotel room the night before, rookie Jim McAnany recalled, "I said a little prayer: 'Dear Jesus, just don't let me screw up.' I remember walking out of the dugout, and Jiminy Christmas, everybody was in a suit and tie, all dressed up. It was just different. It was not just another game. There was a lot of tension, a lot of pressure. I really noticed it."

One who didn't notice was Johnny Callison, who wasn't on the Series roster and had chosen to skip the Series altogether and begin to get ready for his winter-ball assignment in Venezuela.

"I said, 'Why should I have to buy a ticket to watch these guys play? I played with them.' I had a bad attitude. But really, I was going to go to winter ball, so my wife and I figured, 'Let's spend some time at home before we go.' So I ended up wreckin' my car—oh, that was a terrible year. Wrecked the car, turned it over in Cheyenne, Wyoming. No one was hurt. We were on our way to meet up with my in-laws in San Francisco. So we saw them, went back to Bakersfield, then got on a plane to South America."

The center of attention this day in North America was Chicago's South Side. A crowd of 48,103 was gathering for the first Series at Comiskey Park since October 1919, when little Dickie Kerr beat the Cincinnati Reds 3-0 in Game 3 for the Sox's only Series victory at home. Now, 40 years later, Kerr was on hand again, this time with press credentials, reporting his observations for one of his hometown's newspapers, the *Houston Post*. Covering the Series for *Look* magazine was Casey Stengel, who commented: "I never realized that finishing third was so low until I talked to my bosses about a new contract."

There were far more celebrities in the stands. Mayor Daley and his wife—with their four sons— were in their third-base box, and not far away were Illinois Gov. William Stratton, former Gov. Adlai Stevenson, Chief Justice Earl Warren and former commissioner A.B. "Happy" Chandler. From the entertainment world were Joan Crawford, George Gobel, Orson Welles, Joe E. Brown, Danny Thomas and Ralph Edwards of "This Is Your Life." There were Roy Campanella, Joe DiMaggio and DiMag's pal, New York restaurateur Toots Shor. And, hard by the Sox dugout, former Sox VP John Rigney, his wife Dorothy and ex-Sox slugger Zeke Bonura—plus a couple more Rigney guests.

"John had two Catholic priests with him," remembered Al Lopez. "And I was in the dugout, and he hollered over at me, wanted to introduce me to the priests and wish me luck. He said, 'Hey Al, we've got some help here.' I said, 'Thanks, John—we need all the help we can get.' About 20 minutes later, over on the first-base side, Walter

O'Malley walks in with four priests. And I looked over at John and said, 'John, we're outnumbered over there.'"

On this day, that did not matter.

GAME 1: THURSDAY, OCTOBER 1— WHITE SOX 11, DODGERS 0

The 1917 world championship battery of "Red" Faber and Ray Schalk performed the first-pitch ceremony, and the White Sox took the field. That's when the enormity of the moment hit Ted Kluszewski. "It was the first Series game I'd ever been in," he remembered. "And you run out onto the field, and you suddenly realize that this is the only game in the country and a lot of people are watching. In fact, up in the millions. And I got a big thrill out of it. In fact, even if I had had a bad Series, it still would've been the greatest moment of my life."

Tony Martin sang the National Anthem as the Stars and Stripes moved up the flagpole in center field. Trouble is, about halfway up, the flag got stuck. Wrote Bill Veeck in his autobiography: "We hastily called around for a steeplejack and learned that the steeplejack had apparently disappeared from the American scene. You turn your head away for 10 or 20 years and, all of a sudden, no more steeplejacks."

Fortunately, an expert at untangling flags was eventually located that evening, by which time White Sox fans were seriously talking of a four-game sweep. What had happened? Essentially, the Ted Kluszewski of the early- and mid-'50s had been reborn. But it was more than that. Wrote *New York Herald Tribune* columnist Red Smith: "Generally lacking in size, sinew and gristle, the White Sox are noted for the shell game they play, winning by guile, speed and trickery in a park that distinctly handicaps power hitters. Yet they simply slugged the National League champions to jelly."

It all began in the home half of the first inning. Nellie Fox walked and raced to third on Jim Landis' line single to right. Kluszewski grounded a single to right to score Fox and send Landis to third, and Sherm Lollar's sacrifice fly sent in Landis to make it 2-0.

In the Chicago third, Fox lined a one-out double to right, and Landis again singled to make it 3-0. Landis—with the big crowd yelling 'Go! Go! Go!'—took off for second as Roger Craig fired a pitch to Kluszewski. Klu swung and hit a long fly ball that nestled into the first row of seats near the right-field foul pole, a home run that gave Early Wynn an insurmountable 5-0 lead and turned Comiskey Park into a madhouse. Walter Alston replaced Craig with a rookie named

Clarence Nottingham Churn Jr., known as Chuck. Other than exhibition games, this inning, and the next, would be the last major-league action Churn would experience. The White Sox, and Churn's fielders, made it unforgettable.

First, Duke Snider and Wally Moon collided on Lollar's fly to left-center, Snider dropping the ball for a two-base error. Billy Goodman singled to score Lollar, and it was 6-0. Al Smith then doubled over Moon's head in left, and when Snider's return throw toward the infield got past Gil Hodges for another error, Goodman scored and Smith ended up on third. Jim Rivera sent a grounder to second baseman Charlie Neal, whose throw home to get Smith hit the bat Rivera had dropped in front of catcher Johnny Roseboro and caromed away for yet another error, Smith scoring to make it 8-0. Wynn capped the inning with an RBI double to left-center.

Churn's trials weren't quite over. In the fourth, with Landis on base again, Kluszewski launched one off the upper-deck railing in right for his second homer and fourth and fifth RBIs of the game. The Sox led 11-0—that was the final score—and Klu had tied the single-game Series RBI record set by the Yankees' Tony Lazzeri and Bill Dickey in 1936. And out in Argo and Summit, Klu's old friends and neighbors were beside themselves. In Chester's Tavern at 6255 Archer Ave., owner Chester Strzelzyk, who had known Kluszewski since the two were kids, shouted, "Drinks on the house!" after Klu's second home run. Summit Police Chief John Van Ort, after the second homer, was reported ready to turn on the town's air-raid sirens, a move that certainly would have had Robert Quinn feeling somewhat vindicated. "It was a real temptation to press every siren button in sight," Van Ort said. "But I decided we didn't need any more noise. People were wild enough already."

Twenty years later, standing behind the batting cage at Wrigley Field as he watched his Cincinnati "pupils" go through their paces, Kluszewski, by then the Reds' hitting instructor, remembered that day of triumph, the completion of his comeback from the back miseries that had threatened to end his career. "By World Series time," he said, "I was back to about 80 percent of my old swing. The back is kind of a crazy thing. Even though it hurts, the more you work at it the better off you are, because you're finally starting to loosen up. When your back is bothering you, you have a tendency to stiffen, and everything shortens and you don't swing the bat the way you normally would. So the more I played, the better I swung the bat, and finally it culminated with the Series. I was hitting the ball as well as you could hit it by that particular time."

He had hit the jackpot, too. Jim Moran, "the Courtesy Man" from
Courtesy Motors in Chicago, had offered a new Ford to any Sox player
hitting a home run during the Series. So Moran announced that
Kluszewski would be getting two free cars. However, Commissioner
Ford Frick, with his mighty powers, ruled against the publicity stunt.
Then, to make himself look more foolish, he reversed himself the next
day, saying it was OK with him as long as the White Sox weren't paying
any part of the cost.

That night, while baseball fans and celebs crowded into the downtown restaurants and Rush Street clubs, Ted Kluszewski and his wife,
Eleanor, enjoyed a quiet steak dinner at their Hyde Park "home," the
Shoreland Hotel on South Shore Drive. Klu's Series success was just
beginning, but the White Sox's was just about over.

GAME 2: FRIDAY, OCTOBER 2 — DODGERS 4, WHITE SOX 3

Johnny Podres, a lefty who absolutely loathed his home stadium,
the Los Angeles Coliseum, was chosen to start Game 2 for the Dodgers
by manager Walter Alston. The reason for Podres' abhorrence of the
place was simple. Opposing managers stocked their lineups against lefthanded pitchers with delighted righthanded hitters, who took careful
aim on the Coliseum's 42-foot-high left-field fence, which was only 251
feet down the line and a mere 320 to left-center. Knowing this, Alston
preferred to use his lefty in Comiskey Park, the left-field area of which,
to Podres, must have looked like an airport compared to the Coliseum's.

With the White Sox having won Game 1, there was speculation
now among the national media that veteran lefty Billy Pierce, rather
than young righthander Bob Shaw, would get the Game 2 start, because
surely Al Lopez would not want Pierce to start a game in the lefties'
graveyard that was the Coliseum. Lopez, however, still basing his
verdict on how Pierce had pitched in that final Series tuneup in Detroit,
had long since decided on Shaw as his man for Game 2, a decision that
even one of his bosses, Chuck Comiskey, could not reverse.

"We were gonna go out to play the middle three games out in L.A.,
in that Mickey Mouse ballpark," Comiskey recalled. "I know you've
got to have righthanded pitching out there. You don't want lefthanded pitching, not with that 250-foot fence in left field. Well, I
spent 'til 2 o'clock in the morning at the Del Prado Hotel with Al Lopez
and Tony Cuccinello—Ray Berres wasn't there—pushing and promoting for Pierce to pitch the second game. Al figured we had to have the

righthanders against the Dodgers, basically a righthanded-hitting ballclub. I said, 'Yeah, but here's a guy who deserves a start. Here's a fella who's contributed to this ballclub year in and year out. Here's been our quote-unquote mainstay, he's been our so-called hero. Here's Mr. White Sox, he and Fox. You're not gonna be able to start him in that Mickey Mouse ballpark out there, so why not the second game here?'

"Well, I can see Al's thinking. He wanted to get a two-game jump on 'em on his home field, with his two big winners. I can't argue with him on that point. But I was very disappointed that I wasn't able to get him to change his mind. I'm not gonna override Al. I'm not Steinbrenner or somebody like that who says, 'Goddamn it, you're gonna pitch him whether you like it or not.' I didn't operate that way. But I did plead Billy Pierce's case, 'til 2 o'clock in the morning—still had to drive back out to Hinsdale afterward. Because I thought Pierce deserved the second-game start. In Chicago, a big ballpark, the hoopla of the World Series. Now you've got your other righthanders—Shaw and Donovan—well-rested for the first two games out there, and then you can come back with Wynn in the last game out there, with four days' rest."

But, as Pierce remembered, "Al was a man who, if he made a decision, he was not going to back off that decision for anything in the world. That's just the way he was. Veeck told me later that he and Hank Greenberg tried to get Al to start me in the sixth game. And they couldn't win out on that one, either."

"A lot of people were talking about a matter of personalites, or that so-and-so's in the doghouse," Lopez said. "To me, that's the most asinine statement anybody could make. If there was anybody I didn't like on my club, he wouldn't be on my club. I'd try to get him off the club, because I wouldn't want to pick on a guy. What the hell, Billy Pierce was a great pitcher in Chicago and a great favorite and a great kid. But when you get in a short series like that, you've got to give 'em your best. Go with the best you've got."

By midseason 1960, Pierce, as he had been before, was again the best Lopez had. But this was October 1959, and it was Shaw who got the call in Game 2. A crowd of 47,368 was treated to partly sunny skies and temperatures in the low 60s, an appearance by Democratic presidential hopeful John F. Kennedy—seated alongside Mayor Daley—and a rather unusual rendition of the National Anthem by Nat "King" Cole, who was to open that night at the Chez Paree.

"He forgot the lyrics," remembered Bill Veeck, smiling, one day many years later in the Comiskey Park Bards Room. "We sat up here before the game with Nat and his agent, and we had the lyrics printed up on cards for him. I'd known him a long time. He said, 'Now, come on—no problem.' 'Well,' I said, 'take them along—once in a while you might forget them.' 'He said, 'No no. No way.' So he forgot them. And he went right on fine with different lyrics. And he made up better ones than the ones we have. I thought so, anyway."

The White Sox gave Shaw a quick 2-0 lead. Luis Aparicio, who had led off the first inning with a ground double past first base, scored on Ted Kluszewski's infield out, and Jim Landis, who had walked, scored on Sherm Lollar's single to right. Both Kluszewski's ball and Lollar's were misplayed by second baseman Charlie Neal, but Neal began making up for his fielding blunders with two out and the bases empty in the Dodger fifth with a shot into the lower deck in left. Al Smith backed up to the wall, and, as he watched the ball sail into the stands, the contents from a jostled cup of beer came pouring down upon him.

"At first I was angry," he remembered, "because I thought some-body had thrown the beer at me. I was ticked. But the umpire down the left-field line told me what had happened, that a fan had lost it trying to catch the baseball."

The *Chicago Tribune* ran an eight-picture photo sequence the next day, showing the incident, right down to the very last drop. That off-season, Smith, put to work by Veeck as a season-ticket salesman, journeyed with Sox representative Ira Hutchinson to the front office of Virgin Steel Co. on South Commercial Avenue. "I went in to help them renew their tickets," Smith said, "and all these people start laughing at us." Smith wondered why. "I thought maybe my fly was open or something. I looked, but it wasn't. I looked at Ira, but he was OK, too."

The two men were then led to the office of the company's vice president for public relations. There, on his wall, was a blowup of the *Tribune* photo sequence. "The guy who spilled the beer," Smith realized, "was this vice president. Now we knew why all those people had been laughing."

The Dodgers' seventh inning had been no laughing matter. First, Chuck Essegian, batting for Podres with two out, blasted a pitch 417 feet into the left-field upper deck to tie the game. Said teammate Ron Fairly afterward: "The last time I saw Essegian hit a ball that far was at a driving range." Indeed, Essegian, in just 85 previous at-bats that season with the Cardinals and Dodgers, had hit just one home run. Perhaps that was a sign that Shaw was losing it. He lost Junior Gilliam, walking him, and then Neal lost another of Shaw's pitches, driving this one into the center-field bullpen, some 425 feet away, where Billy Pierce, seeing some Game 2 action after all, made a backhanded catch. Suddenly, the Dodgers led 4-2.

"We were pitching Neal away," Shaw recalled, "because that's what the scouting reports said to do. But in all honesty, in all fairness, I did make a mistake. On one of those home run balls, I didn't get the ball away enough. But you know, it's funny how every pitcher can be a little different. One might be able to get a guy out one way, and you might get him out another way. It might be completely against the book. But I know I was trying to pitch him away, and the results weren't very good. Then I found out later, talking to some other people, they suggested pitching him inside. And so by the time he got to the Mets, and I was in the National League, I just jammed him, and he never hurt me at all.

"Of course, he may have started going downhill then, too. I think he fell off fast. But the point is, I had very good success against him. It was just a little bit too late."

It was getting late now for the Sox, especially after Larry Sherry, who had replaced Podres, retired them in order in the seventh. But in the eighth, Kluszewski looped a single to center and Lollar smashed a hit off Gilliam's glove at third. The decibel level soared. The Sox had rattled the kid reliever, Sherry. Now Lopez sent in Earl Torgeson to run for Kluszewski but chose not to use Sammy Esposito, who was expecting the assignment, to run for Lollar.

Explained Lopez: "I didn't want to pull Lollar out of the game because I wanted to keep some power in the lineup. I didn't want to take Klu out, either, but since it was a bunting situation, I wanted a faster man (Torgeson) in there so we have a chance to get him to third. Al Smith was bunting until they got two strikes on him. Then, if he hits into a double play, having a faster man at first base instead of Lollar wouldn't make any difference anyhow. He'd be out just the same."

Smith did not hit into a double play. Smith, who had worked the count to 3-2 after twice failing to get a bunt down, drilled a long drive beyond Wally Moon's reach in left-center, the ball hitting the wall on one hop. Torgeson scored easily, but Lollar, who had hesitated a moment at second base, fearing Moon might make the catch, did not. Third-base coach Tony Cuccinello, who hadn't noticed Lollar's brief pause, waved him home, ignoring the time-honored baseball commandment: Never get thrown out at third base or home plate for the first out of an inning. (Especially, goes the corollary, when it's the tying run in the eighth inning of a World Series game with a rookie relief pitcher on the ropes.) Cuccinello, and the Sox, paid fully for the gaffe: Lollar was out at the plate by 10 feet, Moon to Maury Wills to John Roseboro. He was so far out he didn't even bother to slide.

It was now 4-3, but instead of runners at second and third with nobody out and the place up for grabs, there was a man at third with one out and a suddenly subdued audience, not to mention a newly confident Sherry. The righthander struck out Billy Goodman and got Jim Rivera, who had taken over defensively for Jim McAnany in right, to pop out weakly. Threat, inning, ballgame and, many will argue, World Series over.

"The Go-Go White Sox," wrote Red Smith, "lost this game on the bases, the domain where they excel, the speedway where they won the American League pennant. They are a running team. But Sherm Lollar is a catcher, with honest feet."

After Sherry stopped the Sox in order in the ninth to close out Los Angeles' 4-3 victory, Cuccinello bravely faced his interrogators. "With the count 3-2 and the men running," he explained, "I thought Sherm would score, and then I'd have Smitty at third with the winning run."

Lopez, rushing to his pal Cuccinello's support, blamed Lollar for his hesitation near second base: "He had no business stopping. The play was right in front of him. He should've been able to see that Moon wasn't gonna catch the ball." By the late 1990s, he had absolved his former catcher. "Moon made a real good fake on the play, as if he was going to catch the ball, and Lollar stopped a little bit to be sure he wasn't gonna catch it. And then, by the time he got started again, Moon had relayed the ball, and that's what threw off the timing on the play. But Tony had to send him in because the other guy, Smith, was right on top of him."

Smith, too, still defends Cuccinello. "To get Sherm, it's got to be like a perfect throw. But I keep running. When I get to second base and I see Cuccinello waving in Sherm, I keep running so that maybe they'll cut it off and try to get me. Well, they get Sherm. But I go into third base, so we still have the tying run on third with one out. And Billy Goodman's comin' up, and he always makes contact. Who would've thought Billy would strike out?"

Most of Smith's teammates thought then that Cuccinello's decision was wrong. They still think it was wrong.

Jim Landis: "I'm saying, 'Oh, my God.' Right away, there's no decision. There's no way there's a decision to send him home. No question he stays at third. Everybody on our club was deflated, 'cause we had something going. Boom! That's sad."

Billy Pierce: "See, they blame Sherm for slowing down around second base, but why Cuccinello sent him in, I'll never know."

Sammy Esposito: "When did I think Sherm was gonna be out? About when he hit third base."

Chuck Comiskey had a different version than most witnesses but still believes Cuccinello must shoulder the blame. "To this day, I seriously feel Cuccinello did not see Lollar trip over second base, or he'd never have sent him home. But he tripped goin' around second, so he loses a stride, and he's slow anyway. By the time he regains his stride, and gets his Olympic-class speed back up and going, he's a dead goose. Should never have been sent."

John Romano, who was watching the play from beyond the fence in center field, blames Lopez more than Cuccinello. "Sending Lollar," he said, "wasn't the problem. The problem was Al put in a runner for Kluszewski at second base but not for Lollar, who was slower than Kluszewski. I mean, he had me sitting in the bullpen and he had Battey sitting in the bullpen. Two catchers. It's the eighth inning. I mean, the two of us had played all year. What the hell was one game? That's what really hurt. Anybody else probably would've scored. I couldn't believe it. I'm sayin' to myself, 'Why the hell put a runner in for Kluszewski, who's faster than Lollar? Lollar's the tying run.'

"And then, if we beat 'em two in a row, they don't beat us. Because they'd be so down, it wouldn't be funny."

Instead, the Dodgers were up, and making fun of the Sox. Third-base coach Charley Dressen, agreeing with Romano's assessment, laughed as he called out to a couple of reporters: "They put in a runner for the wrong guy!"

Clem Labine smiled and said: "Go-Go Sox? Suddenly, they're the slow-slow Sox."

GAME 3: SUNDAY, OCTOBER 4 — DODGERS 3, WHITE SOX 1

The first World Series game played west of St. Louis was to be played before the largest crowd—92,294—to see any World Series game since 1948, when 86,288 showed up at Cleveland's Municipal Stadium to watch Bill Veeck's Indians defeat the Boston Braves. But

Veeck would have been the first to point out that while Municipal Stadium was suitable for both football and baseball, the Los Angeles Coliseum certainly was not suitable for baseball.

In addition to the aforementioned left-field screen, the Coliseum baseball layout contained other oddities, such as a distance down the right-field line of 300 feet, which almost immediately became 390 feet a few yards out from the foul pole. The distance to center field was 420, and the distance to the poor souls who had purchased tickets for seats in right-center was more like 550 or 600.

"There were 92,000 people at each ballgame, and those 92,000 people were way out there," remembered Billy Pierce. "It wasn't like if you could somehow have gotten 92,000 into Comiskey Park, where they'd be right on top of you. Those people were way, way out there."

And they all seemed to be wearing white shirts. "The reason we had problems in L.A.," said John Romano, "was you couldn't see the ball coming from those two guys, Drysdale and Koufax. It'd scare the hell out of ya. I didn't play, but even in batting practice, you couldn't see the ball from the batting-practice pitcher. And I could see how Koufax and Drysdale throwing that sucker out there, how that would scare ya."

On this day, it was Don Drysdale doing the throwing, against the Sox's Dick Donovan. Given the white-shirted background, the fact that both these right handers, when on their game, could be difficult to hit, and that the Sox once again had rediscovered their talent for leaving runners on base (they stranded 11 all told, five in the first two innings), it should not have been surprising that the game was still scoreless in the seventh inning.

"Even in the curve of the oval, in dead center field, at least two city blocks from the plate, all seats were occupied in the area that should have been curtained off in green, out of fairness to the batters," Red Smith wrote. "It seemed incredible that a man at the plate could see a pitch coming out of this background, or an outfielder judge a fly ball against the coatless crowd."

Infielders, too, could have disquieting moments dealing with the background, as Luis Aparicio was soon to discover. With one on and two out in the Dodgers' seventh, Donovan walked Norm Larker and Gil Hodges to fill the bases. Walter Alston called upon Carl Furillo, 37, the former emperor of right field in Brooklyn's Ebbets Field but now strictly a pinch-hitter, to bat for centerfielder Don Demeter. Al Lopez pulled Donovan, plainly unhappy to be lifted after throwing a two-hitter for 6 2/3 innings, and brought in Gerry Staley. Furillo took ball one, then swung and hit a ground ball to Aparicio's left. Most everyone figured Looie would turn it into a forceout, but the ball took a last-second hop over his glove and went on into the outfield for a two-run single.

"I saw the ball a little late," Aparicio remembered. "I saw it when he hit it. But I lost it between the time he hit it and when I was just a couple steps from it. By the time I saw it again, I just had no time to do anything. I got close to it, but the ball just jumped over my glove. It took a hop. But I could've had it if I could've seen the ball all the way."

The two-run advantage stood up, again because the Sox failed in the clutch against Larry Sherry. Drysdale gave up singles to Ted Kluszewski and Sherm Lollar to start the eighth, and Alston summoned Sherry, who with his first pitch hit Billy Goodman in the knee, forcing Goodman from the game but loading the bases with nobody out. This time Sherry did a better job on Al Smith, who rapped into a short-to-second-to-first double play that scored a run but killed the rally. Jim Rivera popped to catcher John Roseboro, and the inning was over. When, in the home eighth, Charley Neal smashed an RBI double past Sammy Esposito, Goodman's replacement at third base, the game was all but over, too. The cheering was not.

"I had like 54 tickets to the Series," said Los Angeles native Earl Battey. "All my family was out there. And my mother was sitting there in the White Sox section, rooting for the Dodgers. And after that first game in Los Angeles, Glen Miller, our farm director, came into the clubhouse and asked, 'Whose family is that, sitting in our section and cheering for the Dodgers?' And I knew my leather-lunged mother was one of them.

"So when I got home that night, I told her how embarrassing it was to have her sitting up there in the White Sox section and cheering for the Dodgers. And she politely told me that she was a Dodger fan long before I got into baseball, and just because I was with the White Sox she wasn't going to change her allegiance. So I told her to think about me —that there was about a four- or five-thousand-dollar difference between the losing team's share and the winning team's share. And she told me she didn't care, she was gonna get it all anyway."

GAME 4: MONDAY, OCTOBER 5—DODGERS 5, WHITE SOX 4

In front of another record Series crowd, 92,650, Early Wynn opposed Roger Craig in a rematch of the Game 1 starters. Al Lopez, attempting to rouse his offense from its repose, tried a new lineup, with Jim Landis leading off followed by Luis Aparicio and Nellie Fox, who never before had batted third. Whatever, the new configuration seemed on the verge of actually producing results when the White Sox loaded the bases with one out in the first inning. But then Sherm Lollar grounded into a 6-4-3 double play, and the momentum swung back to the Dodgers.

It took them, though, till the third inning to do anything with it. With two out, Wally Moon singled to left and, on Norm Larker's single to center, Moon raced for third. Landis made a terrific throw, except the ball glanced off Moon's leg and bounced away from third baseman Billy Goodman, enabling Moon to score and Larker to advance to second. Gil Hodges then sent a soft fly ball to left field that would have been an easy out anywhere else. But, said Al Smith, "I didn't see the ball until it was almost in front of me. By then, it was a base hit." Larker scored to make it 2-0.

Don Demeter followed with a bloop to center, Hodges taking third, and when a low pitch got past Lollar, who was charged with a passed ball, Hodges came home and Demeter was standing on second. Now came another bloop single, this one by Johnny Roseboro to right field, dropping in front of Jim Rivera, and Demeter scored for a 4-0 lead. Lopez, deciding right there and then that if this Series were to go to a sixth game he needed Wynn to start it, pulled Ol' Gus and brought in Turk Lown. Lown got the final out and then Lopez, likely against his better judgment, decided to try Billy Pierce in this lefthanders' chamber of horrors. All Pierce did was turn in three hitless innings to keep the Sox in the ballgame. Actually, his effectiveness shouldn't have been so shocking: Only three weeks earlier, Art Ceccarelli, a Cub lefty of somewhat less than Hall-of-Fame stature, had shut out the Dodgers in this same place.

Pierce's perfection paid off in the seventh, when the White Sox suddenly awoke. Landis singled with one out before Luis Aparicio was thrown out trying to bunt for a hit. Fox came through with his third hit, but Landis' run meant little, so Tony Cuccinello held him at third. Ted Kluszewski singled to right to score Landis and send Fox to third, and Lollar followed by golfing one over the left-field fence to tie the game at 4-4. The tie did not last long. Gerry Staley, having disposed of the Dodgers in the seventh, now faced Hodges, an old rival from the National League, leading off the eighth. Hodges sent a routine fly ball to left-center, but Al Smith,who had not run very far, quickly ran out of room. The ball went over the so-called "Chinese Wall" at the 320-foot marker for the game-winning homer, a drive of maybe 350 feet tops.

"No, it wouldn't have been a home run in Comiskey Park," Staley remembered, chuckling. "That would've been just a nice, easy fly ball. Looking back, I could've made other pitches against him. But I'd had fairly good luck against him before. I beat the Dodgers quite a few times, you know, when I was with the Cardinals."

This time, he was stuck with the loss, and Larry Sherry, working his magic again—two hitless innings—got the win. L.A. had won three games, and the L.A. native had saved two of them and won the other. And Walter Alston, not without a hint of sarcasm, wrote this message on his clubhouse chalkboard: "One more to Go-Go-Go."

GAME 5: TUESDAY, OCTOBER 6—WHITE SOX 1, DODGERS 0

White Sox fans generally have little about which to boast. But they can always say proudly that their team not only played in front of the largest crowd ever to see a regular-season or postseason baseball game, 92,706, but that the Sox also won the game—and they beat Sandy Koufax in doing so.

This was a baseball game for the ages. It was one the Sox—again wearing their normal socks rather than the odd, all-white ones issued to them by Bill Veeck for Game 1—had to have to bring the Series back to Chicago. Fortunately, Bob Shaw, Dick Donovan, Jim Rivera and the rest were up to the task, doing whatever it took to get out of the Coliseum and back to a real ballpark.

"It was," as Red Smith put it, "a struggle that gripped attention, tormented emotions and illustrated with shocking clarity the appalling inadequacy of the Memorial Cow Pasture for any baseball use except to make money. Fair balls bounced off the bamboo curtain in the China-town section called left field; pop fouls fell safe against the screen that crowds home plate. Batters risked sudden death at the plate when Sandy Koufax's fastball came whistling out of a background of dazzling white, and blinded outfielders cringed in terror as fly balls buzzed out of the sun like bombs."

Somehow, in the fourth inning, Nellie Fox pulled one of those Koufax fastballs into right field for a single, and Jim Landis followed with a hit-and-run single to right to move Fox to third. With the infield playing back, Sherm Lollar tapped into a double play, but Fox scored, and Shaw had the only run he was to get.

"They went for the double play," Shaw remembered, "and you can't fault their decision. In that ballpark, you don't figure you're gonna have a 1-0 game, not with that fence in left field. I did a little after-dinner speaking that winter in Chicago, and I used to kid that when I reached real far back for the good fastball that day, I'd scrape my hand on that fence."

After Fox scored, the game was rather uneventful till the home seventh. With one out, Shaw walked pinch-hitter Chuck Essegian for reasons obvious (see Game 2), and Don Zimmer ran for him. Duke Snider batted for Koufax and slapped into a force play, and Johnny Podres ran for Snider. Junior Gilliam's fourth hit of the afternoon, a liner off the screen in left, put runners at first and second for Shaw's nemesis, Charlie Neal. Out of the dugout on the third-base side came Al Lopez, and everyone's eyes turned toward the bullpen. But Lopez wished only to speak to the umpires: He was going to change outfielders, not pitchers. Jim Rivera entered the game to play right field. Al Smith, who had been in right, moved over to left, and Jim McAnany, who'd been in left, came out of the game.

Lopez figured Neal would pull the ball, so he wanted Smith, who'd had more experience with the Coliseum fence, in left field. There was another reason for the move, Lopez explained decades later. "McAnany was playing out there, and again, I knew he had a tough time with the sunglasses."

Just as in Baltimore, when he was pulled out of the sun field for the same reason, McAnany was not upset with Lopez's move. "That didn't make me feel bad at all," he said, "because whatever was best for the team, that's what mattered. Now today, guys would piss and moan about it, but we didn't look at it that way. I didn't have a problem with that."

Nor did Smith, as it turned out. For, with all the concern over the likelihood that Neal would hit the ball to left field, he instead laced a pitch to right-center. After a wild pitch enabled the runners to advance to second and third, Neal crushed one that was earmarked for three bases. "I was watching Landis," Shaw remembered. "I figured if anybody could catch that ball, Landis could. And he was running and running, and then, all of a sudden, here comes Rivera out of nowhere and grabs it over his shoulder. Thank God he did."

Recalled Rivera: "I knew Charlie Neal from the winter league in Puerto Rico, and his long ball is to left-center and right-center. And that's where the ball was hit, to right-center. And I never thought I had a chance to catch the ball—I'll be honest with you. Oh, he hit the heck out of it. But I just ran as hard as I could and stuck my glove out, and there it was."

Added Smith: "Lopez knew I still had the tender ankle, so he shifted me over to left. And Jungle Jim caught that ball on the dead run. I would *not* have caught that ball."

Rivera's catch ended that Dodger threat, but there was one more to go. Wally Moon opened the Dodgers' eighth inning with a fly ball to shallow center that Jim Landis simply lost. Moon was on first with a gift single.

"I missed it," Landis said, "because I never saw the darn thing. The sun was there, it was all white shirts. There was no background in that stadium. Actually, people don't realize this, but when I missed that fly ball, I was in some real pain, because it landed right on the toe. No-body knew that. Oh, my God, it hurt."

Shaw and the Sox were almost hurting moments later when Gil Hodges, after Norm Larker had been retired, hit a drive to left field that, at the last second, sailed just to the left of the foul pole. "It went foul by maybe a foot," Shaw remembered. "If that goes fair, I would've lost two games in the Series, 4-3 and 2-1. And then, you're a loser."

Hodges eventually was the winner of this particular showdown, singling to center. Moon turned for third and just did make it ahead of Landis' laser throw. On the play, Hodges moved into second, putting Dodgers on second and third with one out. When rookie Ron Fairly was announced as a pinch-hitter for Don Demeter, Lopez yanked Shaw and brought in Billy Pierce to get the lefty-lefty matchup. Walter Alston responded by switching to Rip Repulski, a righthanded hitter, First base was open, so Lopez had Pierce walk Repulski intentionally. The bases were loaded for another pinch-hitter, Carl Furillo, the Game 3 hero who was up to bat for lefty-swinging Johnny Roseboro. Now Lopez called for Dick Donovan.

"I'd been in tough spots before," said Donovan afterward, "but this one had to be the toughest, what with the crowd and the money and the whole Series depending on it. In a situation like that, you either do or you don't. All I tried to think of was getting the ball over and getting the guy out."

First he got Furillo out, on a pop-up to Bubba Phillips at third, and then he retired Zimmer, who had stayed in the game to play shortstop, on a fly ball to Smith in left. In the ninth, Donovan mowed down three more Dodgers in succession, all on ground balls. First was Larry Sherry —Alston had run out of pinch-hitters and maybe figured the rookie had done everything else, so why not try hitting, too? Then came Gilliam, retired at last after going 4-for-4, and finally, Neal, who ended it by bouncing out to Luis Aparicio.

At that moment, at exactly 6:28 p.m. central time, Chicago came back to life. There would be another World Series game in Comiskey Park, maybe more than one, which meant more frivolity for the city and its baseball fans. And, promised Bill Veeck, there would be more frivolity for the temporarily angered sportswriters, who were still grumbling because Dodgers boss Walter O'Malley, with all his millions, had closed down his team's hospitality room—where baseball talk plus free food and liquor, especially liquor, were readily available—at what the writers felt was the rather premature hour of 10 p.m.

Vowed Veeck: "When we get back to Chicago, gentlemen, our hospitality room will be open 24 hours a day. You are welcome to have scotch with breakfast or *for* breakfast."

With that announcement, hundreds of journalists joined White Sox fans in wishing for the Series to go seven games.

GAME 6: THURSDAY, OCTOBER 8—DODGERS 9, WHITE SOX 3

The White Sox, ecstatic to be back home and in an actual ballpark again, were optimistic they could repeat the New York Yankees' feat of the previous October in coming back from a 3-1 deficit to win the Series. Al Lopez was going with Early Wynn on two days' rest, noting that his ace had pitched only into the third inning on Monday and thus had not expended too much energy. Wynn more than welcomed the challenge. He hadn't taken kindly to Charlie Neal's judgment that the Sox likely would have finished fourth in the National League ("We intend to make them eat their words," said Wynn), nor had he enjoyed pitching in the Coliseum ("Maybe we should finish the Series in Soldier Field," he slyly suggested).

As it happened, Wynn's spirit may have been up to the task, but his arm was not. On an overcast afternoon and before a crowd of 47,653 (for a total of 420,784, a record for a six- or seven-game Series), the Dodgers made short work of the 39-year-old warrior. In the visitors' third inning, Duke Snider followed a two-out walk to Wally Moon with a shot of more than 400 feet into the lower deck in left-center. In the fourth, Norm Larker singled and, with Walter Alston figuring on a close game, used Don Demeter to run for him and had Johnny Roseboro bunt Demeter to second. Maury Wills singled home Demeter, and when the pitcher, Johnny Podres, launched an RBI double over Jim

Landis' head to the base of the center-field fence, Al Lopez realized that this certainly was not Early Wynn's day.

In from the bullpen came Dick Donovan, who was quickly lit up as well. Junior Gilliam drew a walk, and Charlie Neal slammed a double to deep right-center, scoring Podres and Gilliam. The score was 6-0, and this one was over. Just to make sure, Moon blasted a home run into the seats in right to make it 8-0. That was all for Donovan, and for the White Sox, too, although Turk Lown, Gerry Staley and Billy Pierce blanked the Dodgers over the next 4 2/3 innings, Pierce thus finishing the Series unscored upon in three appearances.

Meanwhile, the Sox had had one big inning, the fourth. With one out, Landis was hit in the helmet by a pitch that apparently was still bothering Podres eight years later when a midseason waiver deal sent Landis from the Houston Astros to the Detroit Tigers for Larry Sherry, of all people. "I went to Detroit in '67," said Landis, "and Johnny was pitching for them. Even then, he apologized so wholeheartedly. 'Believe me, Jim, there's no way in the world I was throwing at you. That ball just got away.' I told him, 'Don't worry. I believe you.'"

Next came a walk to Sherm Lollar, and then Ted Kluszewski woke up Comiskey Park with a long home run against the upper-deck facade in right-center. That cut the L.A. lead to 8-3 and gave "Big Klu" 10 runs batted in, a record for a six-game World Series. When Al Smith followed with a walk, Alston, taking no chances, removed Podres and brought in the man with the hot hand, Sherry. Bubba Phillips greeted him with a single to center, sending Smith to third. Billy Goodman batted for Jim McAnany and quieted the crowd a bit by striking out, but when Earl Torgeson, swinging for Lown, drew a walk, the bases were loaded and the noise was back.

But again, as they had in Sherry's Game 2 appearance at Comiskey Park, the White Sox helped out the young pitcher. Luis Aparicio swung at Sherry's first delivery and popped it up to Wills to end the inning and any flickering Chicago hope. Now the only "drama" remaining was whether or not any of the as-yet-unused White Sox—John Romano, Earl Battey, Ray Moore, Barry Latman, Rodolfo Arias and Ken McBride —would get a chance to play in a World Series. Romano got his in the seventh, when he batted for Staley and grounded out in his one and only Series at-bat. That wasn't how Lopez had planned it.

"Al kept saving me for the right time," Romano recalled, "and we never had the opportunity. That's what he kept telling me. Finally he decided to put me in just so I could get an appearance. He was saving me in case a crucial spot came up (against a lefthander). But we never had a crucial spot."

Moore got his Series opportunity, such as it was, in the ninth and, on his first pitch, was tagged for a homer by Chuck Essegian, who thus set a record for pinch home runs in a World Series—two. That made the score 9-3, and Sherry breezed through the Sox ninth, getting Goodman on a comebacker, pinch-hitter Norm Cash on a liner to center and Aparicio on a pop fly to Moon in short left. The first World Series in Comiskey Park in 40 years was over, with the same result as the last one—a White Sox defeat. And perhaps the man most responsible was Sherry, who gained credit for the Game 6 win to go along with his Game 4 win and his saves in Games 2 and 3, thereby becoming the first pitcher in Series history to either win or save all four of a team's victories. This day, he worked 5 2/3 scoreless innings, giving him a total of 12 2/3 innings for the Series, in which he allowed only eight hits and one run for an earned-run average of 0.71. For his efforts, he was named Series MVP and presented by *Sport* magazine with a new Corvette.

"He had one of those times," Landis remembered. "He threw hard, believe me he threw hard. And he threw all strikes. It was one of those times in his career where he made very good pitches for as hard as he threw. I don't remember him walking anybody (actually, he did walk two). He had very good control, out of nowhere, because I don't remember him being that much of a control pitcher before that or after. I think that's what did it for him: He threw real good and threw strikes with it."

"We didn't have much of a scouting report on him, because he wasn't supposed to be that good," was Lopez's recollection. "But by God, every time he came in there, he stopped us. He stopped us dead."

Recalled Bill Veeck: "Two guys beat us, really: Maury Wills and Larry Sherry. We thought we would have by far the best shortstopping with Aparicio, but it turned out that Wills had a remarkably fine Series in the field. And Sherry, of course, never pitched as well before that and never pitched as well after that. You always have that, for some reason. One reason, I suppose, is that element of the unexpected. You anticipate that if it's a Lefty Grove or a Rich Gossage coming in from the bullpen, that he'll be phenomenal. But you don't anticipate that a Larry Sherry is going to close the door on you."

Sherry's performance had made the World Series experience that much more difficult for his former Fairfax High School teammate,

Barry Latman. Not only had Latman sat out the entire Series, here was his old buddy basking in the spotlight. "It did hurt," Latman said, "but there's nothing you can do about it. You had nothing to say in those days. But after the games, Larry and I were always together. In fact, I still see Larry. He's a 'private pitching coach.' That's what he tells me. Actually, what it is, parents pay him to teach their kids how to pitch."

Another Los Angeles product chagrined at being left out of this first Los Angeles World Series was Earl Battey. "Barry, McAnany and I were the only players on that team from Los Angeles," he said. "And we had all grown up competing against each other, and the same scouts had signed us—Hollis Thurston and Doc Bennett. And the other thing was, I had a lot of friends on that Dodger team: Wills, Johnny Roseboro and Charlie Neal. And Larry Sherry—I'd known him almost all my life. And we had made All-City a couple times together."

McAnany, who was about to begin a six-month hitch in the Army at Ft. Leonard Wood in Missouri, at least had gotten the chance to play. "But I really felt badly that we lost," he said, "and I remember the veterans really took it hard. I did, too, but I felt I might have a few more of these. But they had been around for a while. They might not have that chance again."

Perhaps the most disappointed veteran of all was Billy Pierce. "That was a very tough day for me, when the Series ended," he said. "I remember how Ted Lindsay—remember Ted, the hockey player? He was a good friend of mine, and we came home from the ballpark that last day and he helped me pack. And I got the car and I was out of town, heading home to Detroit, by one hour after the ballgame had ended.

"You didn't want to lose and you wanted to see if you could help 'em win. Maybe I couldn't, but you wanted to try. That's the way it goes sometimes. And as the years go by, you forget about those things."

What helped him forget was the success he had three years later for the San Francisco Giants, for whom he went 16-6, beat the Dodgers in the opener of a three-game pennant playoff series and saved the final contest, then went 1-1 in the World Series, defeating the Yankees and Whitey Ford in Game 6 to force a seventh game.

"The best thing for Billy," said Jim Landis, "was when he went to the Giants in '62, had a hell of a year there and they won the pennant. That took away a lot of the thoughts he'd had about what happened in Chicago. That more than took the sting out of it for him."

Pierce agreed: "Sixty-two canceled out the disappointment of not starting in the World Series in '59. There's no doubt it made me feel a lot better."

But at that particular moment, as he drove toward Michigan, he was not a happy camper. "See, I had been in six or seven All-Star Games by that time," he said, "and I'd started three of 'em. And the key thing to me is, if you're in an All-Star Game or a World Series, if you're the starting pitcher of that ballgame, all the play is right there. That's what gets the adrenaline going. That's where all the excitement is."

Back at Comiskey Park, meanwhile, Bill Veeck was sending out large hints that the off-season, the first to include interleague trading, would not be lacking for excitement. "We can't be content standing still," he told the press corps. "If we don't improve, we'll surely go backwards, and I don't intend for that to happen. The main thing we're looking for is added power. Klu gave us some, but we need more. We'd like to find an outfielder who can hit the long ball, another good pitcher, a third baseman and a first baseman."

Having said that, Veeck began thinking of ways to address a more immediate problem—how to rid himself of 20,000 roses.

"We had ordered them," he recalled, 20 years later at Comiskey Park, "for the ladies for every game. Including the seventh game, which was never played. So at the end of the sixth game, they were bringing them in for the next day. Well, there was no point in keeping them and letting them die here, so we loaded up a station wagon and went down State Street, asking people, 'Would you like three-four dozen roses to take home?' We got rid of them all, but you'd be amazed at the difficulty of getting people to believe that you were just giving them to them. It was interesting."

The next few months would be far more so.

AFTERMATH

Breaking Up Is Easy to Do

The residue of frustration from the World Series failure began to be cleared away in the weeks that followed, as one award after another came the White Sox's way.

First Al Lopez was honored as American League Manager of the Year, to the surprise of no one. Johnny Callison proved all those pre-season prognosticators wrong by not winning the AL Rookie of the Year award, which went to Washington's Bob Allison, but Bob Shaw did receive the late, lamented Sophomore of the Year honor, and Early Wynn won the Cy Young Award, which at that time was presented to just one pitcher, period, instead of to one in each league. And Wynn, Nellie Fox and Sherm Lollar were voted to *The Sporting News* Major League All-Star team.

Finally, came the announcement that Fox, who had followed his .306 regular season with a .375 mark against the Dodgers, had been voted the American League's Most Valuable Player. It is true that Fox, batting .334 on July 31 with 50 runs batted in, had hit just .247 with 20 RBIs the rest of the way, but the general feeling both nationally and in Chicago was that he had been the heart and soul of the White Sox since 1951. This award, then, was a tribute to Little Nell not just for his efforts in 1959 but for an entire decade. And surely, the White Sox would not have won the pennant without him.

The same could be said for the men who finished second and third in the MVP voting, Luis Aparicio and Jim Landis, although Aparicio, like Fox, had slumped at the plate (.222 after the first All-Star Game on July 7). Landis, who had hit .301 in the second half, was the preferred candidate of the *Sun-Times'* Jerome Holtzman, but bear in mind that Holtzman had not switched over from the Cubs beat to cover the Sox until the first full week of July.

"I don't even remember if I voted," he said, "but if I did, I voted for Landis. I thought Landis was the MVP. But you see, Landis was a younger player, wasn't established—this was only his second full season —and he wasn't that well known in the league. But Landis was the best centerfielder in the league and he was a very good hitter. But you know, there was a mystique about Fox. He was a very colorful guy, he had that big chaw of tobacco in his cheek. And he was a very valuable player. But he wasn't as valuable that year as either Aparicio or Landis."

Whatever, the important matter was that a White Sox player, for the first time, had been named the league's MVP, capping the team's domination of the postseason hardware competition. But then, shortly after the Sox had received, they began to give. And give. And give some more.

"It was kind of a little vengeance toward Charles—it really was," remembered Chuck Comiskey, referring to himself in the third person. "Like getting rid of any players that he was instrumental in bringing into the organization. And the second thing was, Veeck was a 'hole player' type of operator. Bill figured, like the rent-a-player situation you see today: 'If I can get one or two years out of this guy....' He just figured the older heads would improve the ballclub. I'm not saying that approach is right or wrong. I happen to think it's wrong, OK? But that's the way he thought. He thought we'd repeat in '60 and '61, and I don't think he was thinking beyond that. I never worked under that theory. I always figured you should have some mature heads, as well as an influx of young blood coming up to your club at all times."

But now, a good quantity of young blood was about to be spilt. Bill Veeck already had dropped hints here and there as to what he had hoped to accomplish.

"The statement Bill made," remembered Billy Pierce, "was that the '59 team wasn't his team. He wanted to repeat in '60 with *his* team."

Recalled Al Lopez: "Bill made the remark, 'If Lopez could win the pennant with that club, I'm gonna get some hitters in here and he'll win the pennant next year easy.' Veeck wanted to win the pennant again. He was having some health problems, and he didn't know how long he was going to stay, so he wanted to win again real badly."

The health problem, first thought to be cancer, turned out to be a weakened blood vessel near the brain. All that was required in terms of treatment was rest. But that determination was not made until 1961. In late 1959, Bill Veeck, perhaps fearing the worst, was not thinking three, four or five years ahead—not that he ever did anyway. His first move was designed to get Lopez some lefthanded bullpen help, something Lopez had been lacking, given the inability of Rodolfo Arias to do much more than drill Ryne Duren when called upon to do so. To replace Arias, Veeck sent one former bonus baby, big Ron Jackson, to Boston for another, pitcher Frank Baumann, a St. Louis native who had signed for big bucks with the Red Sox when Veeck was running the Browns.

The Sox needed a lefty, and Jackson wasn't getting anywhere in Chicago, not with three first basemen already ahead of him. So this deal, an exchange of 26-year-olds on November 3, made sense. But then, once Veeck arrived in Miami Beach to join Lopez and Hank Greenberg at the winter meetings the first week in December, came deals that did not. Having failed to talk St. Louis Cardinals GM Bing Devine out of first baseman Bill White (for Earl Battey and Ken McBride), and getting a Sherm Lollar-for-Orlando Cepeda proposal laughed off by the San Francisco Giants, Veeck renewed with Frank Lane the Minnie Minoso trade talks that had expired in mid-June. On Sunday night, December 6, a deal was worked out: Minnie, allegedly 37, was returning to his beloved White Sox along with two more left-handed pitchers—Don Ferrarese and rookie Jake Striker—plus backup catcher Dick Brown. (The latter three were gone by June.) To Cleveland went three players brought into the Sox organization by Chuck Comiskey: Bubba Phillips, Norm Cash and a startled John Romano.

"I thought I was gonna be the No. 1 catcher in '60," Romano remembered. "As a matter of fact, I was over at a baseball writers dinner in New York, and when I was there I met Hank Greenberg in the hotel lobby. And he says to me, 'You're gonna be my catcher next year.' I come home, and a week or two later, I get traded to Cleveland."

Romano wasn't alone in his surprise. Not only was the *Chicago Tribune's* David Condon, who was among Veeck's biggest boosters, surprised, he was certain the Sox had been held up by Frank Lane. Wrote Condon: "Back in a White Sox uniform, Minnie Minoso will be an exciting baseball player. For one season, he may be a valuable player. But the White Sox are apt to find that, over the route, they sacrificed too much potential playing talent for a box-office attraction."

Veeck was not concerned. He had the power-hitting outfielder he had sought, and he had added three pitchers. Next on his list was a third baseman, especially now that his depth chart listed only Billy Goodman and Sammy Esposito at that spot. So two days later, Veeck agreed to send Johnny Callison, 20, to the Philadelphia Phillies for 26-

year-old Gene Freese, who with his 23 home runs—four of them grand slams—had displayed that season the kind of pop that Veeck wanted at third base. Never mind that Freese's glove was somewhat suspect and that his arm was a bit on the inaccurate side. He could swing the bat, and offense was what mattered most to his new boss. And never mind that Callison had a chance to be a terrific player three or four years down the road. What mattered was now, not later.

"I read it in the paper in Venezuela," Callison said, recalling how he had learned of the trade. "Nobody called me. All I saw was my picture and Gene Freese's picture. And all the words around it were in Spanish. I said, 'Something's wrong here.' You know, I'd just found my way around the American League. I didn't want to go to the National League. And the Phillies were in last place. I told my wife, 'We're in trouble.' And we were."

Said Al Lopez, who apparently had forgotten his trip to Milwaukee for the Braves-Phillies series the final weekend of the season: "I never had seen Gene Freese. Bill wanted to get him. His report was that Freese was a hell of a player. A good hitter. So we talked to Philadelphia and they insisted on Callison, otherwise they wouldn't let Freese go. So I told Veeck, 'Geez, Bill, give 'em three or four of the other guys and keep Callison.' Veeck says, 'Al, let's just worry about this year. Let's get Freese here, and we've got a great chance to win the pennant again.'"

"When they made that trade," Jerome Holtzman remembered, "Glen Miller, the farm director, who had been monitoring Callison through the system—he was heartsick. He was very upset about it because he knew, or suspected, that Callison was going to be a star of the future."

Some White Sox fans were upset, too, though they seemed to be in the minority. A small band of them, in their late teens, crafted a makeshift dummy and hung it, with a placard attached reading "Bill Veeck," from an oak tree on the northwest corner of 70th Street and Oakley Avenue in Chicago. The youths admired their handiwork but inwardly wondered what was going on with their favorite team.

Meanwhile, Sox players, reading their newspapers back home, were wondering the same thing. Then came part of the answer. Veeck announced plans for baseball's first exploding scoreboard, a $350,000 marvel that was to hail the occurrence of every White Sox home run at Comiskey Park with flashing lights, loud music and, of course, fireworks.

"So, you know," said Bob Shaw, "if you're gonna have a new

exploding scoreboard, you need home runs to make it go off. Bill wanted more home runs and more excitement. So I know what his thinking was: Get a little more power, hit a few more home runs, get the scoreboard to explode. But that was not a good park to hit home runs in. They went for power, and that ballpark was not designed for power."

Nonetheless, Veeck wanted even more of it, particularly when he heard the Yankees, as predicted months earlier by Warren Brown, had acquired lefthanded power hitter Roger Maris from Kansas City in a seven-player deal. Now Veeck's sights shifted again toward Washington and Calvin Griffith, who had spurned his advances the previous June, when Veeck had sought to shower Griffith with money and ballplayers in exchange for Roy Sievers. In 1959, Sievers had slipped to .242 (from .301 in '57 and .295 in '58) and to 21 homers (from 42 and 39) and 49 RBIs (from 114 and 108). At age 33, he didn't figure to suddenly start getting better, but Veeck, who'd had him with the Browns, was con-vinced Sievers would bounce back. So he kept waving money at Griffith until finally, during spring training, an agreement was reached —as the Sox were completing a series of exhibitions in Puerto Rico. Recalled Jack Kuenster, then covering the club for the *Chicago Daily News*: "It was like Veeck waited for us to get as far away as possible before he made the deal."

Here was the deal: Earl Battey, a 22-year-old minor-league first baseman named Don Mincher and $150,000 for Sievers. "Pennant insurance," is how the deal was termed in some newspaper reports, and there were accompanying photos of the quartet of Sievers, Minoso, Freese and Ted Kluszewski, bats in hand and looking fearsome. The deal apparently caught Lopez by surprise. "When I got to the White Sox camp at Sarasota," Sievers remembered, "Lopez said, 'Well, it's nice to have you, but I don't know where you're gonna play.'"

The deal also came as a surprise, and a disappointment, to Battey, who, Kuenster remembers, had tears in his eyes when told of the trade. "That was about the low point of my career," Battey said. "Here I'm going from the first-place team to the last-place team. It was disap-pointing at first, but then I realized, 'Well, here's your chance to find out if you can be an everyday player at the major-league level.'"

What he discovered was that yes, indeed, he could be. So did John Romano, Norm Cash and Johnny Callison. But they weren't the only young 1959 White Sox missing from the 1960 cast. The day before the season opened, Barry Latman, a month away from turning 24, was sitting in a barber shop when he heard the news on the radio: He had been traded to Cleveland for the celebrated lefty, Herb Score, three years his senior. This, however, was an Al Lopez trade, not a Bill Veeck deal. "We didn't want to trade Barry," Lopez remembered, "but we had a chance to get Herb Score. And I thought Herb, even if he wasn't at 100 percent, even if he was just 90 percent, could win some ballgames for us. But Herb never did quite come around."

Thus Latman, Romano, Cash, Callison and Battey—farm products all, with their brightest days ahead of them—were elsewhere when the White Sox raised the 1959 pennant at pregame ceremonies April 19 at Comiskey Park. By May 19, when rosters had to be cut from 28 to 25, two more youngsters, Ken McBride and Jim McAnany, also were gone, to Triple-A San Diego. (Both subsequently were lost to the new Los Angeles Angels in the expansion draft the following off-season.) McAnany, a late arrival at Sarasota because of his Army duty, was not shocked by his return to the minors.

"When I got to spring training," he said, "I felt like I didn't belong. It was just a strange feeling. Lopez didn't say a lot to me—the coaches, too. I got this feeling like, 'It's all sewed up.' I didn't get any extra hitting, stuff like that. The handwriting was on the wall. I knew what was coming."

Some White Sox players feared what might be coming. Recalled Billy Pierce: "We had a ballclub in '59 where we had veterans and young fellows. When we made the trades, we traded youth for age, so in '60, there were no young players around anymore. To the team itself, the trades seemed odd. We thought yes, we'd gotten Minnie, whom everybody liked, and Sievers, who had a good reputation. But it was like, 'What's gonna happen down the road?'"

Bob Shaw was worried not only about the added age but about the lessened defense. "Minnie was at the end of the line. Was not a good outfielder. Sievers couldn't move off a dime. And Freese was a terrible defensive player. So now your defense really went down."

Even so, and even with the Yankees' acquisition of Maris, the White Sox were favored by oddsmakers and most baseball writers to repeat as American League champions. On Opening Day, Minoso celebrated his Chicago return with a grand slam and, in the ninth, with a home run that broke a 9-9 tie and sent 41,661 home thinking repeat. Minoso went on to have a big year (20 homers, 105 RBIs, .311 average and 17 steals), and Sievers, once he wrested the first-base job from Ted Kluszewski in June, sparked the Sox on a July surge that took them from fourth place to the AL lead and ended up with 28 homers, 93 RBIs and a .295 average. Freese, after injury problems in May, did well offensively (17, 79, .273, 10 steals) if not defensively, and Frank Baumann, the new lefty, went 13-6 and led the league in earned-run average (2.67).

Even Score, almost invisible during the first half as Lopez worked tirelessly with him on the sidelines, had his moments during an often-spectacular six-week stretch from mid-July through late August before wildness problems revisited him and rendered him all but useless the final month.

So Veeck's reinforcements did their part. It surely wasn't all their fault that the Sox, two games out with two weeks to go, finished in third place, 10 games behind the champion Yankees. The newcomers' presence, plus Al Smith's big comeback year (.315), had helped the Sox lead the AL in hitting with a .270 batting average. The 1960 Sox also stole 122 bases, nine more than the '59 champs; turned a league-best 175 double plays (compared to 141 by the '59 Sox); led the league in fielding with a .982 percentage (better than the '59 team's AL-best mark of .979) and actually committed 21 fewer errors than the '59 club (109 to 130).

So why the drop from 94-60 and a pennant to 87-67 and 10 games behind? The pitching was not as effective: Though Baumann was outstanding and Billy Pierce came back to have a solid year (14-7), Early Wynn (13-12), Bob Shaw (13-13, 4.06 ERA), Dick Donovan (6-1 but a 5.60 ERA) and Turk Lown (3.88 and only five saves) were far off their 1959 form. Also, Jim Landis (.253), Nellie Fox (.289) and particularly Sherm Lollar (.252 and just seven homers and 46 RBIs) slipped sharply at the plate. But maybe the biggest difference was in one-run games: Whereas the White Sox had gone 35-15 in games decided by a run in '59, they were 22-23 in 1960.

And yet, it was a fun year for White Sox fans, who turned out in record numbers (1,644,460, at that point an all-time Chicago mark), attracted by an exciting pennant race, a team that seldom lost at home (the Sox were 51-26 at Comiskey), the nightly fireworks displays and, without question, the exploding scoreboard. But the season ended without Veeck's hoped-for title repeat—and with Earl Battey (15 homers, 60 RBIs, .270), Norm Cash (18, 63, .286), John Romano (16, 52, .272) and Johnny Callison (9, 30, .260) having settled in as big-league regulars elsewhere. And by midseason 1961, just weeks after Veeck had sold the club to Arthur Allyn Jr., Cash, Romano and Ken

McBride were taking part in pregame introductions at the All-Star Game. So was Barry Latman. Herb Score? He was at Triple-A San Diego, trying to regain his old magic. As for Callison and Battey, they had to wait until 1962 to make their All-Star debuts.

But Bill Veeck, 20 years later, was still defending his trades.

"What happened was that the people we had depended on the year before fell off," he said. "Looie and Nelson didn't have their finest years (though Aparicio did hit .277 with 51 steals). The centerfielder, Landis, had a bad year, and Sherm had a bad year. And that after Al had assured me he was not going to catch either Battey or Romano. So I figured, 'Let's see what we can get for them, rather than leave it on the bench.' That's why I included them in those deals. I could've made them another way, but in any event, we were going to go for broke. I wasn't interested in what was going to happen five years down the road. I wanted to win back to back.

"We had bulwarked the club pretty well, I thought. It was a good ballclub. We hit the ball around a little bit. The only ones who kept us competitive were the new players—Minoso, Freese and Sievers. But the line down the middle, the positions you felt you could count on—center field, shortstop, second base and catcher—is where we were betrayed."

Some people contend Bill Veeck betrayed White Sox fans by dealing away much of their future. "Betray" is a rather strong word. Veeck wanted to win as much as and maybe more than Sox fans. Even as the 1960 season moved along, he kept trying to add the right parts to come up with another winner. Pitcher Russ Kemmerer, stolen from Washington in May, was 6-3 with a 2.98 ERA in 36 games with the Sox; Joe Ginsberg was picked up on waivers to give Al Lopez a left-handed-hitting catcher; and Al Worthington, former Giants pitcher and future Twins bullpen ace, was added in September and helped out in relief—until, upon discovering that the Sox were stealing signs from their center-field scoreboard, the devout righthander quit the ballclub. And then, in the off-season, Veeck partially atoned for the Johnny Callison blunder by sending Gene Freese to Cincinnati for pitchers Cal McLish and Juan Pizarro, the latter of whom became an All-Star just like Callison.

So Veeck cannot be charged with not trying to win. He cannot be charged with not being fan-friendly. Indeed, the fan came first with him, or a close second, anyway, to the sportswriters—even the lowliest of writers from the most obscure newspaper. He was a prince of a man, a brilliant man, a gentle man. Clever, funny, warm, entertaining. He was all of those. He just happened to make some unfortunate trades.

"Veeck," said Jerome Holtzman, "wasn't a great baseball man. He was a good guy who was a great promoter. He just wasn't an expert on player personnel."

Even now, after almost 40 years, former White Sox players have trouble believing the wave of deals that broke up a club that had reached the World Series for the first time in four decades.

Said Earl Battey: "They had built that team on pitching, speed and defense. That's basically what we had. And that was what was the surprising thing about being traded. I thought we had a nucleus of some very good young ballplayers. And then it seemed like they changed their philosophy, that they didn't believe they could win again with pitching, speed and defense. They went for power instead."

The oddity is that the Sox traded away more power than they got in return. By 1961, Battey was hitting 17 home runs with a .302 average for the Minnesota Twins, the transplanted Senators. Cash, that same year, led the AL in hitting with a .361 average and pounded out 41 homers for Detroit, which had heisted him from Cleveland just before the '60 season. His average plunged the next year to .243, but he still belted 39 home runs, a mere 23 more than the Sox's club leader in 1962, Al Smith. Romano hit .299 in '61 with 21 homers and 80 RBIs, then followed up with 25 and 81 in '62. That was the year Callison really hit his stride with the Phillies at age 23, hitting .300 with 23 homers, 10 triples and 83 RBIs. All four, like Latman, became All-Stars, Callison winning the 1964 All-Star Game at Shea Stadium with a two-out, three-run pinch homer in the ninth—against an AL team managed by Al Lopez.

"They traded me and Cash. They traded Johnny Callison. And then they get rid of Earl? I mean, come on," said Romano. "They traded away a bunch of All-Stars. Veeck brought in Minoso, Sievers. Those guys were finished. Is that unbelievable? Couldn't believe that. How the hell could they get rid of all those young guys?"

Billy Pierce still doesn't have an answer.

"The shame of the White Sox was the fall and winter of '59, when we traded all the young fellows away. That was maybe the worst thing that ever happened to the White Sox. That was a tragedy, really. Kluszewski had a bad back, there was no doubt about it. Earl Torgeson had been around for a long, long time. So a young first baseman, like Cash, we needed him. Cash, even in batting practice, nobody ever threw a fastball by him. He could get around on that fastball pretty good.

"Sherman had played for a long time. And Battey was a *good* young catcher. He could hit, he could catch and he could throw. And Johnny Romano wasn't as good a defensive catcher as Battey, but he could hit that ball real good. So the last thing we thought would happen was we'd get rid of our two young catchers.

"You can never tell about trades, but at that time it looked like a young first baseman and a young catcher were two things they were gonna need right away, within a year or two. But Bill wanted more long balls, I guess. And, as it turned out, Cash, Callison, Battey and Romano hit some long balls."

True, they went to clubs whose ballparks were significantly more hitter-friendly, but, for the record: Cash wound up with 377 home runs, 373 after 1959; Callison hit 226 homers, 222 after '59; Romano hit 129, 124 of them after '59; and Battey hit 104 long ones, 91 after '59. And Don Mincher, the throw-in in the Sievers deal, hit an even 200, all after '59. Those were home runs that might well have helped offensively challenged White Sox teams built almost solely around pitching to win pennants in 1964 and 1967, when the Sox fell short by one game (in '64) and by three games ('67). No one is arguing that the White Sox, had Bill Veeck stood pat, would have repeated in 1960. Even Al Lopez admitted it would have been an arduous task. But pennants in subsequent years, with Callison, Cash and either Romano or Battey in the lineup and perhaps Mincher coming off the bench, certainly could have been won.

"No, I don't think we could've repeated," Lopez said. "Shaw had an outstanding year in '59, when we really weren't expecting anything from him. Wynn was 22-10, a great year. See, a lot of things have to fall in place for you to win like we did in '59. We had no power. We had to scratch for runs. We won 35 games by one run. And remember, the Yankees had added Roger Maris from Kansas City, and Yankee Stadium was a good park for him. So it would've been tough to repeat with the same club. But I'd have liked to try it. At least we would've still had those young ballplayers around."

And Jim Landis, Luis Aparicio, and Bob Shaw, all 26 by the end of April 1960, would have had more company among the younger set. But it was not to be.

"With the unity we had on that '59 club," said Landis, "especially among the younger guys who'd come up through the minors together, we *had* to get better. We had one of the best youth movements in baseball going at that time. For another three to five years, what a beautiful blend.

"But the word 'power' takes over in people's minds. But power isn't always the answer. Especially in our ballpark. You didn't hit 30 home runs there, you didn't win with power. If they wanted to make a trade, our pitching was getting older. Why not improve the pitching, for a Cash or a Romano? But instead, they went for power, and I could never understand that.

"That's the sad thing I remember from being on that club. When you win a pennant and are in a World Series, why do you want to change a ballclub that much? I'll never forget that. It was a shame. And all those guys—Cash, Callison, Battey, Romano and Latman—were All-Stars within three years. So it did come back to haunt them."

Like Luis Aparicio's "curse," it has been haunting the White Sox for 40 years. There is this one interesting note, however. Judge Kenesaw Mountain Landis, baseball's first commissioner, broke up the 1919 White Sox with his "Black Sox" suspensions. Bill Veeck broke up the 1959 White Sox with his trades.

Both men are in baseball's Hall of Fame.

It follows then that, for the man who breaks up the next White Sox pennant winner, enshrinement in Cooperstown awaits.

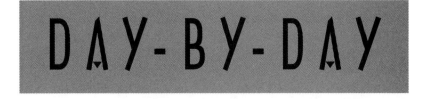

DAY-BY-DAY

The 1959 White Sox

DATE	PLACE	SCORE	STARTING PITCHER	REC.	POSITION (GA/GB)
Fri., 4/10	Detroit	Sox 9, Tigers 7(14)	Pierce	1-0	1
Sat., 4/11	Detroit	Sox 5, Tigers 3	Wynn	2-0	1
Sun., 4/12	Detroit	Sox 5, Tigers 3	Donovan	3-0	1/+1
Tue., 4/14	CHICAGO	Sox 2, A's 0	Pierce	4-0	1/+1 1/2
Wed., 4/15	CHICAGO	A's 10, Sox 8	Latman	4-1	3/-1/2
Thu., 4/16	CHICAGO	A's 6, Sox 0	Wynn	4-2	3/-1
Fri., 4/17	CHICAGO	Sox 6, Tigers 4	Donovan	5-2	3/-1
Sat., 4/18	CHICAGO	Tigers 5, Sox 2	Moore	5-3	3/ -2
Sun., 4/19	CHICAGO	Game vs. Tigers ppd.		5-3	2/-1 1/2
Tue., 4/21	Kan.City	A's 8, Sox 3	Pierce	5-4	3/-2 1/2
Wed., 4/22	Kan.City	Sox 20, A's 6	Wynn	6-4	3/-2 1/2
Fri., 4/24	Cleveland	Indians 6, Sox 4	Donovan	6-5	3/-4
Sat., 4/25	Cleveland	Sox 8, Indians 6	Latman	7-5	2/-3
Sun., 4/26	Cleveland	Sox 6, Indians 5	Wynn	8-5	2/-2
		Sox 5, Indians 2	Pierce	9-5	2/-1
Tue., 4/28	CHICAGO	Game vs. Yankees ppd.		9-5	2/-1
Wed., 4/29	CHICAGO	Yankees 5, Sox 2	Moore	9-6	2/-1 1/2
Thu., 4/30	CHICAGO	Sox 4, Yankees 3(11)	Pierce	10-6	2/-1
Fri., 5/1	CHICAGO	Sox 1, Red Sox 0	Wynn	11-6	2/-1
Sat., 5/2	CHICAGO	Red Sox 5, Sox 4	Latman	11-7	2/-2
Sun., 5/3	CHICAGO	Orioles 4, Sox 2	Donovan	11-8	2/-2 1/2
Tue., 5/5	CHICAGO	Senators 8, Sox 3	Pierce	11-9	2/-3 1/2
Wed., 5/6	CHICAGO	Senators 6, Sox 4	Wynn	11-10	4/-3 1/2
Fri., 5/8	CHICAGO	Indians 3, Sox 1	Donovan	11-11	4/-4 1/2
Sat., 5/9	CHICAGO	Sox 9, Indians 5	Latman	12-11	3/-3 1/2
Sun., 5/10	CHICAGO	Sox 4, Indians 3(11)	Pierce	13-11	2/-2 1/2
		Sox 5, Indians 0	Wynn	14-11	2/-1 1/2
Tue., 5/12	Boston	Sox 4, Red Sox 3(12)	Donovan	15-11	2/-1 1/2
Wed., 5/13	Boston	Sox 5, Red Sox 0	Shaw	16-11	2/-1 1/2
Thu., 5/14	Boston	Sox 14, Red Sox 6	Wynn	17-11	2/-1/2
Fri., 5/15	New York	Sox 6, Yankees 0	Pierce	18-11	2/-1/2
Sat., 5/16	New York	Sox 4, Yankees 3(11)	Moore	19-11	2-1/2
Sun., 5/17	Washington	Senators 4, Sox 2	Donovan	19-12	2
		Sox 10, Senators 7	Shaw	20-12	2/-1/2

Mon., 5/18	Washington	Sox 9, Senators 2	Wynn	21-12	1/+1/2
Tue., 5/19	Baltimore	Orioles 2, Sox 1	Pierce	21-13	2/-1/2
Wed., 5/20	Baltimore	Sox 5, Orioles 2	Donovan	22-13	1/+1/2
Fri., 5/22	Kan.City	Sox 2, A's 1	Shaw	23-13	2/-1/2
Sat., 5/23	Kan.City	A's 16, Sox 0	Wynn	23-14	2/-1/2
Sun., 5/24	Kan.City	A's 8, Sox 6	Pierce	23-15	2/-1
Tue., 5/26	CHICAGO	Indians 3, Sox 0	Donovan	23-16	2/-1 1/2
Wed., 5/27	CHICAGO	Sox 5, Indians 1	Wynn	24-16	2/-1/2
Thu., 5/28	CHICAGO	Game vs.Tigers ppd.		24-16	2/-1/2
Fri., 5/29	CHICAGO	Tigers 4, Sox 1	Shaw	24-17	2/-1
Sat., 5/30	CHICAGO	Tigers 4, Sox 2	Pierce	24-18	2
		Sox 4, Tigers 3	Donovan	25-18	2/-1
Sun., 5/31	CHICAGO	A's 9, Sox 1	Wynn	25-19	2/-1
Mon., 6/1	CHICAGO	A's 3, Sox 1	Moore	25-20	2/-1
Tue., 6/2	CHICAGO	Orioles 3, Sox 2	Shaw	25-21	3/-1
Wed., 6/3	CHICAGO	Sox 6, Orioles 1	Pierce	26-21	2/-1/2
Thu., 6/4	CHICAGO	Sox 6, Orioles 5(17)	Donovan	27-21	1/+1/2
Fri., 6/5	CHICAGO	Sox 5, Red Sox 2	Wynn	28-21	1/+1 1/2
Sat., 6/6	CHICAGO	Red Sox 4, Sox 2	Moore	28-22	1/+1 1/2
Sun., 6/7	CHICAGO	Sox 9, Red Sox 4	Donovan	29-22	1
		Red Sox 4, Sox 2	Pierce	29-23	1/+1
Tue., 6/9	Washington	Senators 7, Sox 4	Shaw	29-24	1
Wed., 6/10	Washington	Sox 4, Senators 1	Wynn	30-24	1/+1
Thu., 6/11	Washington	Sox 3, Senators 1	Pierce	31-24	1/+1 1/2
Fri., 6/12	Baltimore	Game vs.Orioles ppd.		31-24	1/+1 1/2
Sat., 6/13	Baltimore	Orioles 6, Sox 4	Shaw	31-25	1/+1/2
Sun., 6/14	Baltimore	Sox 9, Orioles 6	Wynn	32-25	1
		Sox 3, Orioles 2(10)	Donovan	33-25	1/+1/2
Tue., 6/16	New York	Yankees 5, Sox 1	Pierce	33-26	2/-1
Wed., 6/17	New York	Yankees 7, Sox 3	Moore	33-27	2/-1 1/2
Thu., 6/18	New York	Yankees 5, Sox 4(10)	Shaw	33-28	2/-1 1/2
Fri., 6/19	Boston	Game vs.Red Sox ppd.		33-28	2/-1
Sat., 6/20	Boston	Red Sox 8, Sox 2	Wynn	33-29	
		Red Sox 9, Sox 0	Donovan	33-30	5/-1 1/2
Sun., 6/21	Boston	Sox 3, Red Sox 2	Pierce	34-30	2/-2
Tue., 6/23	CHICAGO	Sox 4, Senators 1	Wynn	35-30	2/-1
Wed., 6/24	CHICAGO	Senators 4, Sox 2	Donovan	35-31	3/-1
Thu., 6/25	CHICAGO	Sox 4, Senators 1	Latman	36-31	2/-1
Fri., 6/26	CHICAGO	Yankees 8, Sox 4	Pierce	36-32	3/-2
Sat., 6/27	CHICAGO	Sox 5, Yankees 4	Shaw	37-32	2/-1
Sun., 6/28	CHICAGO	Sox 9, Yankees 2	Wynn	38-32	2
		Sox 4, Yankees 2	Donovan	39-32	2/-1
Tue., 6/30	Cleveland	Indians 3, Sox 1	Pierce	39-33	2/-2
Wed., 7/1	Cleveland	Sox 6, Indians 5	Latman	40-33	2/-1
Thu., 7/2	Detroit	Tigers 9, Sox 7	Shaw	40-34	2/-1
Fri., 7/3	Detroit	Sox 6, Tigers 5(10)	Wynn	41-34	2/-1
Sat., 7/4	Kan.City	Sox 7, A's 4	Donovan	42-34	2
		A's 8, Sox 4	Pierce	42-35	2/-2
Sun., 7/5	Kan.City	Sox 4, A's 3(10)	Latman	43-35	2/-2

182

******** **ALL-STAR BREAK** ********

Thu., 7/9	CHICAGO	Sox 4, Indians 3	Pierce	44-35	2/-1
Fri., 7/10	CHICAGO	Indians 8, Sox 4	Wynn	44-36	2/-2
Sat., 7/11	CHICAGO	Sox 8, A's 3	Latman	45-36	2/-2
Sun., 7/12	CHICAGO	Sox 5, A's 3	Donovan	46-36	2
		Sox 9, A's 7	Shaw	47-36	2/-1
Tue., 7/14	Boston	Sox 7, Red Sox 3	Pierce	48-36	2/-.002
Wed., 7/15	Boston	Game vs.Red Sox ppd.		48-36	2/-.002
Thu. 7/16	Boston	Sox 4, Red Sox 3	Donovan	49-36	1
		Red Sox 5, Sox 4	Latman	49-37	1/+1
Fri., 7/17	New York	Sox 2, Yankees 0	Wynn	50-37	1/+1
Sat., 7/18	New York	Sox 2, Yankees 1	Shaw	51-37	1/+1
Sun., 7/19	New York	Yankees 6, Sox 2	Latman	51-38	
		Yankees 6, Sox 4	Pierce	51-39	2/-.001
Tue., 7/21	CHICAGO	Sox 2, Red Sox 1	Donovan	52-39	2/-.002
Wed.,7/22	CHICAGO	Sox 5, Red Sox 4	Wynn	53-39	1/+1
Thu., 7/23	CHICAGO	Game vs.Red Sox ppd.		53-39	1/+1/2
Fri., 7/24	CHICAGO	Sox 2, Orioles 1	Pierce	54-39	1/+1/2
Sat., 7/25	CHICAGO	Sox 3, Orioles 2	Shaw	55-39	1/+1/2
Sun., 7/26	CHICAGO	Sox 4, Orioles 1	Wynn	56-39	1
		Orioles 4, Sox 0	Donovan	56-40	2/-1/2
Tue., 7/28	CHICAGO	Sox 4, Yankees 3	Pierce	57-40	1/+1/2
Wed.,7/29	CHICAGO	Tie: Sox 4, Yankees 4	Shaw	57-40	1/+1
Thu., 7/30	CHICAGO	Sox 3, Yankees 1	Wynn	58-40	1/+1
Fri., 7/31	CHICAGO	Sox 7, Senators 1	Latman	59-40	1/+1
Sat., 8/1	CHICAGO	Sox 2, Senators 1	Moore	60-40	1/+2
Sun., 8/2	CHICAGO	Sox 3, Senators 2	Pierce	61-40	1
	CHICAGO	Sox 9, Senators 3	Shaw	62-40	1/+3

******* **SECOND ALL-STAR GAME August 3** *******

Tue., 8/4	Baltimore	Orioles 3, Sox 2	McBride	62-41	1/+2
Wed., 8/5	Baltimore	Sox 2, Orioles 0	Latman	63-41	1
		Orioles 7, Sox 1	Wynn	63-42	1/+2
Thu., 8/6	Baltimore	Tie: Sox 1, O's 1(18)	Pierce	63-42	1/+1 1/2
Fri., 8/7	Washington	Sox 3, Senators 1	Shaw	64-42	1/+1 1/2
Sat., 8/8	Washington	Game vs.Senators ppd.		64-42	1/+1 1/2
Sun., 8/9	Washington	Sox 4, Senators 3	McBride	65-42	1
		Sox 9, Senators 0	Wynn	66-42	1/+3
Tue., 8/11	Detroit	Tigers 8, Sox 1	Pierce	66-43	1/+2 1/2
Wed., 8/12	Detroit	Sox 11, Tigers 6	Latman	67-43	1/+2 1/2
Thu., 8/13	Detroit	Sox 9, Tigers 0	Wynn	68-43	1/+2 1/2
Fri., 8/14	Kan.City	Sox 5, A's 1	Shaw	69-43	1/+3 1/2
Sat., 8/15	Kan.City	A's 2, Sox 1	Pierce	69-44	1/+3 1/2
Sun., 8/16	Kan.City	A's 7, Sox 2	Donovan	69-45	1/+3
Tue., 8/18	CHICAGO	Sox 6, Orioles 4	Wynn	70-45	1/+4 1/2
Wed., 8/19	CHICAGO	Orioles 3, Sox 1	Shaw	70-46	1/+3 1/2

183

Thu., 8/20	CHICAGO	Orioles 7, Sox 6	Latman	70-47	1/+2 1/2
Fri., 8/21	CHICAGO	Sox 5, Senators 4	Donovan	71-47	1/+2 1/2
Sat., 8/22	CHICAGO	Sox 1, Senators 0	Latman	72-47	1/+2 1/2
Sun., 8/23	CHICAGO	Yankees 7, Sox 1	Wynn	72-48	1
		Sox 5, Yankees 0	Shaw	73-48	1/+1 1/2
Mon., 8/24	CHICAGO	Sox 4, Yankees 2	Moore	74-48	1/+2
Tue., 8/25	CHICAGO	Sox 5, Red Sox 4	Donovan	75-48	1/+2
Wed., 8/26	CHICAGO	Red Sox 7, Sox 6	Wynn	75-49	1/+1
Thu., 8/27	CHICAGO	Sox 5, Red Sox 1	Latman	76-49	1/+1 1/2
Fri., 8/28	Cleveland	Sox 7, Indians 3	Shaw	77-49	1/+2 1/2
Sat., 8/29	Cleveland	Sox 2, Indians 0	Donovan	78-49	1/+3 1/2
Sun., 8/30	Cleveland	Sox 6, Indians 3	Wynn	79-49	1/+4 1/2
		Sox 9, Indians 4	Latman	80-49	1/+5 1/2
Tue., 9/1	CHICAGO	Tigers 4, Sox 0	Shaw	80-50	1/+5
Wed., 9/2	CHICAGO	Sox 7, Tigers 2	Donovan	81-50	1
		Sox 11, Tigers 4	Latman	82-50	1/+5 1/2
Fri., 9/4	CHICAGO	Sox 3, Indians 2	Wynn	83-50	1/+6 1/2
Sat., 9/5	CHICAGO	Indians 6, Sox 5	Shaw	83-51	1/+5 1/2
Sun., 9/6	CHICAGO	Indians 2, Sox 1	Donovan	83-52	1/+4 1/2
Mon., 9/7	CHICAGO	Sox 2, A's 1	Pierce	84-52	1
		Sox 13, A's 7	Latman	85-52	1/+4 1/2
Tue., 9/8	CHICAGO	Sox 3, A's 2	Wynn	86-52	1/+5
Wed., 9/9	Washington	Sox 5, Senators 1	Shaw	87-52	1/+4 1/2
Thu., 9/10	Washington	Senators 8, Sox 2	Donovan	87-53	1/+4 1/2
Fri., 9/11	Baltimore	Orioles 3, Sox 0	Pierce	87-54	1
		Orioles 1, Sox 0 (16)	Latman	87-55	1/+4
Sat., 9/12	Baltimore	Sox 6, Orioles 1	Wynn	88-55	1/+4
Sun., 9/13	Boston	Sox 3, Red Sox 1	Shaw	89-55	1/+5 1/2
Mon., 9/14	Boston	Red Sox 9, Sox 3	Donovan	89-56	1/+4 1/2
Tue., 9/15	New York	Sox 4, Yankees 3	Pierce	90-56	1/+5 1/2
Wed., 9/16	New York	Yankees 3, Sox 1	Wynn	90-57	1/+5 1/2
Fri., 9/18	CHICAGO	Sox 1, Tigers 0	Shaw	91-57	1/+5 1/2
Sat., 9/19	CHICAGO	Tigers 5, Sox 4	Donovan	91-58	1/+4 1/2
Sun., 9/20	CHICAGO	Tigers 5, Sox 4	Pierce	91-59	1/+3 1/2
Tue., 9/22	Cleveland	Sox 4, Indians 2	Wynn	92-59	1/+4 1/2
Fri., 9/25	Detroit	Tigers 6, Sox 5	Pierce	92-60	1/+3
Sat., 9/26	Detroit	Sox 10, Tigers 5	Wynn	93-60	1/+4
Sun., 9/27	Detroit	Sox 6, Tigers 4	Shaw	94-60	1/+5

******* END OF REGULAR SEASON *******

STATISTICS

Batting

PLAYER	G	AB	R	H	2B	3B	HR	RBI	SB	AVG	OBP	SA
Mueller	4	4	0	2	0	0	0	0	0	.500	.500	.500
Hicks	6	7	0	3	0	0	0	0	0	.429	.429	.429
Fox	156	*624	84	191	34	6	2	70	5	.306	.383	.389
Kluszewski	31	101	11	30	2	1	2	10	0	.297	.355	.396
Romano	53	126	20	37	5	1	5	25	0	.294	.407	.468
McAnany	67	210	22	58	9	3	0	27	2	.276	.339	.348
Landis	149	515	78	140	26	7	5	64	20	.272	.376	.379
Lollar	140	505	63	134	22	3	22	84	4	.265	.348	.451
Phillips	117	379	43	100	27	1	5	40	1	.264	.320	.380
Aparicio	152	612	98	157	18	5	6	*51	56	.257	.319	.332
Goodman	104	268	21	67	14	1	1	28	3	.250	.304	.321
Martin	3	4	0	1	0	0	0	1	0	.250	.250	.250
Doby	21	58	1	14	1	1	0	9	1	.241	.267	.293
Cash	58	104	16	24	0	1	4	16	1	.240	.378	.375
Boone	9	21	3	5	0	0	1	5	1	.238	.429	.381
Smith	129	472	65	112	16	4	17	55	7	.237	.312	.396
Rivera	80	177	18	39	9	4	4	19	5	.220	.270	.384
Torgeson	127	277	40	61	5	3	9	45	7	.220	.363	.357
Battey	26	64	9	14	1	2	2	7	0	.219	.306	.391
Ennis	26	96	10	21	6	0	2	7	0	.219	.250	.344
Jackson	10	14	3	3	1	0	1	2	0	.214	.313	.500
Simpson	38	75	5	14	5	1	2	13	0	.187	.228	.360
Callison	49	104	12	18	3	0	3	12	0	.173	.271	.288
Esposito	69	66	12	11	1	0	1	5	0	.167	.286	.227
Skizas	8	13	3	1	0	0	0	0	0	.077	.250	.077
Carreon	1	1	0	0	0	0	0	0	0	.000	.000	.000

*indicates led league.

STATISTICS

Pitching

PLAYER	G	GS	CG	IP	H	R	ER	SO	BB	HRA	W	L	ERA	SV
Peters	2	0	0	1	2	0	0	1	2	0	0	0	0.00	0
Rudolph	4	0	0	3	4	0	0	0	2	0	0	0	0.00	1
Staley	*67	0	0	116.1	111	39	29	54	25	5	8	5	2.24	14
Shaw	47	26	8	230.2	217	72	69	87	54	15	18	6	2.69	3
Lown	60	0	0	93.1	73	32	30	63	42	12	9	2	2.89	*15
Wynn	37	*37	14	*255.2	202	106	90	179	*119	20	*22	10	3.17	0
McBride	11	2	0	22.2	20	11	8	12	17	1	0	1	3.18	1
Stanka	2	0	0	5.1	2	2	2	3	4	1	1	0	3.38	0
Pierce	34	33	12	224	217	98	90	114	62	26	14	15	3.62	0
Donovan	31	29	5	179.2	171	84	73	71	58	15	9	10	3.66	0
Latman	37	21	5	156	138	71	65	97	72	15	8	5	3.75	0
Arias	34	0	0	44	49	23	20	28	20	7	2	0	4.09	2
Moore	29	8	0	89.2	80	46	41	49	46	10	3	6	4.12	0
Raymond	3	0	0	4	5	4	4	1	2	2	0	0	9.00	0

*indicates led league.

NOTE: Shaw's .750 winning percentage also led league.

186

BIBLIOGRAPHY

BASEBALL BOOKS

Condon, David. *The Go-Go Chicago White Sox*. New York: Coward McCann, 1960.

Halberstam, David. *October 1964*. New York: Villard Books, 1994.

Kahn, Roger. *A Season in the Sun*. New York: Harper and Row, 1977.

Kahn, Roger. *Memories of Summer*. New York: Hyperion, 1997.

Kahn, Roger. *The Era: 1947-57*. New York: Ticknor and Fields, 1993.

Lindberg, Richard. *Who's on 3rd? The Chicago White Sox Story*. South Bend, Ind.: Icarus, 1983.

Minoso, Orestes, with Herb Fagen. *Just Call Me Minnie: My Six Decades in Baseball*. Champaign, Ill.: Sagamore, 1994.

Nemec, David, et al. *20th Century Baseball Chronicle*. Montreal: Tormont, 1992.

Official Baseball Guide. St. Louis: *The Sporting News*, 1955-64.

Peary, Danny. *We Played the Game: 65 Players Remember Baseball's Greatest Era*, 1947-64. New York: Hyperion, 1994.

Reichler, Joseph L. (ed.). *The Baseball Encyclopedia*, 6th Edition. New York: MacMillan, 1985.

Sox: Complete Record of Chicago White Sox Baseball. New York: MacMillan, 1984.

Vanderberg, Bob. *Minnie and The Mick: The Go-Go White Sox Challenge the Fabled Yankee Dynasty, 1951-1964.* South Bend, Ind.: Diamond Communications, 1996.

Vanderberg, Bob. *Sox: From Lane and Fain to Zisk and Fisk.* Chicago: Chicago Review Press, 1982.

Veeck, Bill, with Ed Linn. *Veeck As In Wreck.* New York: Putnam's, 1962.

Veeck, Bill, with Ed Linn. *Hustler's Handbook.* New York: Putnam's, 1965.

NEWSPAPERS

Baltimore Evening Sun, May 1959.

Chicago American, Chicago Daily News, Chicago Sun-Times, ChicagoTribune, 1956-1964.

New York Times, New York Herald Tribune, June-Sept. 1959.

The Sporting News, 1958-1960.